MOMENTS *of* ENLIGHTENMENT

STORIES FROM ANCIENT AND MODERN MASTERS

ROBERT ULLMAN AND
JUDYTH REICHENBERG-ULLMAN

MJF BOOKS
NEW YORK

We dedicate this book to Baba Hari Dass, a silent yogi who has patiently guided and inspired us and is a living example of what it means to be liberated.

Published by MJF Books
Fine Communications
322 Eighth Avenue
New York, NY 10001

Moments of Enlightenment
LC Control Number 2002106259
ISBN 1-56731-539-9

Previously published as *Mystics, Masters, Saints, and Sages*

This edition published by arrangement with Conari Press

Manufactured in the United States of America on acid-free paper ∞

MJF Books and the MJF colophon are trademarks of Fine Creative Media, Inc.

BG   10 9   8   7   6   5   4   3   2   1

Acknowledgments

Foreword XIII

Introduction

ACKNOWLEDGMENTS

WE THANK all of those beings, known and unknown, who have had the sincerity, courage, and unfaltering dedication to put finding God above all else. We express profound gratitude for having the exceptional fortune to have met personally or to have sat with the following spiritual teachers.

Adyashanti, Ammachi, Avatar Adi Da, Baba Hari Dass, Byron Katie, Chagdud Rinpoche, His Holiness the Dalai Lama for his wonderful foreword, Deepa Kodikal, Eckhart Tolle, Gangaji, Guru Mayi, Jean Klein, Kalu Rinpoche, Karunamayi, Kriyananda, Tsering Everest, Mother Hamilton, Mother Teresa, Pir Kalimi, Pir Vilayat Inayat Khan, Ram Dass, Ramesh Balsekar, Reshad Feild, Sant Keshavadas, Satya Sai Baba, Seung Sahn, Shantimayi, Sheikh Suleiman Dede, Shlomo Carlebach, Shree Maa, Shri Shivabalayogi, Shri Shri Anandamurti, Swami Chidananda, Swami Ganapati Satchidananda, Swami Krishananda, Swami Muktananda, Swami Satchidananda, Tony Parsons, Yogi Bhajan.

BY HIS HOLINESS THE DALAI LAMA

AS HUMAN BEINGS, we all want happiness, peace, and release from suffering. We often think that the enlightened ones are somehow special, different from us, with a state of mind that is unattainable to an ordinary person. And yet, each human being has an equal opportunity to attain wisdom, happiness, and enlightenment by cultivating a correct motivation—a sincere aspiration to benefit all sentient beings—and engaging in diligent practice.

Whether in the course of one lifetime or many, it is possible for each of us to overcome ignorance and delusion and find release from the cycle of life and death. The Buddha, like many of the individuals described in this book, was born an ordinary person. He was brought up as a prince, married, and had a son. Then, after observing the suffering of human beings—that they grow old, fall sick, and die—he totally renounced the worldly way of life in his determination to find a solution to human suffering. Having undergone severe physical penance, he purified and illumined his mind through intense meditation, and attained supreme enlightenment.

In this way the Buddha set an example for his followers. Purifying the mind is not easy. It takes time and hard work. But this is true of any human enterprise. You need tremendous willpower and determination right from the start, accepting that there will be many obstacles and resolving that despite them all you will continue until you have attained your goal. But having attained enlightenment, the Buddha did not retire into isolation. Moved by a spontaneous concern to help others, he spent the rest of his life as a homeless monk, sharing his experience with everyone who wished to listen.

His entire doctrine can be presented with the Four Noble

Truths, the subject of his first discourse. What we seek is happiness; happiness is the effect of a cause; what we do not want is suffering, which has its own causes. The Buddha's view of dependent arising and his advice not to harm anyone, but to help whomever you can, both emphasize the practice of nonviolence. The practice of nonviolence remains one of the most potent forces for good in the world today, for such practice is service to our fellow beings.

In this valuable, inspiring book you will find the stories of people known and unknown who have experienced and realized some aspect of the enlightened mind. The rich diversity of their experiences is vast, yet their realizations have a universal quality. From each of their stories, we can develop a greater awareness and appreciation of their spiritual journeys, the positive qualities they embodied, and the understanding and realization of the nature of life that they experienced. It is important to understand that each of these saints and sages was born an ordinary person. Some underwent intensive spiritual practices, including fasting, meditation, physical hardships, and great sacrifices in pursuit of Truth. Others were spontaneously awakened, perhaps as a result of positive spiritual merit accumulated from previous births.

All the world's spiritual traditions have provided us with examples of persons who sought wisdom and practiced compassion in their lives. We can see that the illumination of mind is a universal phenomenon. It can happen in the East and West, North and South, among all races and religions, even among people who have no religion.

We must think of ourselves as human beings first and forget the distinctions that in our imagination divide us. In this era of great change and upheaval, we must work urgently and diligently to ensure that everyone has the basic necessities for life, to ensure that everyone has political and religious freedom, and to protect the Earth from environmental exploitation and devastation.

June 16, 2001

WHAT IS ENLIGHTENMENT?

TO "ENLIGHTEN" means, literally, to provide knowledge or spiritual insight, to illuminate what was previously dark or obscured. Those who describe enlightenment experiences recount a shift out of their ordinary frames of reference. Their worldviews become markedly different from what they had been before the experience. Many individuals report never again being the same and that their sense of individuality and separateness evaporated, often permanently. This alteration leaves these enlightened beings in a state of freedom. They are still themselves, and yet they are not. They continue to live out their lives in their physical bodies, yet their identification is no longer confined to the body or the mind. For some, even the world itself as anything more than an illusion disappears. Those who attain enlightenment become liberated, released from the attachment to suffering and limitation of any kind. They are absolutely free, and extraordinarily awakened.

Enlightenment is an aspiration of many seekers regardless of religion or birthplace, often pursued over the course of decades or lifetimes. There are those who believe enlightenment occurs primarily at birth. Some say whether or not one attains enlightenment during the course of his or her lifetime is a matter of destiny or karma. Others describe it as a natural outcome of serious and diligent spiritual practice, and still others say it can happen to anyone anytime, by realizing what has always been one's true nature. In fact, some teachers of nondualism would go so far as to say there is no one to be enlightened because there are no separate beings. The focus of this book is on those beings who were not fully awakened at birth but went through a describable process of transformation. This process is for some blissful and ecstatic, for others arduous or terrifying.

There is something palpably different about someone who has undergone an experience of revelation and transformation that leads to enlightenment. His or her countenance may exhibit serenity, humor, and innocent joy, or the severe features of years of austerity, or even apparent insanity. There is a profound realization of living fully in the present moment: a deep sense of relaxation that arises from the understanding that there is nowhere else to go and nothing else to do. A magnanimity and spaciousness is observed as compared to the finite, limited nature of the individual self, and a complete sense of apparent indifference or nonattachment to the world or social norms may also be present. Enlightened beings often exude a sweetness that draws others to them like bears to honey, or contrarily, some may display a crusty, obnoxious, or obscene isolationism that drives away all but the most persistent and worthy aspirants. Though many enlightened beings seek seclusion and remain unknown, others attract thousands of seekers who come to them for blessings and teachings, the answers to their innermost questions, freedom from their worldly problems and concerns, and, ultimately, their own liberation. Enlightenment appears mysterious and elusive to the unawakened yet the ordinary and natural state of being for those who are liberated.

The mystics, masters, saints, and sages here, drawn from the world's spiritual traditions or from their own individual paths, have expanded their human experience to embrace the cosmic or universal aspects of human life. They have achieved, or at least tasted, that which is desired but eludes the vast majority of human beings: profound peace, extreme happiness, and a deep understanding of truth. Although these masters and saints can inspire us, teach us, and show us the way they found peace, each of us in our own way must ultimately discover our own paths to self-realization, peace, and happiness. May we all awaken to who we truly are.

Characteristics of the Enlightenment Experience

The actual experience of enlightenment is unique to the individual and is colored, to some degree, by her prior experience, spiritual tradition, and culture temperament. Though this is hardly surprising, there do seem to be, however, certain features that are common to all of those who share the phenomenon of awakening.

To consider enlightenment as an experience at all can seem to contradict our notions of no-mind, absorption into the infinite, and emptiness, yet something indeed has happened to those individuals to change them, as difficult or impossible as it may be to describe the event or the process of transcendence. Even so, some qualities do seem common to the enlightenment experience:

INTERCONNECTEDNESS AND EGO TRANSCENDENCE. A fundamental shift in consciousness from the individual to the whole appears to typify the enlightenment experience. This shift may be described as the dissolution of the self, a merging of the wave in the ocean, union with the infinite, abdication of the personal sense of doership, or the loss of a separate identity. There remains no identification with the individual ego or isolated, differentiated self. The individual, ego, and personality all continue to exist, but the identification with them is eliminated.

TIMELESSNESS AND SPACIOUSNESS. No thing or concept remains fixed in time and space. Enlightenment sets into play a moment-to-moment existence. In the words of the Buddha, the only thing that is constant is change. There is a realization of the present moment as all there is and a sense of fluidity that pervades all of life.

ACCEPTANCE. This is a relaxation or surrender, a revelation or insight that all is transpiring according to a plan or randomness that surpasses the individual will. Struggle ends and gives way to acceptance of a reality free of bondage from and attachment to personal desires, thoughts, and feelings.

BEYOND PLEASURE AND PAIN. Those who have experienced enlightenment describe rapture, ecstasy, love, or simply a contentment that transcends suffering. In the midst of transformation, however, fear, confusion, disorientation, pain, torment, and even madness are not uncommon, sometimes lasting over extended periods of time. This has been described by some, such as Saint John of the Cross, as the "dark night of the soul." Disease and pain inevitably arise and many enlightened ones, such as Ramana Maharshi and Ramakrishna, have died of cancer. Suffering exists but the personal identification with it does not.

CLARITY. The enlightened mind is spontaneous, immediate, and flexible. Thinking is clear and unencumbered by extraneous and limiting thoughts and emotions. Thoughts are purposeful, direct and in the moment, free of extraneous mind chatter.

SHATTERING OF PRECONCEIVED NOTIONS. Rigidity, expectations, preconceived ideas and personae give way to a vaster reality and even to a profound realization of emptiness, vastness, or nothingness.

The Enlightenment Stories

The stories of enlightenment in this book are collected from a wide variety of sources, various spiritual traditions, and from a few who followed no tradition. The intent is to capture the experience of enlightenment as clearly and succinctly as possible. We have attempted to find the subject's core experience that produced the greatest transformation in consciousness from individual to transpersonal, although we recognize the process may extend over a longer period of time. For most of the stories, the subject's own words are used, usually from published autobiographical writings, or new selections created for this work. For a few selections, such as Saint Catherine of Siena, or Abulafia, the report of a close contemporary associate or disciple was all that was available to reflect the experience of the saint or master. In some cases, such as with Rumi, Kabir, Saint John of the Cross, and the Second Dalai Lama, the experiences are recounted in verse.

What Can We Learn from These Stories?

Each person's experience and process of the spiritual and transpersonal aspects of enlightenment is, of course, unique. No two experiences are ever the same, yet stories such as these may inspire us, give us clues to the process of awakening, or act as signposts for our own spiritual seeking and explorations of enlightenment. The diversity of experiences in this book attests to our individuality as human and spiritual beings, while the commonality in consciousness in those who have crossed over from individual to cosmic is just as marked. Paths are many but the goal is one. We hope the reader will find models in our mystics, masters, saints, and sages, and pointers to attitudes and methods that may be of benefit in their own spiritual process. We all have much to learn from these spiritual adepts who continually manifest to grace us with their presence and transcendence.

Who Is Included and Who Is Not

No one religion, country, socioeconomic class, or gender has laid special claim to enlightenment. Men and women, bankers and renunciates, saints and sinners, the worldly and the otherworldly have all experienced enlightenment. Enlightenment is not dependent on lineage or on the number of scriptures one has read, and it is equally within reach of the least or most educated. Our most difficult task in writing this book has been deciding whom to include and whom to exclude.

Many wonderful beings have been left out for a variety of reasons, including space limitations, the need for diversity of traditions and gender, and a desire to include beings from past and present, known and relatively unknown. We were intrigued by those who achieved their transformations in ordinary places: a cannery, a classroom, or in bed. It is these stories, perhaps more than the others, that illustrate how enlightenment is available to any of us.

Our criteria have been to include the best descriptions of the actual enlightenment experience that we could find. There are undoubtedly great beings unknown to us whom we might have included. We were unable to obtain permission for others. A number of our most powerful teachers, including Baba Hari Dass, Hazrat Inayat Khan, Anandamayi Ma, Chagdud Rinpoche, and the Dalai Lama do not talk openly about their experiences of awakening. Hindu tradition is by far the most prolific source of writings on enlightenment, which explains its apparent overrepresentation in our book. We tried to include as many women as possible, and there are a number of others we would have included had we found their stories of awakening. We recognize that it is possible for a person to undergo a transient experience of illumination without remaining in a permanent state of oneness and present these accounts of enlightenment without judging who has remained permanently in such a state.

We believe that these transcendent experiences are best presented at face value, without interpretation, and with the barest of introductions, serving mainly to place their subjects in a context of birthplace and years in which they lived. We have aimed for diversity and balance, though the final list is skewed by our own biases, familiarity, and experience. We hope you find these stories to be as uplifting, inspiring, and fascinating as we have

MOMENTS *of* ENLIGHTENMENT

THE BUDDHA

ONE

GAUTAMA, THE BUDDHA

624–544 B.C.E., NEPAL

ONE MIGHT SAY that the Buddha needs no introduction, as he is undoubtedly the most famous of all the enlightened ones included in this book. Yet his story remains an enduring classic and model of the spiritual search and its successful completion.

The pampered prince, Siddhartha, had a beautiful wife and son, dancing girls, sumptuous food, and three palaces for his own use, and was completely sheltered from the world. One day he left the palace surreptitiously and witnessed, for the first time in his life, disease, suffering, old age, and death. This led the prince to renounce his worldly treasures and family to find Truth and a release from suffering for himself and all sentient beings. For six years he pursued ascetic practices in the forest, reducing himself through meditation and fasting to a mere skeleton, at the point of death. At the last moment, he accepted rice milk from a cowherd girl and was revived. Abandoning the ascetic life of the forest for the middle path between indulgence and asceticism, he nevertheless vowed not to move from his meditation seat beneath the Bodhi tree until he reached enlightenment. Defeating Mara, the incarnation of ignorance and evil, all of his past lives appeared before his eyes, and he fell deeply into contemplation of the nature of life and suffering. He sought to transcend birth, suffering, and death. And he succeeded, ultimately attaining the perfect peace of Nirvana. He was absolutely free, liberated while alive.

By means of his exalted state, the Buddha went on to acquire disciples, found an order of monks that persists today, and spread great wisdom and compassion throughout Asia and beyond. Over the past 2,500 years, the Buddha's story and example have inspired countless others to dedicate their entire lives and renounce all the aspects of worldly life to

1

attain Nirvana for the benefit of everyone. Even those who have not yet given up the world have been deeply affected by the Buddha's insights, compassion, and teachings. The Buddhist concepts of the middle path, the four noble truths, the eightfold path, the bodhisattva ideal, and the ultimate release from the sufferings of countless human lifetimes have captivated entire cultures. Throughout Asia, Buddhism is deeply engrained in the fabric of society and forms a primary basis for religious expression. Buddhists throughout the world form what is known as the Sangha, or community of those following the Buddha's example.

The Dharma, as Buddhist teaching is called, has become increasingly popular in the past fifty years in the West as well, as the great diaspora of Buddhist teachers has captivated new generations of spiritual seekers looking beyond their own cultures for Truth. The Buddha did not set out to found a religion and did not even have a concept of God in his teaching. His only mission was to share the truth of his experience, to enlighten others as he had been enlightened, and to save others from the fear and sufferings of old age, sickness, and death. He wandered and taught for forty-five years, giving instruction even on his deathbed, to guide seekers to self-realization. With his dying breath he instructed those by his bedside: "Decay is inherent in all component things, but the truth will remain forever. Work out your salvation with diligence!" His compassion was unbounded, his wisdom supreme. Now read the culmination of the story in which Prince Siddhartha became Gautama, the Buddha, the Awakened One.

The Buddha's story was originally oral history told to his disciple Ananda, approximately 2,500 years ago, and recorded in various sources including the *Pali Canon*, the *Lalitavishtara Sutra*, and the *Buddhacharita*. The material has been collected and presented here by Sherab Chodzin Kohn, a modern Western Tibetan Buddhist author.

FROM SUFFERING TO NIRVANA

The Buddha's Liberation

THE BODHISATTVA had triumphed over Mara. The air cleared and was still. The full moon rose in the sky and shone softly. The bodhisattva, unmoving, entered into the first level of meditation. The night was utterly silent; even insects made no murmur. As the moon continued to rise, the bodhisattva's composure deepened, and one by one he mastered the levels of meditation until he reached the fourth. His concentration was bright and unblemished, full and balanced. Then through great confidence and trust, he relinquished the watcher, and his mind entered into a fathomless openness untroubled by content. Here the bodhisattva naturally rested until a profound contentment pervaded him. But as one who already knew the way, he did not become caught up in this. Rather, with utter clarity and tenderness, he turned his mind to untying the knot of birth, old age, sickness, and death.

He saw that the condition for old age, sickness, and death is birth. Once birth happens, the rest follows inevitably. He saw that the condition for birth lay in processes of becoming already set in motion; that the condition for this was grasping or craving; that the condition for this was desire; and the condition for desire, feelings of happiness, suffering, or indifference; and the condition for these, sensual contact; and the condition for sensual contact, the fields of the senses; the condition for sense fields, the arising of mind-body; the condition for mind-body, consciousness. He saw that mind-body and consciousness condition each other to make a rudimentary sense of self. He saw that the condition for consciousness was volitional impulses, and finally that the condition for volitional impulses was ignorance.

Thus he saw that the whole process ending in old age and death begins when basic intelligence slips into unawareness of its own nature. In this way all-pervading intelligence strays into the sense of a self.

After the bodhisattva had penetrated the nature of the process of birth, old age, sickness, and death, the clarity and openness of his mind increased yet further. Then in the first watch of the night, his inner vision became completely unobstructed. This is called the opening of the divine eye. Then he turned his attention to the past, and he saw his and others' countless past lives stretching back over many eons and ages of the world. Even back through world ages separated from the present one by long intervals of universal destruction, he knew that at a certain time he had been thus and such a person. He had been this kind of being, of this sex, of this race, had eaten this food, and had lived this long. Then he had been born again this or that way and once more lived through certain circumstances, and thus had been born and had died and been reborn again an incalculable number of times. This he saw in relation to himself and all other beings.

Then, in the second watch of the night, moved by compassion, he opened his wisdom eye yet further and saw the spectacle of the whole universe as in a spotless mirror. He saw beings being born and passing away in accordance with karma, the laws of cause and effect. Just as, when one clears one's throat, one is next ready to speak, past deeds create a certain inclination. When the basic condition of ignorance is present, the inclination takes shape in a certain kind of volitional impulses, which engender a certain consciousness, and so on up to old age and death, and then once more into ignorance and volitional impulses. Seeing birth and death occurring in accordance with this chain of causality, the bodhisattva saw the cyclic paths of all beings. He saw the fortunate and the unfortunate, the exalted and the lowly going their various ways. He saw how, ignorant and suffering, they were tossed on the stormy waves of birth, old age, sickness, and death.

In the third and last watch of the night, he applied himself to the task of rooting out this suffering once and for all. He had clearly understood the wheel of dependent arising in which each stage follows from a preceding cause, beginning with ignorance.

And he saw how beings were driven on it by the powerful motive force of karma. Now his divine eye sought the means of liberation. He saw that through the cessation of birth, old age and death would not exist; through the cessation of becoming, there would be no birth; through the cessation of grasping, no becoming—and so back through the sequence of causation to ignorance. He saw suffering, the cause of suffering, the cessation of suffering, and at last also the path to cessation.

At the end of the third watch, at the first light of dawn the bodhisattva saw through the very last trace of ignorance in himself. Thus he attained complete and utter enlightenment and became the Buddha. The first words that came to him were these:

> Seeking but not finding the House Builder,
> I traveled through the round of countless births:
> O painful is birth ever and again.
> > House Builder, you have now been seen;
> > You shall not build the house again.
> > Your rafters have been broken down;
> > Your ridge pole is demolished too.
> My mind has now attained the unformed nirvana
> And reached the end of every kind of craving.

Then he thought: "I have attained the unborn. My liberation is unassailable. This is my last birth. There will now be no renewal of becoming."

A compilation from the *Pali Canon*, the *Lalitavishtara Sutra*, and the *Buddhacharita*.

HUI-NENG

H UI-NENG is one of the most beloved teachers in Zen Buddhism and exemplifies that neither wealth nor formal education is a prerequisite for enlightenment. He was the
last in a line of founding teachers in the Zen tradition and served as inspiration for the Southern School of Zen. The title of *sutra* (scripture)
given to the documents of Hui-Neng's life and teachings, traditionally
reserved for the Buddha himself, give evidence to the high degree of respect accorded this woodcutter turned enlightened master.

The T'ang dynasty, considered by many to be the culmination of
Chinese culture, provided the backdrop for Hui-Neng's life. During this
era tremendous progress was made in the development of Chinese Buddhist teachings and writings. Legend has it that at the moment of Hui-
Neng's birth, in Chou of Kwangtung, beams of light illuminated the air
and the room was blanketed with an unusual fragrance. At dawn, two
mysterious monks are said to have paid a visit to the newborn's father,
instructing him to give his child the auspicious name of Hui-Neng. His
childhood was that of a simple, uneducated peasant. An illiterate woodcutter, Hui-Neng was said to have attained enlightenment (as told in
the accompanying selection) in a momentary flash. His teachings provide immediate and direct insights regarding the nature of awareness at
its very essence.

As a result of his sudden enlightenment while still a young man,
Hui-Neng inherited the title of Grand Master of Zen. That a simple man
lacking name, fame, and riches was chosen for this appointment over
others far more learned and influential was a threat to the old guard.
Persecuted by those who were envious of his attainment, Hui-Neng fled
to the mountains. He did not reappear until his middle-age years, at

which time he resumed his mission of spreading the knowledge of Zen to the masses. His mode of expression was simple and to the point, placing the wisdom of Zen within the reach of many who would have otherwise been excluded from such teachings. The disciples of Hui-Neng were many, including common folk and Confucian scholars alike. It was not uncommon for him to offer teachings to over a thousand scholars, officials, monks, nuns, and laypeople at a time.

Instructing students and disciples to seek equanimity and understanding of the true or essential nature, Hui-Neng cautioned against stagnation. He emphasized humility rather than self-aggrandizement, detachment from thoughts, and remaining true to one's essential nature. Shaving one's head and receiving ordination as monks and nuns was fruitless without evenness of mind and straightforwardness of action. The way to enlightenment or buddhahood, advised Hui-Neng, was through purification of the mind and recognition of the Pure Land within the body. Rebirth without enlightenment, he counseled, is a long road. Better, he taught, to realize the "birthless reality of immediacy."

Hui-Neng had a tremendous impact on revitalizing the quiet asceticism of his own Buddhist section and on the spread of Zen in China. His successors were numerous, and countless thoughtful students continue to benefit from his teachings.

This story is told in first person by Hui-Neng as part of what is known as the *Altar Sutra*. It was translated by Thomas Cleary from a version by a monk named Tsung-Pao that was compiled in 1291 from earlier sources, including a version from Hiu-Neng's disciple, Fahai.

FROM ILLITERATE WOODCUTTER
TO SIXTH ZEN PATRIARCH

AFTER HAVING gotten my mother settled, I left right away and reached Huang-mei within thirty-odd days. There I paid respects to the Fifth Grand Master.

The Grand Master asked, "Where are you from, and what do you want?"

I replied, "I am a peasant from Hsin Province in Ling-nan. I have come from far away to pay my respects to you only because I seek to be a buddha, nothing else."

The Grand Master said, "You are a southerner, and an aborigine; how can you be a buddha?"

I said, "People may be southerners or northerners, but the buddha-nature originally has no south or north. As an aborigine, my social status is not the same as yours, but what difference is there in our buddha-nature?"

The Grand Master wanted to talk with me more, but he saw that his followers were all around, so he had me do chores with the workers.

I said to him, "My own mind always produces wisdom. Not being alienated from one's own essential nature is itself a field of blessings. What work would you have me do?"

The Grand Master said, "This aborigine is very sharp! Don't say any more. Go work in the mill."

So I retired to a back building, where a worker had me splitting firewood and pounding rice. I spent over eight months at this, when the Grand Master saw me one day and said, "I think your insight is reliable, but I was afraid bad people would harm you, so I didn't talk to you. Do you realize this?"

I said, "I do know your intention. That is why I didn't dare walk in front of the auditorium, lest one be careless."

One day the Grand Master called all his disciples to him and said, "I tell you, for people in this world the matter of birth and death is serious. You lot just seek fields of blessings all day long, and do not seek to get out of the ocean of misery of birth and death.

"If your own nature is confused, how can blessings save you? Let each of you look into your own wisdom, grasp the insightful nature of your own basic mind, and compose a verse to show me. If you have understood the great meaning, I will bequeath to you the robe and the teaching, and make you the Sixth Grand Master.

Other people hearing this all set their minds to rest, saying, "We will rely on Master Shen-hsiu after this; why bother to compose a verse?"

Shen-hsiu reflected, "The reason the others won't present verses is that I am their mentor. I must compose a verse to present to the teacher—if I do not present a verse, how will the teacher know the depth or shallowness of the insight and understanding within my mind? If my intention in presenting a verse is to seek the teaching, then it is good; if it is to seek the rank of Grand Master, that is bad—it would be the same as the ordinary mentality. How would it be different from usurping the rank of a sage? If I do not present a verse, I'll never get the teaching. This is very difficult, very difficult."

In front of the Fifth Grand Master's auditorium was a hallway three rooms long, where they were going to have an artist paint a mural of the projection of the *Lankavatara-sutra* and the succession of the five Grand Masters of Ch'an. After Shen-hsiu had composed his verse, several times he got as far as the front of the auditorium intending to present it, but each time he felt faint and broke out in a sweat. Unable to bring himself to present his verse, over a period of four days he made thirteen unsuccessful attempts.

Finally Shen-hsiu thought, "It would be better if I wrote the verse in the hallway, where the teacher can see it. If the teacher says it is good, I will respectfully come forth and declare it to be my composition. If he says it won't do, I have been wasting years in the mountains accepting respect from others—what further path would I practice?" That night, in the middle of the night, letting no one know, he took a lamp and wrote his verse on the wall of the south hallway, presenting his insight.

The verse said,

> The body is the tree of enlightenment,
> The mind is like a clear mirror-stand.
> Polish it diligently time and again,
> Not letting it gather dust.

Having written this, Shen-hsiu went back to his room, totally undetected by anyone.

Two days later, a boy passing by the mill was chanting that verse. As soon as I heard it, I realized this verse did not yet reveal the fundamental essence. Although I had not received instruction, I already knew the main idea, so I asked the boy, "What verse is that you're chanting?"

The boy said, "You aborigine! Don't you know that the Grand Master said for people in this world the matter of birth and death is serious—if they want to get transmission of the robe and the teaching, he had the disciples compose verses. If anyone has realized the great meaning, he will transmit the robe and the teaching and make him the Sixth Grand Master. The senior monk Shen-hsiu wrote this formless verse on the wall of the south hallway; the Grand Master had everyone memorize it, saying that if one puts this verse into practice one will avoid falling into evil ways, and if one puts this verse into practice one will gain great benefit."

I said, "I have been here pounding rice for over eight months, and have never been to the auditorium. Please take me to where the verse is, so I can pay my respects."

When the boy had led me to the verse to pay respects, I said, "I am illiterate; please read it for me." At that time the lieutenant military inspector of Chiang Province was there, a man named

Chang Chih-yung; he read the verse aloud. After I'd heard it, I said I had a verse too, and asked the lieutenant inspector to write it for me.

The lieutenant inspector said, "How extraordinary that you too would compose a verse!"

I said to the lieutenant inspector, "If you want to learn supreme enlightenment, don't slight beginners. A person of the lowliest rank may have the very highest knowledge, while a person of the highest rank may lack practical wisdom. If you slight people, you will have done incalculable wrong."

The lieutenant inspector said, "Recite your verse, and I will write it for you. If you attain the teaching, you should liberate me. Don't forget these words."

My verse went this way:

> Enlightenment originally has no tree,
> And a clear mirror is not a stand.
> Originally there's not a single thing—
> Where can dust be attracted?

After this verse had been written down, the whole community was amazed, and everyone wondered. They said to each other, "How odd! You can't tell about people by their appearance! How could we have employed him, a living bodhisattva, as a servant for so long?"

Seeing the surprise and wonder of the crowd, the Grand Master feared someone might do me harm, so he erased the verse with his shoe and said, "This is still not yet perception of essence."

Everyone thought it was so, but the next day the Grand Master surreptitiously came to the mill, where he saw me pounding rice, a stone at my waist. He said, "People who seek the Way forget their bodies for the sake of the teaching; will he be like this?" Then he asked me, "Is the rice ready yet?"

I replied, "The rice has been ready for a long time, but it still wants sifting."

The Grand Master knocked the mortar three times with his cane. Immediately understanding the Grand Master's meaning, I went to his room at the third watch [in the middle of the night]. Using his vestment as a screen so no one could see us, he explained the *Diamond Sutra* to me. When he came to the point where it says, "You should activate the mind without dwelling on anything," at these words I had the overwhelming realization that all things are not apart from inherent nature.

I then said to the Grand Master, "Who would have expected that inherent nature is originally intrinsically pure? Who would have expected that inherent nature is originally unborn and undying? Who would have expected that inherent nature is originally complete in itself? Who would have expected that inherent nature is originally immovable? Who would have expected that inherent nature can produce myriad things?"

Knowing I had realized original nature, the Grand Master said to me, "If one does not discern the original mind, it is of no benefit to study the teaching. If you discern your own original mind and see your own original essential nature, you are what they call a great man, a teacher of humans and angels, a buddha."

I received the teaching in the middle of the night, unbeknownst to anyone. He then handed on the doctrine of immediacy, as well as the bowl and robe, saying, "You are the sixth-generation Grand Master. Be conscientious and spiritually liberate beings everywhere, popularizing the teaching so that it will not die out in the future. Listen to my verse:

"Those with sense plant seeds;
The fruits grow from the ground.
Since there is no seed without sense,
There is no nature, no life."

The Grand Master also said, "When the great teacher Bodhidharma first came to this land a long time ago, people did not yet believe in him, so he handed on this robe as an embodiment of faith, and it has been inherited through the generations. As for the teaching, it is transmitted mind to mind, enabling all to awaken themselves and understand themselves.

"Since olden times, the buddhas have only communicated the original reality; the teachers have intimately imparted the original mind. The robe is a bone of contention; let it stop with you and not be passed on. If you were to pass on this robe, your life would be in danger. You must go away immediately, for I fear people may harm you."

I asked, "Where should I go?"

The Grand Master said, "Stop when you meet Huai; hibernate when you encounter Hui."

Taking the robe and bowl in the middle of the night, I said, "I am originally a southerner, unfamiliar with the mountain roads here. How can I get out to the mouth of the river?"

The Fifth Grand Master said, "Don't worry. I'll take you there myself." The Grand Master than took me right to Nine River Station, where he had me get onto a boat. The Fifth Grand Master himself took up the oars and rowed.

I asked the Grand Master to sit down and let me row, but he said, "It is appropriate that I ferry you across."

I said, "When people are at a loss, the guide ferries them over; when one is enlightened, one ferries oneself over."

The Grand Master said, "So it is. It is so. Hereafter Buddhism will become very popular through you. Three years after you go, I will depart from this world. Now you should go; make your way to the South. It is better not to speak out too quickly; it is hard to promote Buddhism."

After I had bade farewell and left the Grand Master, I set out southward.

From the *Altar Sutra* by Hui-Neng, Sixth Grand Master of Zen.

THREE

YESHE TSOGYAL

757–817, TIBET

YESHE TSOGYAL, whose name means "Ocean of Primordial Wisdom," is considered to be the mother of Tibetan Buddhism. She is best known for her role as consort and biographer of Padmasambhava (Lotus-Born), the Vajrayana Buddhist guru who is credited with bringing Buddhism from India to Tibet. This great woman, however, deserves to be recognized for her own profound spiritual attainments. In addition to being a historical figure, Yeshe Tsogyal's story has been mythologized over the centuries and she has assumed the status of a deity, the Queen of Great Bliss.

In the mundane world, Yeshe Tsogyal was the young wife of Emperor Trisong Detsen, who invited Padmasambhava to teach and build monasteries in Tibet. However, she had no interest in married life in the emperor's harem, and sought only spiritual wealth and experiences. When Yeshe Tsogyal became the student and tantric consort of the Indian spiritual teacher, quite a scandal erupted at the emperor's court, and she was forced into exile.

Keith Dowman, in his book *Sky Dancer,* relates the story of her first tantric encounter with the Lotus-Born Lord:

> I, the girl Tsogyel, sank beneath mundane appearances, and having slipped into the nakedness of pure pleasure, I anointed my mandala of delight with the five sacred substances, and made further petition:
>
>> Buddha Hero of Pure Pleasure, do as you will.
>> Guru and Lord of Pure Pleasure,
>> With true energy and joy, I implore you to inject
>> The seed into the inner mandala.
>> And I will guard the secret of the method with my life.

Painting *Aro Ter Khandro Chenmo Yeshe Tsogyel* by Khandro Dechen, Courtesy Aro Gar.

YESHE TSOGYEL

Then with three fingers stirring the pollen dust of the lotus, I offered my mandala to the mandala of the Guru's Body with an intense snake-like dance. The mandala of dynamic space having gathered into itself the nature of the Great Pema Heruka himself by means of the hook of the lower member's focal point, the Absolute Heruka, his magnificent flaming vajra in a state of rapacity and violent abuse, his wrinkles uncreased, projecting his full emanation, took command of the lotus throne with a roar of scornful laughter that flooded appearances with glory, transmuting them into pure pleasure. Thus he revealed to me the Mandala of the Blazing Sun of Radiant Inner Space, conferring power upon me.

Throughout her life, Yeshe Tsogyal wandered and performed advanced spiritual practices in many caves and monasteries throughout Tibet and Nepal. Her attainments and spiritual prowess were legendary, nothing short of miraculous. She is credited with raising the dead, defeating demons, and controlling the elements of nature and the energies of millions of gross and subtle worlds. Yeshe Tsoygal's wisdom and compassion were reputed to be beyond compare. As an eighth-century woman and spiritual adept in an era when women were not highly valued in society or in religious endeavors, she is quite remarkable. This great teacher served as a model for a host of later yoginis, including some of her own future incarnations.

Known for her infallible memory, Yeshe Tsogyal collected and spread the teachings of Padmasambhava throughout Tibet. She also preserved and interred them securely for future generations of spiritual aspirants in hidden mystical emplacements known as *termas* (treasures), to be rediscovered hundreds of years later by special treasure finders known as *tertons*. Indeed, her own autobiography was found as a terma in the sixteenth century by the terton Taksham Nuden Dorje.

Whether woman or deity, Yeshe Tsogyal left a remarkable legacy of marvels that are unparalleled today, but worthy of emulation by those aspirants, women and men, who wish to discover the secret treasures of Tibetan Buddhism.

This poem in which Yeshe Tsogyal recounts her remarkable spiritual achievements is from an eighth-century manuscript, mystically hidden by herself and found in the sixteenth century by the terton Taksham Nuden Dorje. The translation is by Padmakara Translation Group.

LADY OF THE LOTUS-BORN

Signs of Accomplishment

Stirred, in Tidro by the allegorical display of Dakinis,
I undertook the eight austerities,
Extracting certain tokens of attainment.

Residing at a place where snow and moraines meet,
I came upon the heat of tummo fire,
And threw away the clothing of the world.
In the Trysting Place of Dakinis
The fourth empowerment's warmth was mine,
And all that I beheld was cleansed,
Becoming thus the presence of the Teacher.

In Nepal I brought a dead man back to life
And by this means my Atsara I ransomed
To gain the essence of the path profound.
My speech was vibrant with the melody of Brahma
My body journeyed like a rainbow in celestial fields;
My mind became the Wisdom of the triple time.

In Senge-Dzong I took the sap of healing herbs
And saw the vision of the deities of medicine.
In Nering I subdued and quelled the uproar
Of a host of demons and attained accomplishment.
I beheld the face of all the deities I practiced,
And I attained accomplishments with ease.

At Paro Taktsang, with my three companions
I trod the path profound and deep
And I, Heruka of Great Bliss,
Controlled and brought within my power
The subtle veins, the essence drop and energies,
And likewise the five elements I tamed.
My body, speech and mind transfigured
As the Triple Kaya,
The Prophecies of Amitayus came to me.
From Vajravarahi inseparable,
I then became the mistress of all Mandalas.

At Onphu Taktsang I attained Kilaya
And seized the life force of the gods and spirits
Of a thousand million worlds.
The deities of Amitayus' mandala I saw
And reached the level of a deathless vidyadhara,
Diamond-like, invincible and indestructible.

Throughout the far-flung regions of Tibet
In every hill and dale,
The places where I practiced are uncountable.
And not a single clod of earth that hands may grasp
Is now without my blessing,
And time the truth of this will show—
The proof will be the taking out of Treasures.
In lesser sites, so many that the mind cannot encompass
The imprints of my hands and feet now fill the rocks.
And mantras, syllables, and images,
I placed and set to be
The stay and basis of the future faithful,
And prayed that, linked with them,
They might derive great profit.
These are the signs of my attainment:
Demons and the evil-minded were subdued,

The five-fold elements were brought beneath my sway,
And everywhere I filled the earth with Treasures.

Since unfailing memory I gained,
The whole of Padma's teaching I collated.
Since intrepid Confidence is mine,
The future I predict, and shield the fortunate.
Since I am the peer of all Buddhas,
I bring their labor to completion—
The work of those who in past, present, and future time
Are gone to bliss.
And thus I am adorned with all attainments.

In brief, to tell my ordinary accomplishments,
I hold phenomena beneath my sway.
I have the power of fleet-footedness,
The universal remedy and the balm of magic sight,
And entry to the hidden lands
Concealed within the sky and earth and secret zones.

Then to tell of my supreme attainment.
I possess the threefold concentration.
The wisdom mind, Samantabhadri's vastness,
Is not hid from me.
And Ultimate Reality is but my jewel and plaything.
I do not hope for Liberation
And of the pains of hell I have no fear.
Far from the nihilism of non-believers,
Such is the calm assurance of profound Dharmata!
The Great Perfection, which no action may accomplish,
Is indeed the fruit I have won,
The all-pervading Presence of the Atiyoga.

Wherever space pervades, my wisdom mind is present.
My compassion now outshines the sun.
Greater are my blessings than the following clouds,
And swifter than the rain I bring accomplishments.

My faithful ones, who follow me in future times,
Your prayers to me are thus of highest moment,
For I have forged the links that bind us.

Know that I will guide you even in the states of sorrow,
While those who turn away, forsaking me,
Will turn their backs on all the Buddhas.
Only suffering can be the fruit of such an error.
Yet even then, my love will not forsake them,
And when their karma is exhausted, they will come to me.
  Samaya Gya Gya Gya

From *The Secret Life and Songs of the Tibetan Lady Yeshe Tsogyal.*

JALAL UD·DIN RUMI of PERSIA

JALALUDDIN RUMI

FOUR

JALALUDDIN RUMI

1207–1273, AFGHANISTAN

J ALALUDDIN RUMI, founder of the Mevlevi order of Sufi dervishes, was without a doubt one of the most open-hearted and ecstatic consorts of the Beloved of all time. Born in the remote village of Balkh (now part of Afghanistan), Rumi spent most of his life in Konya, Turkey, which in the thirteenth century lay at the western edge of the Silk Road and was a mingling spot for merchants and mystics alike. There Muslims, Christians, Hindus, and even Buddhists crossed paths. In his late thirties, Rumi, a respected scholar of theology, started a school of divinity. He was a consummate Sufi, or seeker of God. Some consider Sufism to be the mystical branch of Islam; others hold it to be the pursuit of truth and communion with the Divine in any aspirant of any tradition. There is no reality, exhort the Sufis, but God; only Love, Lover, and Beloved; mere emptiness to be filled with all that is God.

Without a doubt, the defining moment of Rumi's life was his meeting, in those same streets of Konya, with Shams (meaning "sun") of Tabriz. A wandering dervish with no school of his own, Shams sought no great or subservient following. He merely sought one receptive soul spacious enough to contain his teachings and to be a companion in Divine ecstasy. As Rumi rode his donkey through the market stalls of Konya, he was pierced by the penetrating glance of Shams, and would never again be as he was. "Who," challenged Shams, "was greater—Mohammed or Bestami [a renowned Sufi master claiming to have merged with God]?" Immersed in the question, Rumi came to the realization in that very moment that he need search no further. He stood face to face with God.

Shams and Rumi became inseparable, engaging in shared communion with the Divine, sometimes spoken, often in silence. Their spirits commingled, immersed in contemplation, meditation, revelation, and celebration. Rumi's students came to be quite jealous of Shams and, in 1247, murdered him, leaving no trace of his body. Rumi was devastated, but eventually came to know that Shams was ever with him; they remained inseparable, in spirit as in body. His sublime odes to Love, Lover, and Beloved, the Sufi trinity, may be considered an ongoing dialogue with his precious teacher and companion.

The Mevlevi order has spread throughout the world, and Rumi's ecstatic verses continue to set many a heart and soul aflame. *Intoxication* is the word that most aptly describes Rumi's love affair with the Divine. Imbibing the delicious nectar of the spirit, turning 'round and 'round in absolute harmony with the music of the spheres, Rumi celebrates the dance of the spirit. A Sufi, filled with ecstasy, remarked to his companion that his cup overflowed with the wine of the spirit. So bursting was he with his Beloved that there was no room left for even one more drop of wine. "Never," the other replied, "can one have too much of God, as he floated a rose petal atop the full-to-the-brim goblet." So is the bursting heart and spirit of Jalaluddin Rumi.

The following poems and writings are all by Jalaluddin Rumi, drawn from various sources (indicated if known) and translated from the Persian by several translators, including Coleman Barks. (See the bibliography for more details.)

INTOXICATED WITH THE BELOVED

Say I Am You

I am
dust particles in sunlight.
I am the round sun.

To the bits of dust I say, *Stay*.
To the sun, *Keep moving*.

I am morning mist,
and the breathing of evening.

I am wind in the top of a grove,
and surf on the cliff.

Mast, rudder, helmsman, and keel,
I am also the coral reef they founder on.

I am a tree with a trained parrot in its branches.
Silence, thought, and voice.

The musical air coming through a flute,
a spark off a stone, a flickering in metal.

Both candle and the moth
crazy around it.

Rose and the nightingale
lost in the fragrance.

I am all orders of being,
the circling galaxy,

the evolutionary intelligence,
the lift and the falling away.

What is and what isn't.
You who know Jalaluddin,
you the One in all,
say who l am.
Say I am you.

No one knows what makes the soul
wake up so happy

Maybe a dawn breeze has blown the veil
from the face of God.

A thousand new moons appear.
Roses open laughing.

Hearts become perfect rubies
like those from Badakshan.

The body turns entirely spirit.
Leaves become branches in this wind!

Why is it now so easy to surrender,
even for those already surrendered?

There's no answer to any of this.
No one knows the source of joy.

A poet breathes into a reed flute,
and the tip of every hair makes music.

Shams sails down clods of dirt from the roof,
and we take jobs as doorkeepers for him.

Become the Sun Itself

A TRUE SEEKER must transcend those joys and delights that
are just the ray and reflection of the glory of God. He must not
let himself grow content with such things, even though they are
of God, come from God's grace, and are of the radiance of God's
beauty, for they are not eternal; with reference to God they are
eternal: with reference to man, they are not.

Think of the rays of the sun shining into houses. They are
rays of the sun, and they are light, but they are attached to the
sun and not the houses. When the sun sets, their light no more
remains.

What we have to do, then, is to *become* the Sun itself, so all
fear of separation can forever be ended.

—*Letters*

Busy Yourself with That Head

It is the time of Union, of Vision, the time of
Resurrection and Eternity.

It is the time of grace and generosity,
the sea of perfect purity.

The treasure of gifts has arrived,
the shining of the sea has flashed out.

The dawn of blessing has arisen.
Do I say dawn? No, the Light of God.

What is this "figure," this "face"?
Who is this "Emperor" and "Prince"?

What is this "ancient knowledge"?
All these are only veils—

Only ecstasies like this one
can transport you beyond them.

The source of such live waters is in your head,
and in your eyes:

Busy yourself with that head—
yet, in reality, you have two!

Your clay head comes from earth,
your pure head from heaven.

How many pure heads have rolled in the bloody dust
So you can know that it is on that head that this
    depends!

Your original head's hidden,
your derived one's manifest:
Behind this world opens an infinite universe.

—*Odes*

The Real Work

THERE IS one thing in this world that you must never forget to do. If you forget everything else and not this, there's nothing to worry about; but if you remember everything else and forget this, then you will have done nothing in your life.

It's as if a king has sent you to some country to do a task, and you perform a hundred other services, but not the one he sent you to do. So human beings come to this world to do particular work. That work is the purpose, and each is specific to the person. If you don't do it, it's as though a priceless Indian sword were used to slice rotten meat. It's a golden bowl being used to cook turnips, when one filing from the bowl could buy a hundred suitable pots. It's a knife of the finest tempering nailed into a wall to hang things on.

You say, "But look, I'm using the dagger. It's not lying idle." Do you hear how ludicrous that sounds? For a penny, an iron nail could be bought to serve the purpose. You say, "But I spend my energies on lofty enterprises. I study jurisprudence and philosophy and logic and astronomy and medicine and all the rest." But consider why you do those things. They are all branches of yourself.

Remember the deep root of your being, the presence of your lord. Give your life to the one who already owns your breath and your moments. If you don't, you will be exactly like the man who takes a precious dagger and hammers it into his kitchen wall for a peg to hold his dipper gourd. You'll be wasting valuable keenness and foolishly ignoring your dignity and your purpose.

FIVE

A DISCIPLE OF THE KABBALISTIC
SCHOOL OF ABRAHAM ABULAFIA

1240–1291, SPAIN

ABRAHAM BEN SAMUEL ABULAFIA, a Sicilian Kabbalist born in Saragosa, Spain, in 1240, is considered one of the most colorful figures in Jewish mysticism. A foremost figure in ecstatic, or prophetic, Kabbalism, Abulafia developed his own theory of Jewish mysticism. He sought a state of mystical union with God beyond the individual self. It is not surprising that this unconventional wandering prophet, apparently influenced by the Sufis during his travels, attracted quite a following.

This passionate prophet predicted the coming of the Messiah in 1295, then declared himself to be this very Messiah (messenger), calling himself the Son of God. Abulafia's rejection by the rabbis of his day did not, however, dampen his spirit and commitment. Seven hundred years before the establishment of the State of Israel, in 1280 this bold visionary addressed Pope Nicholas III in Rome to convince him of the unity of all religions and to request that the Jews be returned to their homeland. Thrown into prison and sentenced to death for his heresy, Abulafia survived and was set free after the sudden death of the pope. Never accepted by the traditional Jewish community, who refuted his audacious claims, Abulafia was exiled to the island of Malta, where he died in 1291.

Prophecy, in the eyes and heart of Abulafia, served as an expression of the love of God. Everyone who knew the name of God, according to Abulafia's teachings, embodied the Holy Spirit and was beloved by God. It was the hunger and thirst for Divine wisdom that was capable of overcoming all earthly hindrances. To love God with all one's heart, to recognize that all are created in God's sacred image, to strive day and night to meditate on the Torah, and to understand that the sacred names reflect the angels of all being sent to all those of pure devotion in order to raise them higher and higher: This was the message of Abulafia.

Abulafia offered an original technique designed to elevate the practitioner in the progressive stages of love in order to become beloved and delightful while on Earth. This method was based first on purification, then on contemplation of the letters of the name of God: YHWH. It was by constant meditation on these letters that Heaven could be attained.

Day, and especially night, Abulafia urged his disciples to detach all thoughts from the vanities of the world, to don white garments and a prayer shawl, and to partake of the gladness of the heart through deep introspection and concentration.

The combinations and permutations of the letters, undertaken with a warm heart filled with yearning for God, would then invoke the presence of the holy on high and of the exalted angels. The entire body, predicted Abulafia, would be seized with a trembling so powerful as to resemble a death rattle. Then the soul, overjoyed and filled with ecstasy, would instead be overcome with an influx of God's spirit and love

The story is the testimony of an unnamed disciple of Abulafia, who applied the method of his teacher diligently and with great success. It first appeared in 1295 in a book called *Sha'arei Zedek*. The translation, by G. Scholem, is from *Major Trends in Jewish Mysticism*.

KABBALAH:
THE SECRET NAMES OF GOD

I returned to my native land and God brought me together with a Jewish philosopher with whom I studied some of Maimonides' *Guide of the Perplexed* and this only added to my desire. I acquired a little of the science of logic and a little of natural science, and this was very sweet to me for, as you know, "nature attracts nature." And God is my witness: If I had not previously acquired strength of faith by what little I had learned of the Torah and the Talmud, the impulse to keep many of the religious commands would have left me although the fire of pure intention was ablaze in my heart. But what this teacher communicated to me in the way of philosophy (on the meaning of the commandments), did not suffice me, until the Lord had me meet a godly man, a kabbalist who taught me the general outlines of the Kabbalah. Nevertheless, in consequence of my smattering of natural science, the way of Kabbalah seemed all but impossible to me. It was then that my teacher said to me: "My son, why do you deny something you have not tried? Much, rather, would it befit you to make a trial of it. If you then should find that it is nothing to you—and if you are not perfect enough to find the fault with yourself—then you may say that there is nothing to it." But in order to make things sweet to me until my reason might accept them and I might penetrate into them with eagerness, he used always to make me grasp in a natural way everything in which he instructed me. I reasoned thus within myself: There can only be gain here and no loss. I shall see; if I find something in all of this, that is sheer gain; and if not, that which I have already had will still be mine. So I gave in and he taught me the method of the permutations and combinations of letters and the mysticism of numbers and the other "Paths of the book Yezirah." In each path he had me wander for two weeks until each form had been engraven in my heart, and so he led on for four months or so and then ordered me to "efface" everything.

He used to tell me: "My son, it is not the intention that you come to a stop with some finite or given form, even though it be of the highest order. Much rather is this the 'Path of the Names.' The less understandable they are, the higher their order, until you arrive at the activity of a force which is no longer under your control, but rather your reason and your thought are in its control." I replied: "If that be so [that all mental and sense images must be effaced], why then do you, Sir, compose books in which the methods of the natural scientists are coupled with instruction in the holy Names?" He answered: "For you and the likes of you among the followers of philosophy, to allure your human intellect through natural means, so that perhaps this attraction may cause you to arrive at the knowledge of the Holy Name." And he produced books for me made up (of combinations of) letters and names and mystic numbers, of which nobody will ever be able to understand anything, for they are not composed in a way meant to be understood. He said to me: "This is the 'Path of the Names.'" And indeed, I would see none of it, for my reason did accept it. He said, "It was very stupid of me to have shown them to you."

In short, after two months had elapsed and my thought had disengaged itself (from everything material) and I had become aware of strange phenomena occurring within me, I set myself the task at night of combining letters with one another and of pondering over them in philosophical meditation, a little different from the way I do now, and so I continued for three nights without telling him. The third night, after midnight, I nodded off a little, quill in my hands and paper on my knees. Then I noticed that the candle was about to go out. I rose to put it right, as oftentimes happens to a person awake. Then I saw that the light continued. I was greatly astonished, as though, after close examination, I saw that it issued from myself. I said: "I do not believe it." I walked to and fro all through the house and, behold, the light is with me; I lay on a couch and covered myself up, and behold, the light is with me all the while. I said: "This is truly a great sign and a new phenomenon which I have perceived."

The next morning I communicated it to my teacher and I brought him the sheets which I had covered with combinations of letters. He congratulated me and said: "My son, if you would devote yourself to combining holy Names, still greater things would happen to you. And now, my son, admit that you are unable to bear not combining. Give half to this and half to that, that is, do combinations half of the night, and permutations half of the night." I practiced this method for about a week. During the second week the power of meditation became so strong in me that I could not manage to write down the combinations of letters (which automatically spurted out of my pen), and if there had been ten people present they would not have been able to write down so many combinations as came to me during the influx. When I came to the night in which this power was conferred on me, and midnight—when this power especially expands and gains strength whereas the body weakens—had passed, I set out to take up the Great Name of God, consisting of seventy-two names, permuting and combining it. But when I had done this for a little while, behold, the letters took on in my eyes the shape of great mountains, strong trembling seized me and I could summon no strength, my hair stood on end, and it was as if I were not in this world. At once I fell down, for I no longer felt the least strength in any of my limbs. And behold, something resembling speech emerged from my heart and came to my lips and forced them to move. I thought—perhaps this is, God forbid, a spirit of madness that has entered into me? But behold, I saw it uttering wisdom. I said: "This is indeed the spirit of wisdom." After a little while my natural strength returned to me, I rose very much impaired and I still did not believe myself. Once more I took up the Name to do with it as before and, behold, it had exactly the same effect on me. Nevertheless I did not believe until I had tried it four or five times.

When I got up in the morning I told my teacher about it. He said to me: "And who was it that allowed you to touch the Name? Did I not tell you to permute only letters?" He spoke on: "What happened to you represents indeed a high stage among prophetic degrees." He wanted to free me of it for he saw that my face had changed. But I said to him: "In heaven's name, can you perhaps impart to me some power to enable me to bear this force emerging from my heart and to receive influx from it?" For I wanted to draw this force towards me and receive influx from it, for it much resembles a spring filling a great basin with water. If a man (not being properly prepared for it) should open the dam, he would be drowned in its waters and his soul would desert him. He said to me: "My son, it is the Lord who must bestow such power upon you, for such power is not within man's control."

That Sabbath night also the power was active in me in the same way. When after two sleepless nights, I had passed day and night in meditating on the permutations or on the principles essential to a recognition of the true reality and to the annihilations of all extraneous thought—then I had two signs by which I knew that I was in the right receptive mood. The one sign was the intensification of natural thought on very profound objects of knowledge, a debility of the body and strengthening of the soul until I sat there, myself all soul. The second sign was that imagination grew strong within me and it seemed as though my forehead was going to burst. Then I knew that I was ready to receive the Name. I also, that Sabbath night, ventured at the great ineffable Name of God (the name YHWH). But immediately that I touched it, it weakened me and a voice issued from me saying: "Thou shalt surely die and not live! Who brought thee to touch the Great Name?" And behold, immediately I fell prone and implored the Lord God saying: "Lord of the universe! I entered into this place only for the sake of heaven, as Thy glory knoweth. What is my sin and what my transgression? I entered only to know Thee, for has not David already commanded Solomon: "Know the God of thy father and serve Him"; and has not our master Moses, peace be upon him, revealed this to us in the Torah saying: "Show me now Thy way, that I may know Thee, that I may there find grace in Thy sight?" And behold, I was still speaking and oil like the oil of the anointment anointed me from head to foot and very great joy seized me which for its spirituality and the sweetness of its rapture I cannot describe.

All this happened to your servant in his beginnings. And I do not, God forbid, relate this account from boastfulness in order to be thought great in the eyes of the mob, for I know full well that greatness with the mob is deficiency and inferiority with those searching for the true rank which differs from it in genus and in species as light from darkness.

From the testament of an unknown Spanish disciple
of the Kabbalist, Abraham Abulafia.

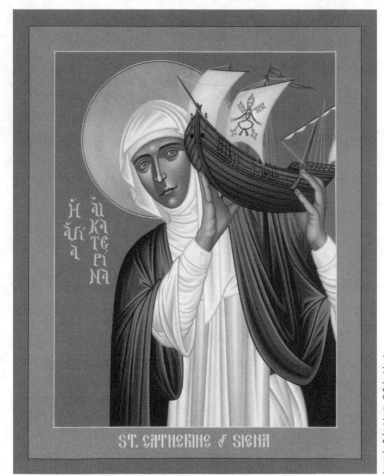

Image by Robert Lentz, © Robert Lentz.

ST. CATHERINE OF SIENA

SAINT CATHERINE OF SIENA

SIX

SAINT CATHERINE OF SIENA

1347–1380, ITALY

ATERINA BENINCASA was born in 1347, the twenty-fifth child of an Italian family of modest means. Enjoying sublime visions and practicing extreme austerities from a tender age, Catherine consecrated her virginity to Christ at the age of seven. When her parents attempted to betroth her at sixteen, she incurred their wrath by cutting off her hair. In turn, they deprived her of a private prayer space, dismissed the maid, and placed Catherine in charge of the household work. Imagining her father to be Jesus, her mother the blessed Mary, and the rest of the family to be the disciples of Jesus, she toiled blissfully. It was when her father witnessed a white dove hovering above her head as she prayed that he finally recognized his daughter's destiny as a nun.

At sixteen, Catherine joined the Third Order of Saint Dominic in Siena and, shortly after, experienced several years of celestial visitations, intimate conversations with Christ, and what she considered to be her marriage to Jesus. Three years later, after rejoining her family, Catherine became known for her remarkable gift of contemplation and her loving devotion to the plague-stricken and the destitute. Austerities were an integral part of Catherine's practice, inspired perhaps by the example of Mary Magdalene, who spent thirty-three years (the age at which Catherine died) rapt in contemplation in her cave retreat, taking little or no food. Just as Mary Magdalene was said to have been lifted by the angels seven times daily, so enraptured was Catherine in the mysteries of God that her body was frequently lifted into the air, her soul in ecstatic communion with her Beloved. Oblivious to physical suffering, material needs, and persecution by friars and sisters of her own order, Catherine attracted a following of disciples drawn by her radiance and simplicity.

Catherine spent much of her time in sublime contemplation of her Lord, the angels, and the heavens. Once, while engaged in fervent prayer, Catherine begged Him to purify her spirit by removing her heart and will. So thoroughly convinced was she that her Heavenly Bridegroom had granted her wish that she insisted that she was living without a heart. Days later, upon emerging from profound contemplation, she beheld herself embraced in light. There appeared her Lord, holding in His holy hands a bright red, glistening, human heart. Just as he had taken away her own heart, he now offered her His own forever. As proof of the miracle, a scar remained in the flesh of her chest.

Dedicated tirelessly to the reformation of the church, and continuing to serve the poor and afflicted, Catherine's strength was quickly depleted. Following a three-month period of mysterious agony and ecstasy, Catherine succumbed at the age of thirty-three. Several weeks before her death, while praying fervently in St. Peter's Basilica, she had a vision of St. Peter's fishing boat. It came out of a mosaic and landed on her shoulder, crushing her to the floor. She became nearly paralyzed until her untimely death at such a tender age. In the year of her death, 1380, the church reconciled its differences, the goal for which Catherine had so tirelessly devoted herself. Canonized in 1461, Saint Catherine's feast day is April 29.

The passages are excerpted from *The Life of Saint Catherine of Siena* by Blessed Raymond of Capua, a Dominican priest who was Catherine's dear friend and confessor. He speaks of his experiences with her in the first person.

THE BRIDE OF CHRIST

Ecstasies and Revelations

AT THIS TIME, when the Lord had granted His bride a particular way of living as regards the body, he likewise comforted her soul with great and extraordinary revelations, and the supernatural vigor of her body certainly resulted from this abundance of spiritual graces. And now that we have described in the utmost detail Catherine's bodily life, it is requisite to go on to recount the vigor of her spirit.

Know then, reader, that from the time when this virgin drank the water of life from the Lord's side, she abounded in such fullness of graces that she was almost always in a state of contemplation, and her spirit was so absorbed in the Creator that she spent most of her time in a region beyond sense. This . . . I experienced personally time and time again, and so did others, who saw and touched, as I did, her arms and hands, which remained so numb while she was in a state of contemplation that it would have been easier to break them than to get them to move. Her eyes remained tightly shut, her ears could not hear the loudest noise, and none of her bodily senses performed its accustomed functions. You will not find this astonishing if you follow carefully all that follows.

The Lord began to appear to His bride not only privately, as He had done at first, but in public too, in fact before everyone's eyes and quite familiarly, both when she was walking about and when she was standing still, and He set such a fire blazing within her heart that she herself told her confessor that she could not find words to express the divine experiences she had.

Once, when she was praying to the Lord with the utmost fervor, saying to Him as the Prophet had done, "Create a clean heart within me, O God, and renew a right spirit within my bowels,'" and asking Him again and again to take her own heart and will from her, He comforted her with this vision. It appeared to her that her Heavenly Bridegroom came to her as usual, opened her left side, took out her heart, and then went away. This vision was so effective and agreed so well with what she felt inside herself that in confession she told her confessor that she no longer had a heart in her breast. He shook his head a little at this way of putting it, and in a joking way reproved her; but she repeated it and insisted that she meant what she said. "Truly, Father," she said, "in so far as I feel anything at all, it seems to me that my heart has been taken away altogether. The Lord did indeed appear to me, opened my left side, took my heart out and went away." Her confessor then pointed out that it is impossible to live without a heart, but the virgin replied that nothing is impossible to God, and that she was convinced that she no longer had a heart. And for some time she went on repeating this, that she was living without a heart.

One day she was in the church of the Preaching Friars, which the Sisters of Penance of Saint Dominic in Siena used to attend. The others had gone out, but she went on praying. Finally she came out of her ecstasy and got up to go home. All at once a light from heaven encircled her, and in the light appeared the Lord, holding in His holy hands a human heart, bright red and shining. At the appearance of the Author of Light she had fallen to the ground, trembling all over, but He came up to her, opened her left side once again and put the heart He was holding in His hands inside her, saying, "Dearest daughter, as I took your heart away from you the other day, now, you see, I am giving you mine, so that you can go on living with it for ever." With these words He closed the opening He had made in her side, and as a sign of the miracle a scar remained on that part of her flesh, as I and others were told by her companions who saw it. When I determined to get to the truth, she herself was obliged to confess to me that this was so, and she added that never afterwards had she been able to say, "Lord, I give you my heart."

After the reception of this heart, then, in such a gracious and marvelous way, from the abundance of its graces poured forth Catherine's great works and her most marvelous revelations. In point of fact she never approached the sacred altar without being shown many things beyond the range of the senses, especially when she received Holy Communion. She often saw a baby hidden in the hands of the priest; sometimes it was a slightly older boy; or again, she might see a burning fiery furnace, into which the priest seemed to enter at the moment when he consumed the sacred Species. When she herself received the most adorable Sacrament, she would often smell such a strong sweet smell that she almost fainted. Seeing or receiving the Sacrament of the Altar always generated fresh and indescribable bliss in her soul, so that her heart would very often throb with joy within her breast, making such a loud noise that it could be heard even by her companions. At last, having noticed this so often, they told her confessor Fra Tommaso about it. He made a close inquiry into the matter and on finding it was true, left the fact in writing as an imperishable record.

This noise bore no resemblance to the gurgling that goes on naturally in the human stomach; there was nothing natural about the noise at all. There is nothing surprising in the fact that a heart given in a supernatural way should act in a supernatural way too, for, as the Prophet says, "My heart and my flesh have rejoiced in the Living God," that is to say, "They have jumped out, into the Living God."

The Prophet says, "the living God," to signify that this special beating or heart action, being caused by the true Life, does not bring death to the person to whom it happens as it would in the ordinary course of nature, but Life.

After the miraculous exchange of hearts the virgin felt a different person, and she said to her confessor Fra Tommaso, "Can't you see, Father, that I am not the person I was, but am changed into someone else?" And she went on, "If only you could understand how I feel, Father! I don't believe that anyone who really knew how I feel inside could be obstinate enough not to be softened or be proud enough not to humble himself, for all that I reveal is nothing compared to what I feel." She described what she was experiencing, saying, "My mind is so full of joy and happiness that I am amazed my soul stays in my body." And she also said, "There is so much heat in my soul that this material fire seems cool by comparison, rather than to be giving out heat; it seems to have gone out, rather than to be still burning." And again, "This heat has generated in my mind a renewal of purity and humility, so that I seem to have gone back to the age of four or five. And at the same time so much love of my fellow-men has blazed up in me that I could face death for them cheerfully and with great joy in my heart." All this she told her confessor alone, in secret; but from others she hid as much as she could.

Words and happenings like this give some idea of this abundance the Lord had infused into the holy virgin's soul at this time, in a way far beyond the ordinary. But if I tried to describe everything in detail it would mean writing several books; so I have decided to collect together only a few things that nevertheless provide extraordinary evidence of Catherine's sanctity.

You must now know then, dearest reader, that while this abundance of graces was being poured from on high into Catherine's soul, many remarkable visions were being revealed to her from heaven, and it would be a sin to pass them all over in silence.

First of all the King of Kings appeared to her with the Queen of heaven, His Mother, and Mary Magdalene, to comfort and strengthen her in her holy intentions. The Lord said to her, "What do you want?" And she, weeping, said to Him, as Peter had done, "Lord, you know what I want; you know, because I have no will but yours and no heart but yours." At that moment she remembered how Mary Magdalene had given herself wholly to Christ when she had wept at His feet; and she began to feel something of the delightful sweetness and love that the Magdalene must have experienced at that time; and so she turned her eyes towards her. The Lord, as though to satisfy Catherine's desire, said to her, "Sweetest daughter, for your greater comfort I give you Mary Magdalene for your mother. Turn to her in absolute confidence; I entrust her with a special care of you." The virgin gratefully accepted this offer, commended herself with great humility and veneration to the Magdalene, and begged her earnestly and passionately to take care of her now that she had been entrusted to her by the Lord. From that moment the virgin felt entirely at one with the Magdalene and always referred to her as her mother.

In my view this had a very serious significance. As Mary Magdalene spent thirty-three years—a period of time which equals the Savior's own age—in her cave in continual contemplation without taking any food, so, from the time of this vision until the time she was thirty-three, when she died, Catherine devoted herself with such fervor to the contemplation of the Most High that, feeling no need of food, she found nourishment for her mind with the abundance of graces she received. And as Mary Magdalene was taken up into the air by the angels seven times a day so that she could listen to the mysteries of God, so Catherine was for most of the time taken out of the world of the senses by the power of the Spirit, to contemplate heavenly things and praise the Lord with the Angels. The result was that her body was frequently lifted into the air, as many people, both men and women, claim to have seen. But we shall discuss this in more detail later.

During these raptures, while she was contemplating the marvels of God, she would be all the while muttering wonderful phrases and the most profound sayings, some of which were written down, as we shall explain when the time comes.

On the feast day of the Apostle's conversion our virgin was rapt in ecstasy and her spirit ascended so high that for three days and nights she gave not the slightest sign of life. Those present believed her dead, or on the point of death. A few, however, who understood what was happening considered that she had been taken up by the Apostle into the third heaven. Time passed, and the ecstasy came to an end; but her spirit, drunk with the heavenly things it had seen, seemed so reluctant to return to the things of earth that she remained in a sort of daze, like a drunkard who is stupefied but not asleep.

I went off to see her in a state of the utmost concern, and did all I could to find out what she was thinking, imploring her to tell me the truth. Instead of answering me, she burst into tears. After a while she said, "Father, would you feel sorry for a soul that had been freed from a dark prison, seen a light that made her blissfully happy, and then was once again locked up in darkness? That unhappy person is me! And it all happened to me because of my own fault, God's providence having so decreed." These words increased my curiosity to know how anything so portentous had happened to her, and I said, "Mother, was your soul really separated from your body?" She replied, "The fire of Divine Love and the longing to be united with Him I love had burned so high that even if my heart had been made of stone or steel it would have been split apart in just the same way.

"I am convinced that no created thing could have made my heart proof against the violence of that love. So you can take it as certain that my heart broke from top to bottom and split apart, solely as a result of the violence of that love, and I still seem able to feel the wound that splitting apart made. This will give you some idea whether my soul was separated from my body. And I saw divine mysteries that no living soul can utter because memory has no hold over them and there are no words capable of describing things so sublime: any words that were used would be like mud compared with gold. One thing I do retain from the experience, however, is this; that whenever I hear people talking about what happened to me I get very upset, because it reminds me of what a worthless state I have been reduced to after rising to such heights of nobility; and the only way my disappointment can express itself is in tears."

On hearing this, desirous as I was to learn the most minute details of what had happened to her, I said, "Mother, you never keep any secrets from me; well, then, I beg you, describe this miraculous event to me down to the last detail." She said: "In those days, after many ecstasies and visions and after receiving many spiritual favors from the Lord, I fell ill, entirely overcome by love of Him, and had to go to bed, where I prayed to him continuously to take me from the body of this death, that I might be more closely united with Him. I did not obtain this, but I did finally manage to get Him to communicate the pains that He had felt to me, in so far as I was able to bear them."

Then she told me what I have related above about the Lord's Passion. She went on: "From these teachings about His Passion I got a much clearer idea of how much my Creator had loved me, and this so increased my love that I languished to the point of wanting only one thing, that my soul should depart from my body. Each day He himself increased the fire that He had lit within my heart until It could bear it no longer, and the love became as strong as death: then the heart broke in two, as I said, and my soul was set free from this flesh of mine. But unfortunately for all too short a time!"

"How long," I asked, "did your soul remain outside the body?" "Those who saw my death," she answered, "say that four hours elapsed between the time I expired and the time I came back to life. Quite a lot of people in the neighborhood went and told my mother and family the sad news. But my soul, which believed it had entered eternity, lost all account of time."

"And during those hours, Mother, what did you see," I asked. "How did your soul come back into the body? Tell me all about it: don't hide anything from me."

"Father," Catherine said, "my soul saw and understood everything in the other world that to us is invisible: that is to say, the glory of the Saints and the pains of sinners. I have already told you: the memory cannot keep anything of it and words are not adequate to describe it; but as far as I can I will try to tell you about it. You can be certain, then, that my soul contemplated the Divine Essence; that is why I am now always so discontented with being in the prison of the body. If I was not sustained by love of Him and love of my fellow-men, for whom He sent me back into the world, I should die of misery. Nevertheless, it is infinite comfort to me to know that I suffer what I do suffer: it is through suffering that I shall enjoy a more sublime vision of God. For this reason alone, my tribulations do not weigh on me; in fact they bring comfort to my soul, as you and the others who are with me can witness daily.

From *The Life of St. Catherine of Siena* by Blessed Raymond of Capua.

Image courtesy of the American Institute of Indian Studies. Original (1825) is in the Government Museum, Jaipur, India.

KABIR

SEVEN

KABIR

CIRCA 1440–1518, INDIA

KABIR, a weaver by trade, was simple and uneducated, yet he had little patience for narrow-mindedness of spirit, whether Hindu or Muslim. Rather, he sought to dance in pure rapture with the infinite, the fathomless. This heart-filled mystic spoke to the common folk of his day: the priests and the warriors, tradesmen and barbers, washwomen and carpenters, *sadhus* (wandering spiritual seekers) and beggars. An ecstatic poet, artisan, musician, husband, and father, Kabir rejected austerities and found little virtue in asceticism.

Born in the most sacred Hindu city of Benares (Varanasi), at an early age Kabir was drawn to a renowned Hindu guru, Ramananda. Convinced there was no way that a Hindu teacher would accept a Muslim disciple, Kabir hid on the steps of the river Ganges, knowing that Ramananda would soon need to cross his path on the way to the bathing *ghat*, where Hindus performed their daily ablutions. As the master inadvertently stepped on Kabir, Ramananda shouted "Ram," a Hindu name for God. Kabir claimed this to be his mantra of initiation.

Bound by neither Hinduism nor Islam, Kabir courted the Beloved in its infinite, eternal, limitless form. Kabir's ecstatic expressions bear great similarity to those of Rumi and other Sufi poets. Proclaiming himself to be "the child of Allah and of Ram," he urged sadhus and monks to rejoice rather than retreat. "There is nothing but water at the holy bathing places; and I know that they are useless, for I have bathed in them." For Kabir, the mystical search lay beyond images, rituals, or scriptures.

Kabir's poetry celebrates his sublime love affair with the Divine. His heart dances with joy, unstruck music resounds, streams of light flow in all directions, and the fragrance of sandalwood and flowers permeates the atmosphere. The Beloved gleams like a flash of lightning, a chorus of music fills the heavens day and night. An overflowing heart drunk with Divine spirit, a swan having taken flight to the lake beyond the mountains, the ravished eyes of the Lover united with the Beloved. These are the passionate reveries of one who has himself become intoxicated with and ravished by God. For Kabir, a moment engaged in anything less than the most passionate devotion to ultimate union was a wasted one, full of misery and unfulfilled longing.

It is of little surprise that such an outspoken, free thinker was the object of persecution by his contemporaries. Ultimately banished from Benares around the age of sixty, Kabir spent the next eighteen years pursuing ever more passionately his longing for oneness with his beloved God. The story goes that, after Kabir's death, the Muslims insisted on burying his body and the Hindus on cremating his remains. Amidst their arguing, Kabir appeared before them, instructing them to lift the shroud and examine what lay beneath it. There they found only flowers, half of which were buried according to Islamic tradition, the other half burned in Benares. Even in death, Kabir's spirit would not be bound by the limitations of a single creed.

These Kabir poems are the famous Indian poet and writer Rabindrath Tagore's translation from the original Hindi. The first line from the Hindi leads each piece.

BEYOND DOGMA TO DIVINITY

grah candra tapan jot varat hai
The light of the sun, the moon, and the stars shines bright:
The melody of love swells forth, and the rhythm of love's
    detachment beats the time.
Day and night, the chorus of music fills the heavens; and Kabir
    says
"My Beloved One gleams like the lightning flash in the sky."

Do you know how the moments perform their adoration?
Waving its row of lamps, the universe sings in worship day and
    night,
There are the hidden banner and the secret canopy:
There the sound of the unseen bells is heard.
Kabir says: "There adoration never ceases;
there the Lord of the Universe sitteth on His throne."

The whole world does its works and commits its errors:
but few are the lovers who know the Beloved.
The devout seeker is he who mingles in his heart the double
    currents of love and detachment, like the mingling of the
    streams of Ganges and Jumna;
In his heart the sacred water flows day and night;
and thus the round of births and deaths is brought to an end.

Behold what wonderful rest is in the Supreme Spirit!
and he enjoys it, who makes himself meet for it.
Held by the cords of love, the swing of the Ocean of Joy
sways to and fro; and a mighty sound breaks forth in song.
See what a lotus blooms there without water!
and Kabir says "My heart's bee drinks its nectar."

What a wonderful lotus it is, that blooms at the heart of the
    spinning wheel of the universe! Only a few pure souls know
    of its true delight.
Music is all around it, and there the heart partakes of the joy of
    the Infinite Sea.
Kabir says: "Dive thou into that Ocean of sweetness: thus let all
    errors of life and of death flee away."

Behold how the thirst of the five senses is quenched there!
and the three forms of misery are no more!
Kabir says: "It is the sport of the Unattainable One:
look within, and behold how the moon-beams of that Hidden
    One shine in you."

There falls the rhythmic beat of life and death:
Rapture wells forth, and all space is radiant with light.
There the Unstruck Music is sounded;
it is the music of the love of the three worlds.
There millions of lamps of sun and of moon are burning;
There the drum beats, and the lover swings in play.
There love-songs resound, and light rains in showers;
and the worshiper is entranced in the taste of the heavenly nectar.
Look upon life and death; there is no separation between them,
The right hand and the left hand are one and the same.
Kabir says: "There the wise man is speechless;
for this truth may never be found in Vedas or in books."

I have had my Seat on the Self-poised One,
I have drunk of the Cup of the Ineffable,
I have found the Key of the Mystery,
I have reached the Root of Union.

Traveling by no track, I have come to the Sorrowless Land:
very easily has the mercy of the great Lord come upon me.
They have sung of Him as infinite and unattainable:
but I in my meditations have seen Him without sight.

That is indeed the sorrowless land, and none know the path
    that leads there:
Only he who is on that path has surely transcended all sorrow.
Wonderful is that land of rest, to which no merit can win;
It is the wise who has seen it, it is the wise who has sung of it.
This is the Ultimate Word: but can any express its marvelous
    savor?
He who has savored it once, he knows what joy it can give.
Kabir says: "Knowing it, the ignorant man becomes wise, and
    the wise man becomes speechless and silent,
The worshiper is utterly inebriated,
His wisdom and his detachment are made perfect;
He drinks from the cup of the inbreathings and the out-
    breathings of love."

There the whole sky is filled with sound, and there that music
    is made without fingers and without strings;
There the game of pleasure and pain does not cease.
Kabir says: "If you merge your life in the Ocean of Life, you will
    find your life in the Supreme Land of Bliss."

What a frenzy of ecstasy there is in every hour!
and the worshiper is pressing out and drinking the essence of
    the hours:
he lives in the life of Brahma.
I speak truth, for I have accepted truth in life;
I am now attached to truth, I have swept all tinsel away.
Kabir says: "Thus is the worshiper set free from fear;
thus have all errors of life and of death left him."

There the sky is filled with music:
There it rains nectar:
There the harp-strings jingle, and there the drums beat.

What a secret splendor is there, in the mansion of the sky!
There no mention is made of the rising and the setting of the sun;
In the ocean of manifestation, which is the light of love, day
    and night are felt to be one.
Joy for ever, no sorrow, no struggle!
There have I seen joy filled to the brim, perfection of joy;
No place for error is there.
Kabir says: "There have I witnessed the sport of One Bliss!"

I have known in my body the sport of the universe: I have
    escaped from the error of this world.
The inward and the outward are become as one sky, the Infinite
    and the finite are united: I am drunken with the sight of
    this All!
This Light of Thine fulfils the universe: the lamp of love that
    burns on the salver of knowledge.
Kabir says: "There error cannot enter, and the conflict of life
    and death is felt no more."

santo, sahaj samadh bhali
O Sadhu! the simple union is the best.
Since the day when I met with my Lord, there has been no end
    to the sport of our love.
I shut not my eyes, I close not my ears, I do not mortify my body;
I see with eyes open and smile, and behold His beauty everywhere:
I utter His Name, and whatever I see, it reminds me of Him;
    whatever I do, it becomes His worship.
The rising and the setting are one to me; all contradictions are
    solved.
Wherever I go, I move round Him,
All I achieve is His service:
When I lie down, I lie prostrate at His feet.

He is the only adorable one to me: I have none other.
My tongue has left off impure words, it sings His glory day and
    night:
Whether I rise or sit down, I can never forget Him; for the
    rhythm of His music beats in my ears.
Kabir says: "My heart is frenzied, and I disclose in my soul
    what is hidden. I am immersed in that one great bliss which
    transcends all pleasure and pain."

tirath men to sab pani hai
There is nothing but water at the holy bathing places;
and I know that they are useless, for I have bathed in them.
The images are all lifeless, they cannot speak;
I know, for I have cried aloud to them.
The Purana and the Koran are mere words; lifting up the
    curtain, I have seen.
Kabir gives utterance to the words of experience; and he knows
    very well that all other things are untrue.

murali bajat akhand sadaye

The flute of the Infinite is played without ceasing, and its sound
    is love:

When love renounces all limits, it reaches truth.

How widely the fragrance spreads! It has no end, nothing stands
    in its way.

The form of this melody is bright like a million suns:

incomparably sounds the vina, the vina of the notes of truth.

---

sil santosh sada samadrishti

He who is meek and contented, he who has an equal vision,
    whose mind is filled with the fullness of acceptance and
    of rest;

He who has seen Him and touched Him, he is freed from all
    fear and trouble.

To him the perpetual thought of God is like sandal paste
    smeared on the body, to him nothing else is delight:

His work and his rest are filled with music: he sheds abroad the
    radiance of love.

Kabir says: "Touch His feet, who is one and indivisible, im-
    mutable and peaceful; who fills all vessels to the brim with
    joy, and whose form is love."

From *Songs of Kabir*, translated by Rabindranath Tagore.

The headlines of the poems are from *Shantiniketana: Kabir* by Shri Kshitimohan Sen.

GENDUN GYATSO PALZANGPO

EIGHT

GENDUN GYATSO PALZANGPO

1475–1541, TIBET

KUNGA GYALTSEN, father of Gendun Gyatso Palzangpo, the Second Dalai Lama, was himself a highly respected lama. His wife was recognized as a reincarnation of a thirteenth-century yogini who, from childhood, was able to recall many of her previous incarnations. Both were direct disciples of the First Dalai Lama. Around the time of the death of the First Dalai Lama, Kunga performed intently the practice of dream yoga. First a young boy appeared to him. Then arrived the First Dalai Lama, his body elderly yet emblazoned with light, who flew off with the boy to a meditation cave. In a second dream the First Dalai Lama instructed Kunga to gather his robes and bowl from the monastery. Shortly afterward, his wife dreamed that a tiny blue light entered her womb and shone with great brightness, filling her body and overflowing through her every pore.

The child is said to have been born with exceedingly clear eyes and to have greeted everyone present. Also at birth, legend has it, the infant turned his radiant countenance toward the monastery of his predecessor, placed his palms together, and recited the sacred mantra of the mother of all Buddhas. As a toddler, he showed little interest in games or other typical childhood pastimes, preferring instead to sit on rocks and give imaginative blessings to the multitudes before him.

According to Tibetan tradition, the young boy was ordained as a monk and was given the name Gendun Gyatso Palzangpo, which means "Sublimely Glorious Ocean of Spiritual Aspirants." At the age of thirteen, he was at his mother's bedside when she passed on to the next world and at sixteen, during meditation retreat, he precipitously remembered many hundreds of his previous reincarnations.

Energetic, articulate, and radiant, the Second Dalai Lama taught lamas of all the various sects, although he belonged primarily to the Gelugpa school. Dreams came to him of a lake and of his dharma (duty) to release its powers. And so he constructed the Chokhor Gyal Monastery and empowered the Lake of Visions, which continues to be a very sacred pilgrim destination among Tibetans. The Second Dalai Lama devoted his time to teaching visiting disciples from all over central Asia, coordinating the creation of hundreds of precious statues and paintings, and serving as the head lama of both Drepung and Sera monasteries.

According to the Fourteenth Dalai Lama, Tenzin Gyatso, the Second Dalai Lama was the greatest of all the early Dalai Lamas. He was profoundly realized and was appreciated as both a great Buddhist scholar and a highly advanced spiritual practitioner. His Holiness explains that his predecessor used to call himself a "Mad Beggar," indicative not of insanity or poverty, but rather his complete nonattachment. When an adept gains the experience of *Shunyata,* or Emptiness, as achieved by the Second Dalai Lama, he may appear mad, for he has completely transcended the material world. The Mad Dalai Lama was an extremely prolific writer and teacher. He authored many philosophical treatises, but was especially loved for his more intimate spiritual songs or poems, which spoke of his own experiences.

The poems of the Second Dalai Lama come from the Tibetan manuscript of his original work, *Mystical Verses of a Mad Dalai Lama,* translated by Glen H. Mullin, who borrowed H. H. The Dalai Lama's personal copy to make the translation.

POEMS OF A MAD DALAI LAMA

Ah-oh-la: The Wise They Sing

The ultimate nature of spiritual realization
Is final union of light and the void.
Ah-oh-la, the wise they sing: ya-yi ya-yi,
It is the union of light and the void.

Ah-oh-la, the wise they sing:
The final taste of all that exists
Is voidness empty of self-nature.

Ah-oh-la, the wise they sing: ya-yi ya-yi,
Yet all things in the world and beyond,
Sketches drawn by the conceptual mind,
Still retain a conventional impact.

Ah-oh-la, the wise they sing: ya-yi ya-yi,
This profound nature free from extremes
Is the vision to be accomplished.

Ah-oh-la, the wise they sing: ya-yi ya-yi,
Such is Nagarjuna's and Aryadeva's lineage;
And I, a yogi who follows in their footsteps,
Am delighted to be part of it.

Ah-oh-la, the wise they sing: ya-yi ya-yi,
This mystical dance of the profound view
Flashes in the sphere free from extremes.

Ah-oh-la, the wise they sing: ya-yi ya-yi,
The gentle aspiration to highest enlightenment,
That cares for others more than oneself,
Is the very door opening to the Great Way.

Ah-oh-la, the wise they sing: ya-yi ya-yi,
Wisdom of voidness grasped by this compassion
Is the very essence of the Great Way.

Ah-oh-la, the wise they sing: ya-yi ya-yi,
This, practiced as the six perfections,
Is the mighty bodhisattva path.

Ah-oh-la, the wise they sing: ya-yi ya-yi,
Such is Maitreya's and Asanga's lineage;
And I, a yogi who follows in their footsteps,
Am delighted to be part of it.

Ah-oh-la, the wise they sing: ya-yi ya-yi,
This mystical dance of vast ways is
A dance of method and wisdom combined.

Ah-oh-la, the wise they sing: ya-yi ya-yi,
The yogic methods of tantra's two stages
Are the highest means for producing Buddhahood.

Ah-oh-la, the wise they sing: ya-yi ya-yi,
They transform death, bardo, and rebirth
Into enlightenment's three perfect kayas.

Ah-oh-la, the wise they sing: ya-yi ya-yi,
Such is the lineage of Lama Tsongkhapa;
And I, a yogi who follows in his footsteps
Am delighted to be part of it.

Through it the dance of great bliss and void
Comes to pervade one's every experience.
Ah-oh-la, the wise they sing: ya-yi ya-yi,
It comes to pervade one's every experience.

Song of Tantric Experience

Homage to Vajrasattva, the Diamond Warrior.
The peerless tantric master
Is the source of all spiritual knowledge.
One places his feet on the crown of one's head
And becomes satiated with the ambrosial nectars
Of his blessings and transforming powers.

One begins by filling the vase of one's heart
With the waters of the four tantric initiations,
Which transform the mind into an appropriate vessel
For cultivation of the sublime vajra path.

From that time onward one should always cherish
The commitments of the tantric way

As deeply as one cherishes one's life,
Never letting ourself become like those yogis
Who pretend to be great tantric practitioners
But in fact are little better than dogs and pigs.

First one must gain unmistaken experience in
The methods of taking death, bardo, and rebirth
As the path of the three perfect kayas,
A training that extracts the very essence
Of the profound generation stage yogas.
In this way the divinity of great bliss
Arises from within the sphere of the void.

The flowing energies of sun and moon
Then block the path of darkness,
And one perceives the innate great bliss
Born together with wisdom of the void.

The most subtle aspects of energy and mind
Manifest like a fish rising in a clear pool.
one sends forth a net of mystical emanations
And becomes freed forever from the great abyss
Of conventional birth and death.

The highest bliss and wisdom then shine
Like a sun at the center of the heart, halting
All activity of attachment, aversion, and ignorance.
This is the unmistaken state of mahamudra, the Great
    Seal.

Thus one discovers direct experience
Of the stages of the tantric path;
And every key in highest yoga tantra is seen
Within the context of one's own training.

The experience of the yogi is then this:
The world is seen as the mystical mandala
And all living beings as tantric deities;

And everything that one eats and drinks
Becomes transformed into blissful ambrosia.

All of one's activities become spiritual,
Regardless of how they conventionally appear;
And every sound that one makes
Becomes part of a great vajra song.

I, a tantric yogi, abide in the blissful mind;
I, a tantric yogi, spontaneously generate goodness
In everything that I do.
All male divinities dance within me
And all female divinities channel
Their vajra songs through me.

Thinking of the great kindness of
Lama Tsongkhapa, an incomparable vajra master,
I could not restrain myself from giving voice
To this song of tantric experience,
A melody that I send forth
As an offering to that illustrious sage.

Song of the Tantric Path

The guru is the source of all tantric power;
The practitioner who sees him as a Buddha
Holds all realizations in the palm of his hand.
So devote yourself with full intensity
To the guru in both thought and deed.

When the mind is not first well trained
In the three levels of the exoteric path,
Then any claim to the profound tantric yogas
Is an empty boast, and there is every danger
That one will fall from the way.

The door entering into the peerless Vajrayana
Is nothing other than the four tantric initiations.
Hence it is important to receive these fully
And thus plant the seeds of the four Buddha kayas.

One must learn to relinquish the habit of grasping
At the mundane way in which things are perceived,
And to place all that appears within the vision
Of the world as mandala and its beings tantric forms.
Such are the trainings of the generation stage yogas,
That purify and refine the bases to be cleansed.

Next one stimulates the points of the vajra body
And directs the energies flowing in the side channels
Into *dhuti*, mystic channel at the center,
Thus gaining sight of the clear light of mind
And giving rise to wisdom born together with bliss.
Cherish meditation on these completion stage yogas.

The actual body of the final path to liberation
Is cultivation of the perfect view of emptiness;
The gate entering into illumination's Great Way
Is the bodhimind, the enlightenment aspiration;
And the highest method for accomplishing Buddha-
    hood
Is meditation on the two profound tantric stages.
Hold as inseparable these three aspects of practice.

This poem summarizing the key points of tantra
Is here composed by the monk Gendun Gyatso
For his disciple Chomdzey Sengey Gyatso
While residing at Drepung, a great center of Dharma
    knowledge.

From *Mystical Verses of a Mad Dalai Lama* by Gendun Gyatso, the Second Dalai Lama.

السَّلِيبِي   القَدِيس يُوحَنَّا

SAN IVAN DE LA CRVZ

SAINT JOHN OF THE CROSS

NINE

SAINT JOHN OF THE CROSS

1542–1591, SPAIN

JUAN DE YEPES Y ÁLVAREZ was born in the sixteenth century in Fontiveros, Spain. Inducted as a Carmelite monk at age twenty-one, Juan was ordained as a priest four years later. At this time, he was called upon by his contemporary, Teresa of Ávila, to assist in organizing a fledgling branch of the order. This offshoot, called the Barefoot Carmelites, emphasized a life of austerity and contemplation. Shortly after opening the first such ascetic monastery, John found himself imprisoned for his efforts to transform the Carmelites. It was in his imposed confinement that John wrote some of his most soulful verses.

It was through renunciation of the tasteless material pleasures of the world that the lover (contemplative) attained union with the Beloved (God). John was best known for his concept of the dark, or naked, night of the soul. Only by baring the soul of all desires, instructed John, might the soul be free to soar in the heavens. Even visions of the holy Christ crucified, of God in resplendent majesty, or of the heavenly effulgence must be released in order to reach Divine union. Form, implored John, must yield to the formless in order for the soul to be fully emptied.

It was with a burning thirst for the Divine that the parched John sought nothing less than the ultimate union with God. His pain was so great, his taste for earthly life so insipid, his desire for the Infinite so unquestionable, that there was simply nothing else for him to seek. It was only by dying before death, by cutting all ties to the senses, by transcending the intellect, that the Divine Essence was even thinkable. By unfettering himself from all that bound him to this world, John enabled himself to climb higher and higher until he reached the pinnacle. The journey was in no way easy: There were bleak nights and periods of feeling exhausted and beaten down, as if he could go no further. Yet he persisted unswervingly. The incomparably sweet and tender caresses of the Beloved are described in a way that only one who had reached such a state could know.

John spent his final years in solitude, rapt in contemplation of the Divine. He died at the age of forty-nine and was canonized in 1726.

The poems of Saint John of the Cross have been translated from the original Spanish by Judyth Reichenberg-Ullman, whose first academic love was Spanish literature.

TRANSCENDING THE
DARK NIGHT OF THE SOUL

The Dark Night
(Songs of the soul that rejoices at having reached
the high state of perfection, which is the union with God,
by the path of spiritual denial)

On a dark night,
with the ardent longing for love afire,
oh blessed fortune!
I left without being noticed,
my house put to bed.

In the blessed night,
in secrecy, so that no one saw me,
I looked at nothing,
with no other light and guide
than that which burned within my heart.

This [light] guided me
more surely than the sunlight at noon,
to where there awaited me,

He whom I knew well,
in a place where no one appeared.

Oh, night, you led the way,
oh night, kinder than the dawn of day,
oh, night, who united
lover and beloved,
lover transformed into the Beloved!

In my florid breast,
that kept itself only for him,
there he remained asleep
and found me spiritless;
I said, "No one will attain such a height!"
and I humbled and humbled myself so,
that I chased it and reached the summit.

By some strange manner,
I soared a thousand flights in a single flight alone,
for the promise of the heavens
is that you can reach as high as you expect that you
    will;
I expected this one chance alone
and in such an expectation I did not fall short,
for I soared so very, very high,
that I chased it and reached the summit.

I Entered Knowing Not Where

(Verses on an ecstasy of contemplation)

I entered where I knew not,
and I remained not knowing,
all knowledge transcending.

I had no idea where I was going,
but, when I saw myself there,
great things did I understand;

I will not say what it is that I felt,
for I remained not knowing,
all knowledge transcending.

Of peace and of godliness
was the perfect knowledge,
in profound solitude
understood straight along;
it was something so secret,
that I was left stammering,
all knowledge transcending.

I was so saturated,
so absorbed and remote,
that I was dispossessed of all reason;
and my spirit was endowed with
an understanding of not understanding,
all knowledge transcending.

He who truly arrives in that place,
his self falls away;
however much he knew at first
much less does it now seem;
and his knowledge grows so much,
that he is left not knowing,
all knowledge transcending.

The higher he climbs,
so much less does he understand,
it is the cloud that is obscured
that at night becomes illuminated;
so it is that he who knew
remains forever not knowing
all knowledge transcending.

This knowing without knowing
is of such great dominion,
that the learned men disputing it

can never overcome it;
for their knowledge does not reach
the understanding of not understanding,
all knowledge transcending.

This loftiest knowing
has such great merit,
that there is no university or knowledge
that can undertake it;
he who knows how to triumph
with a mastery of not knowing
will always transcend.

And if you wish to listen,
this highest knowledge
consists of a most excellent sense
of the divine Essence;
it is an act of its clemency
to make us remain there not understanding
all knowledge transcending.

The Living Flame of Love
(Songs of the soul in intimate union with God)

Oh, living flame of love,
that tenderly stabs
my soul at its deepest center!
You are no longer elusive,
finish now, if you will,
rend the veil of this sweet encounter.

Oh, sweet cautery!
Oh, sweet wound that is gifted to me!
Oh, gentle hand! Oh, delicate touch
that is known in life eternal,
and repays all debts;
slaying, you have transformed death into life.

Oh, lamps of fire,
in whose brilliance
the deepest caves of the mind,
previously dark and blind,
with rare beauty,
heat, and light bestowed at the side of the Beloved.

How docile and affectionate,
you awaken in my breast
where in secrecy you alone dwell,
and in your delicious inhalation
overflowing with goodness and glory,
how delicately you love me!

From the poetry of Saint John of the Cross,
from an original translation by Judyth Reichenberg-Ullman.

TEN

HAKUIN

1686–1769, JAPAN

AKUIN EKAKU is one of the central figures of Japanese Zen Buddhism. What is popularly known as "Rinzai Zen" is in large part derived from the teachings of Hakuin. A tireless, dedicated practitioner of the art of zazen, or meditation, Hakuin is also famous for his koans or Zen riddles, especially the now-clichéd, "What is the sound of one hand clapping?" He was also renowned for his poetry, beautiful calligraphy, and humorous caricatures of himself and other Zen masters.

Inspired by a play in which a Buddhist monk survives a trial by fire, Hakuin hoped to transcend the flames of hell depicted in religious services he attended with his mother. At the age of thirteen, he left home to seek ordination as a monk. Determined to ultimately escape a fiery fate, Hakuin took up the religious life with extraordinary zeal. After seeking out various teachers, he found his master in old Shoju, who thought nothing of brutally beating his disciples without warning to enhance their understanding of Zen. Shoju taught Hakuin to meditate on koans [Zen riddles designed to stop the mind]. "I chewed on those koans day and night," he explained. As we shall see, his practice failed to bear fruit until he met a certain old woman who had a knack for setting him straight.

At the hands of the old woman's broom, the young master had his first of many satori (enlightenment) experiences. But Hakuin wasn't satisfied with one satori. He eventually attained eighteen major satoris and countless minor ones. So intense was his dedication that he practiced zazen (sitting meditation) in the midst of the earthquakes, cascading lava, and falling ash during the great eruption of Mt. Fuji in 1707. Although his entire district was destroyed by the rampaging mountain, Hakuin never

Sculpture and photograph by Randy Jewart, "Hakuin," limestone 1997. Collection of Kent and Marjory Halstead.

HAKUIN

wavered. When Hakuin's family came to the rescue and implored him to escape to safety, he replied, "If I attain enlightenment, I'll be protected; if I don't, it's no loss if I perish—I'm entrusting myself to heaven." Heaven indeed must have saved him from harm for the benefit of all beings.

Known for his simplicity and great asceticism, Hakuin persevered despite all obstacles. At one point his severe austerity left him with a severe illness and weakness that he termed "Zen sickness." Ultimately he found an old mountain hermit master who taught him a meditation in which he visualized a golden lump of melting butter permeating his body, bringing softness, warmth, and nourishment to heal the ravages of too much Zen practice. He was promptly cured.

After the death of his teacher, Hakuin returned to the old monastery, by then a shambles. As the new abbot, he lovingly restored it, and during his lifetime of hard work and harder practice, he trained hundreds of monks with the same fierce determination he applied to his own quest for enlightenment. With koan, walking staff, and zazen, he ensured that his students did not settle for trifling attainments, but instead persisted in the same kind of rigorous training that had brought him great realizations and even greater laughter and joy.

The selections are from Zen master Hakuin Ekaku's spiritual autobiography *Wild Ivy* (Japanese, *Itsumadegusa*), translated from the Japanese with commentary by Norman Waddell. They are in the same order as in the original autobiography, but are excerpted from several chapters.

FALLING DOWN LAUGHING

When we arrived at the Shoju-an hermitage, I received permission to be admitted as a student, then hung up my traveling staff to stay.

Once, after I had set forth my understanding to the master during *dokusan* [personal interview], he said to me, "Commitment to the study of Zen must be genuine. How do you understand the koan about the Dog and the Buddha-Nature?"

"No way to lay a hand or foot on that," I replied.

He abruptly reached out and caught my nose. Giving it a sharp push with his hand, he said, "Got a pretty good hand on it there!"

I couldn't make a single move, either forward or backward. I was unable to spit out a single syllable.

That encounter put me into a very troubled state. I was totally frustrated and demoralized. I sat red-eyed and miserable, my cheeks burning from the constant tears.

The master took pity on me and assigned me some koans to work on: Su-shan's Memorial Tower, The Water Buffalo Comes through the Window, Nan-ch'uan's Death, Nan-ch'uan's Flowering Shrub, The Hemp Robe of Ching-chou, Yun-men's Dried Stick of Shit.

"Anyone who gets past one of these fully deserves to be called a descendant of the Buddhas and patriarchs," he said.

A great surge of spirit rose up inside me, stiffening my resolve. I chewed on those koans day and night. Attacking them from the front. Gnawing at them from the sides. But not the first glimmer of understanding came. Tearful and dejected, I sobbed out a vow: "I call upon the evil kings of the ten directions and all the other leaders of the heavenly host of demons. If after seven days I fail to bore through one of these koans, come quickly and snatch my life away."

I lit some incense, made my bows, and resumed my practice. I kept at it without stopping for even a moment's sleep. The master came and spewed abuse at me. "You're doing Zen down in a hole!" he barked.

Then he told me, "You could go out today and scour the entire world looking for a true teacher—someone who could revive the fortunes of 'closed-barrier' Zen—you'd have a better chance finding stars in the midday skies."

I had my doubts about that. "After all," I reasoned, "there are great monasteries all over the country that are filled with celebrated masters: they're as numerous as sesame or flax seed. That old man in his wretched ramshackle old poorhouse of a temple and that preposterous pride of his! I'd be better off leaving here and going somewhere else."

Early the next morning, still deeply dejected, I picked up my begging bowl and went into the village below Iiyama Castle.

I was totally absorbed in my koan—never away from it for an instant. I took up a position beside the gate of a house, my bowl in my hand, fixed in a kind of trance. From inside the house, a voice yelled out, "Get away from here! Go somewhere else!" I was so preoccupied, I didn't even notice it. This must have angered the occupant, because suddenly she appeared flourishing a broom upside down in her hands. She flew at me, flailing wildly, whacking away at my head as if she were bent on dashing my brains out. My sedge hat lay in tatters. I was knocked over and ended heels up on the ground, totally unconscious. I lay there like a dead man.

Neighbors, alarmed by the commotion, emerged from their houses with looks of concern on their faces. "Oh, now look what the crazy old crone has done," they cried, and quickly vanished behind locked doors. This was followed by a hushed silence; not a stir or sign of life anywhere. A few people who happened to be passing by approached me in wonderment. They grabbed hold of me and hoisted me upright.

"What's wrong?" "What happened?" they exclaimed.

As I came to and my eyes opened, I found that the unsolvable and impenetrable koans I had been working on—all those venomous cat's-paws—were now penetrated completely. Right to their roots. They had suddenly ceased to exist. I began clapping my hands and whooping with glee, frightening the people who had gathered around to help me.

"He's lost his mind!" "A crazy monk!" they shouted, shrinking back from me apprehensively. Then they turned heel and fled, without looking back.

I picked myself up from the ground, straightened my robe, and fixed the remnants of my hat back on my head. With a blissful smile on my face, I started, slowly and exultantly, making my way back toward Narasawa and the Shoju-an.

I spotted an old man beckoning to me. "Honorable priest," he said, addressing me, "that old lady really put your lights out, didn't she?"

I smiled faintly but uttered not a word in response. He gave me a bowl of rice to eat and sent me on my way.

On one occasion, the two of us monks engaged in a private session. We pledged to continue it for seven days and nights. No sleep. No lying down. We cut a three-foot section of bamboo and fashioned it into a makeshift *shippei* [a Zen stick for maintaining alertness]. We sat facing each other with the *shippei* placed on the ground between us. We agreed if one of us saw the other's eyelids drop, even for a split second, he would grab the staff and crack him with it between the eyes.

For seven days, we sat ramrod-straight, teeth clenched tightly in total silence. Not so much as an eyelash quivered. Right through to the end of the seventh night, neither one of us had occasion to reach for that cudgel.

One night, a heavy snowfall blanketed the area. The dull, muffled thud of snow falling from the branches of the trees created a sense of extraordinary stillness and purity. I made an attempt at a poem to describe the joy I felt:

> If only you could hear
> the sound of snow
> falling late at night
> from the trees
> of the old temple
> in Shinoda!

I was soon overtaken by a violent rainstorm. The water poured in sheets, turning the road to thick mud, which sucked at my ankles as I walked. But I pushed forward into the mist and pelting rain oblivious to it all, humming as I went.

All at once, I found I had penetrated a verse that I had been working on, Master Ta-hui's "Lotus leaves, perfect discs, rounder than mirrors; Water chestnuts, needle spikes, sharper than gimlets." It was like suddenly seeing a bright sun blazing out in the dead of night. Overcome with joy, I tripped, stumbled, and plunged headlong into the mud. My robe was soaked through, but my only reflection was, "What's a muddy robe, compared to the extraordinary joy I now feel?" I rolled over onto my back and lay there motionless, submerged in the mire.

Some other travelers happening by rushed up and stared with amazement and alarm at the figure lying dead in the mud. Hands grabbed at me and propped me up. "Is he unconscious?" they cried. "Is he dead?" someone asked.

When I returned to my senses, I began clapping my hands together with delight and emitting great whoops of laughter. My rescuers started backing away from me with doubtful grins on their faces. Then they broke and ran, yelling "Crazy monk! Crazy monk!" (It was a repeat performance of the events that had taken place some years before in Iiyama.) I had just experienced one of those eighteen satoris I mentioned before.

I resumed my journey, stepping buoyantly down the road with a blissful smile on my face. I was plastered with mud from head to foot but so happy I found myself laughing and weeping at the same time.

Alone in the hut, I thrust my spine up stiff and straight and sat right through until dawn. All through the night, the room was haunted by a terrifying demonic presence. Since I dislike having to swell the narrative with such details, however, I won't describe it here.

In the morning, I opened the rice pail, reached inside with my left hand, and grasped a fistful of the grains. I boiled these up into a bowl of gruel, which I ate in place of the two regular meals. I repeated the same routine each day. I wonder, was my regimen less demanding than National Master Muso's, with his half persimmon?

After a month of this life, I still hadn't experienced a single pang of hunger. On the contrary, my body and mind were both fired with a great surge of spirit and resolve. My nights were zazen. My days were sutra-recitation. I never let up. During this period, I experienced small satoris and large satoris in numbers beyond count. How many times did I jump up and jubilantly dance around, oblivious of all else! I no longer had any doubts at all about Ta-hui's talk of eighteen great satoris and countless small ones. How grievously sad that people today have discarded this way of kensho as if it were dirt!

As for sitting, sitting is something that should include fits of ecstatic laughter—brayings that make you slump to the ground clutching your belly. And when you struggle to your feet after the first spasm passes, it should send you kneeling to earth in yet further contortions of joy.

From *Wild Ivy*, the spiritual autobiography of Zen master Hakuin.

ELEVEN

THE BAAL SHEM TOV

1698–1760, EASTERN EUROPE

RABBI ISRAEL BEN ELIEZER, the founder of Hasidism, went by the name of the Baal Shem, meaning "The Good Master of the Name," or "Master of the Good Name," depending on the translation. Born in southern Poland, what is now the Ukraine, in 1698, the Baal Shem's earliest years are shrouded in mystery. What is known is that he sought out seclusion in the Carpathian Mountains, immersing himself in contemplation, prayer, and the study of the Torah and Kabbalah.

This kindly rabbi gained a reputation as a friend of the sick and downtrodden as well as a miracle worker. Rather than fasting and asceticism, the Baal Shem encouraged joyous prayer, singing and dancing, and the sharing of community as the means to attain *deveikut* (communion with God). He recommended releasing the sins of the past and discovering the ecstasy in *ahavat HaShem* (the love of God). The Divine, according to the teachings of the Baal Shem, could be found in each and every aspect of the universe and was not limited to synagogues, rabbis, or sacred texts. Prayer and the performance of *mitzvot* (charitable deeds) linked the devotee directly to the Divine.

Imagine a small and simple room, or *stubel,* in which a Hasidic rabbi, or *zaddik,* acted as a mediator between humankind and God, dispensing wisdom to his unswervingly dedicated and obedient disciples. The atmosphere was one of simplicity and heartfelt study. These were humble people—bookbinders, coachmen, tax collectors, innkeepers—seeking holiness in their everyday lives. The tales of the Baal Shem provided hope and inspiration from the drudgery and difficulties of workday existence. The devotion, exuberance, and charisma of the Baal Shem uplifted the masses of the humble, hardworking Polish Jewry, and vibrant hope spread rapidly throughout all of Eastern Europe. Mysterious and mystical, the tales of the Baal Shem were passed by word of mouth, scribbles in notebooks, and in the spirit of narration carried from one generation to the next.

At the heart of the teachings of the Baal Shem are the concepts and experience of *Elohim* (the being of God), the *Shekina* (presence of God), and *avoda* (service to God). Also embodied in the Baal Shem's wisdom are:

Illumination of the mystery of the apparent duality of ecstasy and service, of having versus seeking;

The burning fire of the yearning heart drawn fervently to the light of God;

The rapture and ecstasy of paradise;

Awakening and renewal before the eyes of God;

Holy men and holy spirits;

The purification and sanctification of body, mind, and soul;

The expansion of the soul beyond all limits;

The embracing of God beyond time and space;

Such is the depth of spirit of the wisdom of the Baal Shem.

The Baal Shem Tov never actually recorded his stories. This was left to his disciples, such luminaries as the Alexander Rebbe, Boyaner Rebbe, Gerrer Rebbe, Lubavitcher Rebbe, and Sochatchover Rebbe. The best known of those who carried on the spirit of the Baal Shem is his great-grandson, Rabbi Nachman of Bratslav, Ukraine. These teachings brought to Judaism new life, creativity, and a dynamic energy, making Hasidism a growing and spirited force in the advancement of the Torah and Jewish mysticism.

The selection is excerpted from the *Mystical Epistle of the Baal Shem Tov,* a letter by the Baal Shem Tov to his brother-in-law, Rabbi Abraham

Gershon in Palestine, describing his profound mystical experience. The letter was unfortunately never delivered, as its bearer, Jacob Joseph, was unable to make the journey to the Holy Land. Jacob preserved the letter, however, and published it in 1781 in his book, *Ben Porat Yosef,* more than twenty years after the Baal Shem Tov's death.

THE HEAVENLY HASID

The Mystical Epistle of the Baal Shem Tov

TO MY dear friend and brother-in-law, whom I love as my own self, wondrous Rabbi and Hasid, renowned in knowledge and fear of God, his honor, our teacher, Rabbi Abraham Gershon, may his light shine. . . .

You . . . remark that the new ideas and mysteries I recorded for you by the hand of the scribe, the Rabbi and Preacher of the holy community of Polonnoye, did not arrive. Over this, too, I am greatly distressed for you would undoubtedly have derived much satisfaction from them. Now, however, I have forgotten many of these matters yet I shall write to you very briefly those details I do recall.

For on the day of the New Year of the year 5507 (= September 1746) I engaged in an ascent of the soul, as you know I do, and I saw wondrous things in that vision that had never before seen since the day I had attained maturity. That which I saw and learned in my ascent it is impossible to describe or to relate even from mouth to mouth. But as I returned to the lower Garden of Eden I saw many souls, both of the living and the dead, those known to me and those unknown. They were more than could be counted and they ran to and fro from world to world through the path provided by that column known to the adepts in the hidden science. They were all in such a state of great rapture that the mouth would be worn out if it attempted to describe it and the physical ear too indelicate to hear it. Many of the wicked repented of their sins and were pardoned, for it was a time of much grace. In my eyes too, it was a great marvel that the repentance was accepted of so many whom you know. They also enjoyed great rapture and ascended as mentioned above. All of them entreated me to my embarrassment, saying: "The Lord has given your honor great understanding to grasp these matters. Ascend together with us, therefore, so as to help us and assist us." Their rapture was so great that I resolved to ascend together with them.

Then I saw in the vision that Samael went up to act the part of accuser because of the unprecedented rapture. He achieved what he had set out to do, namely, a decree of apostasy for many people who would be tortured to death. Then dread seized me and I took my life in my hands. I requested my teacher to come with me since there is great danger in the ascent to the higher worlds and since from the day I attained to maturity I had never undertaken such high ascents. I went higher step by step until I entered the palace of the Messiah wherein the Messiah studies the Torah together with all the *tannaim* and the saints and also with the Seven Shepherds. There I witnessed great rejoicing and could not fathom the reason for it so I thought that, God forbid, the rejoicing was over my own departure from this world. But I was afterwards informed that I was not yet to die since they took great delight on high when, through their Torah, I perform unifications here below.

To this day I am unaware of the reason for that rejoicing. I asked the Messiah: "When will the Master come?" and he replied: "You will know of it in this way; it will be when your teaching becomes famous and revealed to the world, and when that which I have taught you and you have comprehended will spread abroad so that others, too, will be capable of performing unifications and having soul ascents as you do. Then will all the *kelippot* be consumed and it will be a time of grace and salvation." I was astonished to hear this and greatly distressed that it would take such a long time, for when will such a thing be possible? Yet my mind was set at rest in that I learned there three special charms and three holy names and these are easy to grasp and to expound so that I thought to myself, it is possible by this means for my colleagues to attain to the stages and categories which I have attained, that is to say, they, too, will be able to engage in ascents of the soul and learn to comprehend what I have done. But no permission was given to me to reveal this secret for the rest of my life. I did request that I be allowed to teach it to you but no permission at all was given to me and I am duty bound on oath to keep the secret.

However, this I can tell you and may God be your help. Let your ways be set before the Lord and never be moved, especially in the holy land. Whenever you offer your prayers and whenever you study, have the intention of unifying a divine name in every word and with every utterance of your lips. For there are worlds, souls, and divinity in every letter. These ascend to become united one with the other and then the letters are combined in order to form a word so that there is complete unification with the divine. Allow your soul to be embraced by them at each of the above stages. Thus all worlds become united and they ascend so that immeasurable rapture and the greatest delight is experienced. You can understand this on the analogy of the raptures of bride and bridegroom in miniature in the physical world. How much more so at this most elevated stage! God will undoubtedly be your help and wherever you turn you will be successful and prosper. Give to the wise and he will become even wiser. Also pray for me, with this intention in mind, that I should be worthy of being gathered into the inheritance of the Lord (= the Holy Land) while still alive and pray, too, on behalf of all the remnant still in the diaspora.

I also prayed there, asking why the Lord had done this and why this great wrath, to hand over so many Jewish souls to be slain by Samael, among them many souls who had apostatized and had still been killed. Permission was granted to me to ask this of Samael himself. I asked Samael why he did this and what could have been his intention in having Jews become apostates and yet still be killed afterwards. He replied that his intention was for the sake of heaven. And afterwards, for our sins, so it happened, that in the holy community of Izyaslav there was a blood libel against many people, two of whom became apostates and yet they still killed them. But the others sanctified the name of heaven in great sanctity, dying by terrible torture. Afterwards there were further blood libels in the holy communities of Shebitovka and Dunayevtsy. But there none of them became apostates having seen what happened in the aforementioned holy community of Izyaslav. They all resisted temptation, suffering martyrdom and sanctifying the name of Heaven. By their merit the Messiah will come to avenge us and to gain atonement for God's land and His people.

On the New Year of the year 5510 (= September 1749) I made an ascent of the soul, as you know I do, and I saw a great accusation so that permission was almost given to destroy whole lands and communities. I took my life in my hands and prayed: "Let us fall into the hands of the Lord but let us not fall into the hands of man." This they granted to me, that there should be great sickness and an epidemic of unparalleled proportions in all the lands of Poland and in other lands adjacent to ours. And so it came to pass. Sickness spread over all so that it could not be counted and also epidemics in other lands. I discussed with my company whether to recite the portion regarding the making of the incense in order to nullify the above-mentioned judgments but they revealed to me in a vision of the night: "Behold, you yourself chose the alternative of falling into the hands of the Lord [as above] and now you wish to nullify it. An accuser cannot become a defender." So I then desisted from reciting the incense portion and from praying for this. But on Hoshana Rabba I went to the synagogue together with the company, uttering the while many conjurations in great dread, and I recited the incense portion just once so that the epidemic should not spread to our districts, and thank God I was successful. . . . Long may you live. Amen. Selah.

Israel Baal Shem Tov of Medzibezh

From a letter by the Baal Shem Tov to his brother-in-law, Rabbi Abraham Gershom.

TWELVE

BAHÁ'U'LLÁH

1817–1892, IRAN

ORN IN Teheran, Iran, in 1817, Bahá'u'lláh descended from a noble and wealthy family whose lineage could be traced to the ruling dynasties of imperial Persia. Trained in the princely arts of horsemanship, calligraphy, swordsmanship, and classical poetry, he married at the age of sixteen. His wife gave birth to three daughters over the course of the next thirteen years. Declining the ministerial position offered to him, Bahá'u'lláh chose instead to devote his time and energy to philanthropy and became known for his generosity and kindness.

His privileged position came to an abrupt end after 1840 when Bahá'u'lláh became one of the leaders of the Babi movement. Founded by a young merchant from Shiraz who took the name of "the Bab," this messianic sect provided a new religion that was independent of Islam. The secular and religious establishments reacted to the movement with tremendous fear and persecution. The authorities issued a death sentence for the Bab, to be carried out by 750 soldiers. Miraculously, the Bab's body disappeared after the first round of bullets, only to be found back in his cell. His luck ran out the second time.

Soon after the Bab's execution, Bahá'u'lláh was arrested, brought in front of the court in shackles, and threatened with death. His personal reputation, family connections, and the protests from Western Embassies saved him. He was cast instead into the notorious "Back Pit," where he remained for four months. It was in the dark, dank confines of his dungeon that Bahá'u'lláh realized the breadth of his mission on Earth. Upon his release, he suffered banishment from Persia.

So began forty years of exile, incarceration, persecution, wandering, and reflection. Bahá'u'lláh announced in 1863 that he was the Promised One that the Bab had foretold.

Beginning in 1867, he addressed the leaders of the world, warning of political upheavals of great magnitude unless they disarmed and joined together to establish lasting peace. The Turkish government responded by exiling Bahá'u'lláh to a dreaded penal colony, home to the most hardened of criminals. So foul was the air that birds soaring overhead would fall dead from the sky. Here Bahá'u'lláh and his family spent the remaining twenty-four years of his life until he died in 1892.

The fundamental message of Bahá'u'lláh was that of one God and one human race. He advocated the union of all people into a peaceful, integrated global society free of prejudice and with full gender, socio-economic, and religious equality. Included in his vision were universal education, a sustainable balance of technology and nature, and a world federation. The fruits of Bahá'u'lláh's forty years of exile were his sacred scriptures, which outlined a plan for the reorganization of human society on all levels. Today the Bahá'í Faith is one of the fastest growing religions of the world, with more than 5 million members in at least 233 countries and territories representing more than 2,000 different ethnic groups. It is only through an unwavering consciousness of the oneness of mankind, say the Bahá'ís, that world peace can be realized.

IN BONDAGE, YET FREE

BAHÁ'U'LLÁH WAS imprisoned with his comrades, the Bábis . . . "amidst the darkness of a subterranean dungeon in Tihrán—an abominable pit that had once served as a reservoir of water for one of the public baths of the city."

He relates his experience there:

We were all huddled together in one cell, our feet in stocks, and around our necks fastened the most galling of chains. The air we breathed was laden with the foulest impurities, while the floor on which we sat was covered with filth and infested with vermin. No ray of light was allowed to penetrate that pestilential dungeon or to warm its icy coldness. We were placed in two rows, each facing the other. We had taught them to repeat certain verses which, every night, they chanted with extreme fervor. "God is sufficient unto me; He verily is the All-Sufficing!" one row would intone, while the other would reply: "In Him let the trusting trust." The chorus of these gladsome voices would continue to peal out until the early hours of the morning. Their reverberation would fill the dungeon, and, piercing its massive walls, would reach the ears of Nasiri'd-Din Sháh, whose palace was not far distant from the place where we were imprisoned. "What means this sound?" he was reported to have exclaimed. "It is the anthem the Bábis are intoning in their prison," they replied. The Sháh made no further remarks, nor did he attempt to restrain the enthusiasm his prisoners, despite the horrors of their confinement, continued to display.

One day, there was brought to Our prison a tray of roasted meat which they informed Us the Sháh had ordered to be distributed among the prisoners. "The Sháh," We were told, "faithful to a vow he made, has chosen this day to offer to you all this lamb in fulfilment of his pledge." A deep silence fell upon Our companions. Who expected Us to make answer on their behalf. "We return this gift to you," We replied, "we can well dispense with this offer." The answer We made would have greatly irritated the guards had they not been eager to devour the food We had refused to touch. Despite the hunger with which Our companions were afflicted, only one among them, a certain Mirzá Husayn-i-Mutivalliy-i-Qumi, showed any desire to eat of the food the sovereign had spread before us. With a fortitude that was truly heroic, Our fellow-prisoners submitted, without a murmur, to endure the piteous plight to which they were reduced. Praise of God, instead of complaint of the treatment meted out to them by the Sháh, fell unceasingly from their lips—praise with which they sought to beguile the hardship of a cruel captivity.

Every day Our gaolers [jailers] entering Our cell, would call the name of one of Our companions, bidding him arise and follow them to the foot of the gallows. With what eagerness would the owner of that name respond to that solemn call! Relieved of his chains, he would spring to his feet and, in a state of uncontrollable delight, would approach and embrace Us. We would seek to comfort him with the assurance of an everlasting life in the world beyond, and, filling his heart with hope and joy, would send him forth to win the crown of glory. He would embrace, in turn, the rest of his fellow-prisoners, and then proceed to die as dauntlessly as he had lived. Soon after the martyrdom of each of these companions, We would be informed by the executioner, who had grown to be friendly with Us, of the circumstances of the death of his victim, and of the joy with which he had endured his sufferings to the very end.

During the days I lay in the prison of Tihrán, though the galling weight of the chains and the stench-filled air allowed Me but little sleep, still in those infrequent moments of slumber I felt as if something flowed from the crown of My head over My breast, even as a mighty torrent that precipitateth itself upon the earth from the summit of a lofty mountain. Every limb of My body would, as a result, be set afire. At such moments My tongue recited what no man could bear to hear.

One night, in a dream, these exalted words were heard on every side: "Verily, We shall render Thee victorious by Thyself and by Thy pen. Grieve Thou not for that which hath befallen Thee, neither be Thou afraid, for Thou art in safety. Ere long will God raise up the treasures of the earth-men who will aid Thee through Thyself and through Thy Name, wherewith God hath revived the hearts of such as have recognized Him."

While engulfed in tribulations I heard a most wondrous, a most sweet voice, calling above My head. Turning My face, I beheld a Maiden—the embodiment of the remembrance of the name of My Lord—suspended in the air before Me. So rejoiced was she in her very soul that her countenance shone with the ornament of the good-pleasure of God, and her cheeks glowed with the brightness of the All Merciful. Betwixt earth and heaven she was raising a call which captivated the hearts and minds of men. She was imparting to both My inward and outer being tidings which rejoiced My soul, and the souls of God's honored servants. Pointing with her finger unto My head, she addressed all who are in heaven and all who are on earth, saying: "By God! This is the Best-Beloved of the worlds, and yet ye comprehend not. This is the Beauty of God amongst you, and the power of His sovereignty within you, could ye but understand. This is the Mystery of God and His Treasure, the Cause of God and His glory unto all who are in the kingdoms of Revelation and of creation, if ye be of them that perceive."

In His Epistle to Nasiri'd-Din Sháh, His royal adversary, revealed at the height of the proclamation of His Message, occur these passages which shed further light on the Divine origin of His mission: "O King! I was but a man like others, asleep upon My couch, when lo, the breezes of the All-Glorious were wafted over Me, and taught Me the knowledge of all that hath been. This thing is not from Me, but from One Who is Almighty and All-Knowing. And he bade Me lift up My voice between earth and heaven, and for this there befell Me what hath caused the tears of every man of understanding to flow. . . . This is but a leaf which the winds of the will of Thy lord, the Almighty, the All-Praised, have stirred. . . . His all-compelling summons hath reached Me, and caused Me to speak His praise amidst all people. I was indeed as one dead when His behest was uttered. The hand of the will of Thy Lord, the Compassionate, the Merciful, transformed Me." "By My Life!" He asserts in another Tablet, "Not of Mine own volition have I revealed Myself, but God, of His own choosing, hath manifested Me." And again: "Whenever I chose to hold My peace and be still, lo, the Voice of the Holy Spirit, standing on My right hand, aroused Me, and the Most Great Spirit appeared before My face, and Gabriel overshadowed Me, and the Spirit of Glory stirred within My bosom, bidding Me arise and break My silence."

From the words of Bahá'u'lláh as recorded by his close associate, Nabil.

RAMAKRISHNA PARAMAHAMSA

THIRTEEN

RAMAKRISHNA PARAMAHAMSA

1836–1886, INDIA

R AMAKRISHNA, a well-known and beloved nineteenth century Indian saint and master, was born to a poor, orthodox Brahman family in a remote village in Bengal, India. His coming had been foretold to his father through a vision. During a spiritual pilgrimage, the Hindu god Vishnu proclaimed to Ramakrishna's father that Vishnu himself would incarnate in the body of his son. While Ramakrishna was still quite young, his father died. Having little interest in school or the material world, young Ramakrishna often drifted off from the outer world into states of ecstasy. In fact, he once lost consciousness while playing the role of the Lord Shiva in a performance at school.

Disillusioned with the material emphasis of academics, Ramakrishna chose to devote himself to a life of spiritual pursuit and, in order to support himself, became a temple priest. It was there, amidst an image of the blissful Mother Kali, that Ramakrishna worshiped. More important, it was in this temple that the boy was seized, to the point of obsession, with a single question: Does Kali (the Divine Mother) truly exist? Kali's dark color, necklace of skulls, and belt of human limbs, symbolizing the death inherent in every birth, is fearsome to many. But to Ramakrishna, she was the gentlest, most loving of mothers.

Ramakrishna's relatives, despairing of his apparent madness, sought to restore him to sanity by betrothing him. Dedicated singly to discovering the truth of Mother Kali, Ramakrishna left the temple, discarded his few possessions, and took a vow of poverty and chastity. His bride, Sarada Devi, threw herself at her husband's feet, giving her life to his service. She desired only to worship and serve Ramakrishna.

Vision upon vision was bestowed on Ramakrishna by his Divine Mother, Kali. Convinced of her existence, he set out to learn the truth about the world religions. A practitioner of Vedanta (a nondualistic approach to Hinduism), in which the belief is that there is only one in the universe, not two, and that one is consciousness, manifesting itself in and as all beings and things, Ramakrishna also undertook practices of Islam, Christianity, and various other sects under the guidance of knowledgeable teachers. He concluded that the goal of all religions is the same: to embody the Divine. Determined to know genuine humility, he cleaned the homes of untouchables, beseeching Kali to make him their servant. In order to experience the feminine principle and to relinquish sexual desire, Ramakrishna, living in a household of women, dressed, spoke, and behaved like they did. Offering humble salutations to the Mother in all forms, he saw only Her image, regardless of the face or the body.

Devotees came by the thousands for the blessing and wisdom of Ramakrishna. Though Ramakrishna lacked advanced education, scholars and villagers alike thronged to experience his presence. Renunciation and the eternal oneness of all religions formed the basis of Ramakrishna's teachings. Known for his intense love for those who sought his wisdom, he made himself available twenty hours a day for months on end. Even when diagnosed with throat cancer, he could not be dissuaded from answering the questions of any and all visitors. Knowing that his time was short, and surrounded by thousands of devotees, Ramakrishna announced one day that he would leave his body. And so he did at the age of fifty. Ramakrishna continues to remain one of India's most beloved saints, and the monks of the Vedanta Society have spread his teachings throughout the world.

The selections that follow are from various discussions that Ramakrishna had with his disciples in which he related his own spiritual experiences. They are drawn from the book *Sayings of Ramakrishna.*

THE ECSTATIC LOVER OF MOTHER KALI

WHEN THE great yearning for God had developed in him, the Master found life unbearable without His vision. He was therefore about to put an end to his life, when the blessed vision dawned on him suddenly. Describing it the Master said: "The room with all its doors and windows, the temple and everything around me, vanished from sight. I felt as if nothing existed, and in their stead I perceived a boundless effulgent ocean of intelligence. Whichever side I turned my eyes, I saw from all quarters huge waves of that shining ocean rushing towards me, and in a short while, they all came, and falling upon me, engulfed me completely. Thus getting suffocated under them, I lost my ordinary consciousness and fell down." Referring to the same experience he said on another occasion: "I fell down on the floor of the room, completely lost in the ecstasy of the vision. I was perfectly unconscious as to what happened outside, and also how that day and the next passed. The one thing which I was internally conscious of was that through my soul was rolling an ocean of ineffable joy, the like of which I had no experience before. At the same time I was also conscious, to the inner core of my being, of the hallowed presence of the Divine Mother."

Soon after the Master's return to Dakshineswar after his marriage, his old divine madness seized him again. About the state of his mind in those days he said: "The ordinary man would have died, if he were to experience even a fourth of the spiritual metamorphosis that my body and mind underwent. And of this body too [meaning himself] the same would have been the fate; but fortunately the major portion of my days was passed in ecstatic oblivion of the Mother's divine vision. Henceforth for six long years not a wink of sleep ever visited my eyes, and the eyelids would never close, try though I might. All sense of time vanished from me, and the body idea was totally obliterated. A terrible fear would seize me at the slightest reversion of the mind from the Mother to the body. Often the fear came whether I had really run mad. I would stand before my image in a mirror, and when on poking my eyes I would find them insensitive, I would burst into tears in terror, and pray to the Mother: 'O Mother, is it that as a result of all my prayers and absolute reliance on Thee, Thou hast brought on me an incurable disease?'

But next, the alternating thought would come: 'O Mother, whatever fate may overtake my body, do Thou never forsake me! Vouchsafe unto me Thy vision and Thy mercy! O Mother, have I not taken complete shelter at Thy hallowed feet? Except Thee, O Mother, I have no other refuge!' And thus praying tearfully, my mind would be filled with a strange enthusiasm, creating an unbounded disgust for the body, and would lose itself in the comfort of the Mother's Divine vision and consoling words."

The Master's pure mind was itself his first and most important teacher. About this the Master said: "Whenever necessity arose, a young Sannyasin [monk] from inside my body, in appearance exactly like myself, would come out and teach me everything. When he came out in this way, sometimes I would retain a little consciousness of external objects and at other times, I would lose all consciousness of the outside world except for the awareness of his presence and doings. When he re-entered the body, I would again become aware of the external world. What I had heard from him before, the same teachings I heard from Brahmani, Totapuri, and others. What I learnt from him before, the same I learnt from these teachers later."

Referring to his Tantrik Sadhana under the guidance of Bhairavi Brahmani the Master said: "The Brahmani would go during the day to places far away from Dakshineswar and collect the various rare things mentioned in the Tantric scriptures as requisites for Sadhana. At nightfall she would ask me to go to one of the seats. I would go, and after performing the worship of the Mother Kali, I would begin to meditate according to her directions. I could hardly tell my beads, for as soon as I began to do so I was always overwhelmed with divine fervor and fell into deep Samadhi. I cannot now relate the varieties of wonderful visions I used to have. They followed each other in quick succession, and the effects of those practices I could feel most tangibly. The Brahmani guided me through all the exercises mentioned in the sixty-four principal Tantric works. Most of these are extremely difficult Sadhanas, which generally cause many a devotee to slip his foot and sink into moral degradation. But the infinite grace of the Mother carried me through them unscathed."

Describing his experience of the awakening of Kundalini, the Master said: "When I realized this state (the state of God-consciousness), one looking exactly like me came and thoroughly shook my Ida, Pingala, and Sushumna nerves. He licked the 'lotuses' of the six 'centers' with his tongue, and the drooping lotuses at once turned their faces upwards. And at last the Sahasrara 'lotus' became full-bloomed."

I had to practice the various religions once, Hinduism, Islam, and Christianity, and I have walked the paths of the different sects of Hinduism again—the Sakta, the Vaishnava, the Vedantic, and others. And I have found that it is the same God towards Whom all are travelling, only they are coming through diverse ways.

Describing his experience of Nirvikalpa Samadhi, the Master said: "After the initiation, 'the naked one' began to teach me the various conclusions of the Advaita Vedanta and asked me to withdraw the mind completely from all objects and dive into the Atman. But in spite of all my attempts I could not cross the realm of name and form and bring my mind to the unconditioned state. I had no difficulty in withdrawing the mind from all objects except one, and this was the all-too-familiar form of the Blissful Mother—radiant and of the essence of Pure Consciousness—which appeared before me as a living reality and would not allow me to pass beyond the realm of name and form. Again and again I tried to concentrate my mind upon the Advaita teaching but every time the Mother's form stood in my way. In despair I said to 'the naked one,' ' It is hopeless. I cannot raise my mind to the unconditioned state and come face to face with the Atman.' He grew excited and sharply said, 'What! You can't do it! But you have to.' He cast his eyes around for something, and finding a piece of glass, took it up, and pressing its point between my eyebrows, said, 'Concentrate your mind on this point.' Then with a stern determination I again sat to meditate, and as soon as the gracious form of the Divine Mother appeared before me, I used my discrimination as a sword and with it severed it into two. There remained no more obstruction to my mind, which at once soared beyond the relative plane, and I lost myself in Samadhi.

"I was for six months in that state of Nirvikalpa from which ordinary mortals cannot return. For after twenty-one days the body drops off like a withered leaf. Days and nights succeeded one another perfectly unnoticed. Flies would enter the mouth and nostrils just as in the case of a corpse without producing any sensation. Hairs became all matted with dust. Sometimes even Nature's calls were answered unawares. Hardly would the body have survived this state but for a Sadhu who happened to come at this time. He at once recognized my condition, and also understood that the Mother had yet to do many things through this body—that many persons would be benefited if it were preserved. So at meal time he used to fetch some food and try to bring me to external consciousness by administering a good beating to the body. As soon as traces of consciousness were perceived, he would thrust the food into the mouth. In this way a few morsels would be swallowed on some days; on other days, not even that. Full six months were thus passed. Later, after some days' stay in this state, I came to hear the Mother's command, 'Remain on the threshold of relative consciousness (Bhavamukha) for the instruction of mankind.' Then appeared blood dysentery. There was acute writhing pain in the intestines. Through this suffering for six months the normal body consciousness slowly reappeared. Or else, every now and then the

mind would, of its own accord, [...]
beyond form) state.

The natural tendency of this (my [...]
the Nirvikalpa state). Once that state is [...]
to come down. For your sake I drag it dow[...]
pull is not strong enough without a lower [...]
some trifling desires, as for instance, for smok[...]
water, for tasting a particular dish, or for seeing a [...]
son, and repeatedly suggest them to my mind. The[...]
mind slowly comes down (to the body). Again, whil[...]
down, it may run back upward. Again it has to be dragged[...]
through such desires."

I do see the Supreme Being as the veritable Reality with my very eyes! Why then should I reason? I do actually see that it is the Absolute Who has become all things around us; it is He who appears as the finite soul and the phenomenal world! One must have an awakening of the spirit within to see this reality. As long as one is unable to see Him as the one reality, one must reason or discriminate, saying, "Not this; Not this." Of course, it would not do for one merely to say, "I have seen beyond the possibility of a doubt that it is He Who has become all!" Mere saying is not enough. By the Lord's grace the spirit must be quickened. Spiritual awakening is followed by Samadhi. In this state one forgets that one has a body; one loses all attachment to the things of the world, i.e., "woman and gold"; one likes no other words than those relating to God; one is sorely troubled if called upon to listen to worldly matters. The spirit within being awakened, the next step is the realization of the Universal Spirit. It is the spirit that can realize the Spirit."

From the words of Sri Ramakrishna Paramahamsa,
as spoken to his disciples during the latter part of the nineteenth century.

...oar to the Nirvikalpa (Samadhi

...mind is upwards (towards

...reached, it does not like

...perforce. Downward

...desire. So I create

...ng, for drinking

...particular per-

...n alone the

...coming

...down

Photograph courtesy of Sri Ramanasramam.

RAMANA MAHARSHI

FOURTEEN

RAMANA MAHARSHI

1879–1950, INDIA

ONE DAY, in the small village of Tiruchuli in South India, a boy of sixteen named Venkataraman "died," never to be the same again. In that moment he realized the impermanence of the body and his identification with the universe. Soon after, the child was inwardly called to a neighboring peak, the red mountain Arunachala, believed to be the embodiment of Lord Shiva of Hindu mythology. Leaving his home for good with just a few rupees for the journey, the child never touched money again. Upon arriving at the town of Tiruvannamalai, at the base of Arunachala, the boy plunged deeply into the peace of meditation in the cellar of the thousand-pillared temple of Shiva. After months of blissful samadhi (absorption in the Self), covered with vermin, the boy was taken from the temple and cared for in a cave beside the mountain. Sri Ramana Maharshi, as he became known, never left the mountain that had inexorably drawn him. Long after his passing, Ramana's abiding presence continues to draw seekers from all over the world to Sri Ramanashram and Arunachala.

Ramana taught primarily in silence, though at times he engaged in conversations with devotees. Paul Brunton, the Western mystical journalist largely responsible for bringing Ramana to the attention of the West, explained, "I cannot turn my gaze away from him. My initial bewilderment, my perplexity at being totally ignored, slowly fade away as this strange fascination begins to grip me more firmly. But it is not till the second hour of the uncommon scene that I become aware of a silent, resistless change that is taking place within my mind. . . . I know only that a steady river of quietness seems to be flowing near me, that a great peace is penetrating the inner reaches of my being, and that my thought-tortured brain is beginning to arrive at some rest."

Ramana encouraged the seeker to examine his own sense of identity through a process called self-enquiry. "As each thought arises, one must be watchful to whom is this thought occurring." When asked a spiritual question, he often replied, "Find out who it is that wants to know." Ramana emphasized that self-enquiry "directly leads to Self-Realization by removing the obstacles which make you think that the Self is not already realized." He directed his disciples to "Learn first who you are. . . . This is simple experience. The state of being is now and here all along."

Though frail of body in his later years, and plagued by the cancer that led to his death, Ramana remained ever present, ever peaceful, and always compassionate to those who sought him out from the corners of the world. Ramana even gave *darshan* (a viewing of the master) when he was too weak to sit up, not wanting to disappoint the crowds of people who filed slowly by to spend a second or two in his presence. In the hours before he passed away, Sri Ramana remarked, "People say I am leaving. Where could I go? I am here."

These stories following come from Ramana's talks with his close disciples or descriptions of his early life by family members. They are from various sources, collected in *Ramana Maharshi: A Pictorial Biography*, prepared for the centennial of his birth.

I AM NOT THE BODY, I AM THE SELF

IT WAS about six weeks before I left Madurai for good that the great change in my life took place. It was quite sudden. I was sitting alone in a room on the first floor of my uncle's house. I seldom had any sickness and on that day there was nothing wrong with my health, but a sudden violent fear of death overtook me. There was nothing in my state of health to account for it, and I did not try to account for it or to find out whether there was any reason for the fear. I just felt "I am going to die" and began thinking what to do about it. It did not occur to me to consult a doctor or my elders or friends; I felt that I had to solve the problem myself, there and then.

The shock of the fear of death drove my mind inwards and I said to myself mentally, without, actually framing the words: "Now death has come; what does it mean? What is it that is dying? 'This body dies,'" and at once dramatized the occurrence of death. I lay with my limbs stretched out stiff as though *rigor mortis* had set in and imitated a corpse so as to give greater reality to the enquiry. I held my breath and kept my lips tightly closed so that no sound could escape, so that neither the word "I" nor any other word could be uttered. "Well then," I said to myself, "this body is dead. It will be carried stiff to the burning ground and there burnt and reduced to ashes. But with the death of this body am I dead? Is the body I? It is silent and inert but I feel the full force of my personality and even the voice of the "I" within me, apart from it. So I am Spirit transcending the body. The body dies but the Spirit that transcends it cannot be touched by death. That means I am the deathless Spirit." All this was not dull thought; it flashed through me vividly as living truth which I perceived directly, almost without thought-process. "I" was something very real, the only real thing about my present state, and all the conscious activity connected with my body was centered on that "I". From that moment onwards the "I" or Self focussed attention on itself by a powerful fascination. Fear of death had vanished once and for all. Absorption in the Self continued unbroken from that time on. Other thoughts might come and go like the various notes of music, but the "I" continued like the fundamental *sruti* note that underlies and blends with all the other notes. Whether the body was engaged in talking, reading or anything else, I was still centered on "I". Previous to that crisis I had no clear perception of my Self and was not consciously attracted to it. I felt no perceptible or direct interest in it, much less any inclination to dwell permanently in it.

The consequences of this new awareness were soon noticed in my life. In the first place, I lost what little interest I had in my outer relationship with friends and relatives and went through my studies mechanically. I would hold an open book in front of me to satisfy my relatives that I was reading, when in reality my attention was far away from any such superficial matter. In my dealings with people I became meek and submissive. Going to school, book in hand, I would be eagerly desiring and expecting that God would suddenly appear before me in the sky. What sort of progress could such a one make in his studies at school!

One of the features of my new state was my changed attitude to the Meenakshi Temple. Formerly I used to go there very occasionally with friends to look at the images and put the Sacred Ash and Vermilion on my brow and would return home almost unmoved. But after the awakening I went there almost every evening. I used to go alone and stand motionless for a time before an image of Siva or Meenakshi or Nataraja and the sixty-three Saints, and as I stood there waves of emotion overwhelmed me.

The soul had given up its hold on the body when it renounced the "I-am-the-body" idea and it was seeking some fresh anchorage; hence the frequent visits to the temple and the outpouring of the soul in tears. This was God's play with the soul. I would stand before Iswara, the Controller of the universe and of the destinies of all, the Omniscient and Omnipresent, and sometimes pray for the descent of His Grace upon me so that my devotion might increase and become perpetual like that of the sixty-three Saints. More often I would not pray at all but silently allow the deep within to flow on and into the deep beyond.

I stopped going out with friends to play games, and preferred solitude. I would often sit alone and become absorbed in the Self, the Spirit, the force or current which constituted me. I would continue in this despite the jeers of my elder brother who would sarcastically call me "Sage" or "Yogi" and advise me to retire into the jungle like the ancient Rishis.

When Nagaswami, Sri Bhagavan's brother remarked, "What use is all this to such a one," the meaning was obvious; that one who wished to live like a *sadhu* had no right to enjoy the amenities of home life. Venkataraman (Ramana) recognized the truth in his brother's remark. Making the excuse that he had to return to school, he rose to his feet to leave the house then and there and go forth, renouncing everything. For him that meant Tiruvannamalai and the Holy Hill Arunachala. Unconsciously providing him with funds for the journey, his brother said, "Take five rupees from the box downstairs and pay my college fees on the way." Calculating the distance in an old atlas, he found that three rupees should suffice for the fare to Tiruvannamalai. Leaving behind a note and a balance of two rupees he started off for the railway station.

A school friend while visiting Sri Bhagavan years later in Sri Ramanashram asked, "Why did you not tell at least me that you were leaving home?" Sri Bhagavan replied: "How could I? I myself did not know."

"Hearken; it stands as an insentient Hill. Its action is mysterious, past human understanding. From the age of innocence it had shone within my mind that Arunachala was something of surpassing grandeur, but even when I came to know through another that it was the same as Tiruvannamalai I did not realize its meaning. When it drew me up to it, stilling my mind, and I came close, I saw it (stand) unmoving."

With quick steps, his heart throbbing with joy, he hastened straight to the great temple. In mute sign of welcome, the gates of the three high compound walls and all the doors, even that of the inner shrine, were open before him. He entered the inner shrine alone and stood overcome before his Father. Embracing the linga, in utter ecstasy, the burning sensation which had begun at Madurai vanished and merged in the linga of light, Arunachaleswara. There, in the bliss of union, was the journey ended.

Immediately upon leaving the temple, someone called out to ask whether he wanted his head shaved. Taking it to be the injunction of Sri Arunachala, he consented and was conducted to Ayyankulam Tank where a number of barbers plied their trade. There he had his head completely shaved. Then, standing on the steps of the tank, he threw away his remaining money—a little over three rupees. He never handled money again. He also threw away the packet of sweets which he was still carrying.

Discarding the sacred thread and wearing only a loin cloth, thus unintentionally completing the acts of renunciation, he returned to the temple. Hindu Scriptures enjoin a bath after a head shave. Although there had been no rain for a very long time, Sri Arunachala Himself came in the shape of a single cloud, which hovered directly overhead. Immediately there was a short, sharp shower so that before entering the temple he was given a bath.

Entering the thousand-pillared mantapam he sat in silent absorption, but being subjected to the pranks of local urchins he did not remain there long. Seshadriswami, a revered ascetic who had arrived at Tiruvannamalai a few years earlier, attempted to protect Brahmana Swami, as he was now known. These efforts were not very successful; in fact, at times they had the opposite effect. So Brahmana Swami sought refuge in the Pathala Lingam, an underground vault in the thousand-pillared hall. The sun's rays never penetrated this cave, which was inhabited by ants and vermin. So absorbed was he in meditation that he was completely oblivious when he was bodily carried out of the Pathala Lingam vault to the Subramanya Shrine. For about two months he stayed in the shrine absorbed in samadhi. Paying no heed to nourishment, food had to be put into his mouth, and he remained immersed in the effulgence of Bliss, barely conscious of his body, not speaking or moving, so that to onlookers it appeared to be the most intense *tapas*. It was not really *tapas* at all. He was simply ignoring the body he had ceased to need. He was already a *Jivanmakta* [liberated while alive] in unwavering consciousness of identity with the Self and had no *karma* left to wipe out, no further goal to attain.

From the Subramanya Shrine he moved to the adjoining flower-garden and banana grove. Also, at this time, he would sometimes be found in the vehicle room, where the large floats used for temple celebrations were stored. He even moved about in this state, for on waking to the world he would sometimes find himself under the wheel of a vehicle, with no recollection of how he got there. Within the temple precincts, by the side of the road which runs along the outside temple wall, he next sat under the shade of a large Illupai tree or in the Mangai Pillayar Shrine, which was nearby. It was here that he was joined by his first regular attendant, Uddandi Nayanar. Brahmana Swami's shining countenance, resulting from his profound realization, began drawing pilgrims in large numbers. To give Brahmana Swami more solitude he was moved to Gurumurtam less than a year and a half after his arrival at Tiruvannamalai.

His body was so neglected that it might not have endured long and he might have effortlessly discarded it. So the story would have ended. Yet the story was just beginning; for his life was to be a perfect example of an ancient *Rishi of Upanishadic* lore. Living in the world, yet completely untouched by it, he was to attract earnest souls from far and near, guiding so profoundly that it would not cease with the body's passing, as is the case of all great sages down through time.

The scene of the young sage, glowing with self-realization as he enters the Arunachaleswara Temple, shall forever remain imprinted on the heart of humanity.

From the words of Sri Bhagavan Ramana Maharshi
and those close to him in his early life.

Photograph courtesy of Anandashram and Premananda Trikannao

SWAMI (PAPA) RAMDAS AND MOTHER KRISHNABAI

SWAMI (PAPA) RAMDAS
MOTHER KRISHNABAI

1884–1963, INDIA ↶ 1903–1989, INDIA

HERE IS perhaps no being who more fully embodies absolute surrender than Swami Ramdas. Born as Vittal Rao to a devout Hindu couple in Kerala, India, he eventually married and led the life of a householder until the age of thirty-six. Having enjoyed the tribulations and suffered the trials of life in the world, Vittal was overcome, in 1920, with a passionate yearning to realize his Divine nature. The attainment of everlasting peace and knowledge of the Supreme Self was all that mattered to him. Influenced by the teachings of Ramakrishna, Vivekananda, and others, he allowed all attachments to family and ordinary life simply to fall away. There was no other choice to Vittal than to wholeheartedly surrender himself to God. His father, realizing Vittal's calling, initiated him with the Ram (God) mantra. This was the turning point of Vittal's life. The name of Ram did not leave his breath or his consciousness from that day forward.

Devoted to life as a *sadhu*, or wandering beggar, Vittal renounced worldly life to wander wherever God led him. The remarkable tales of his journey are recounted in his autobiography, *In Quest of God*. As he traveled, penniless yet blissful, he saw none but God Himself, be it in the form of his fellow *sadhus* or those who sought to rob him of his very few possessions. In fact, Vittal magnanimously invited the thief to take whatever he wanted, assuring him that he must need it more. Reciting perpetually the mantram "Om Sri Ram Jai Ram Jai Jai Ram," which means "Victory to God," Vittal joyously accepted each moment as it unfolded as the fulfillment of the Divine will.

Under the guidance of Ram, Vittal took the name of Ramdas (servant of Ram) and from that time on, no longer referred to himself in the first person. Ramdas' pilgrimage took him far and wide. After receiving the *darshan* (sitting before the teacher and receiving blessing) of Ramana Maharshi, Ramdas, filled with inexpressible ecstasy, undertook a month-long retreat in a cave on the slopes of Tiruvannamalai. Chanting only the name of God in the form of Papa Ram, Ramdas was blessed with the luminous vision that Ram and only Ram was in every form, inner and outer. Permeated with this radiance and bliss and oblivious to his body and surroundings, for Ramdas the experience was at first temporary, then indwelling and permanent.

Papa continued his journey throughout India over the next several years, ultimately settling into a small ashram in Kerala. The present ashram, Anandashram, founded in 1931, has attracted thousands of devotees from India and abroad. Papa was served by Mother Krishnabai, who was drawn to him following the death of her husband in 1928. Initiated also into the Ram mantram, Mother Krishnabai became renowned for her love, devotion, and service. Eternal peace, surrender, joy, purity, and compassion were palpably present in the lives of both Papa Ramdas and Mother Krishnabai. Papa left his body in 1963 and she carried on his work until her death in 1989. Her enlightenment story is also included.

Swami Ramdas' story comes from his own account of his spiritual search, entitled *God Experience*. Mother Krishnabai's story was recorded by a disciple and is reprinted from *Om Sri Ram* newsletter.

THERE IS ONLY RAM (GOD)

WHEN THE Guru gave Ramdas the Ram Mantra, he told him, "If you chant this Mantra always you will attain everlasting joy." After receiving the Mantra Ramdas started chanting it as in-

---

AUTHORS' NOTE: Papa Ramdas always wrote in the third person when referring to himself.

structed by the Guru. He could not do any other work thereafter. Most of his time was spent in chanting the Mantra. Then people asked him, "Is that all the teaching that you have received from the Guru? Did you not ask him any other question?" There was no other question to be asked until Ramdas first put into practice what he was asked to do. The first lesson we must learn well before we proceed to the second lesson. That lesson he was trying to put into practice. After that he found there were no questions left to be asked. All doubts dissolved, all questions disappeared and what the Guru promised he got by chanting the Mantra. The aspiration of everyone is to get happiness—real, lasting happiness; and that goal was reached by chanting Ramnam. Then there was nothing left to be attained and so there were no questions to be asked at all.

When he was chanting Ram Mantra, God took him out of Mangalore on a wandering life. In the course of his wanderings he went to Ramana Maharshi. There too he did not ask any question. He stood before him and prayed only for grace. And grace was granted, not by talk but by look. Ramdas left that place and came to Siddharudha Math. There he got the Darshan of the sage, did Pranams [prostrations] to him and sat before him, especially during the morning and afternoon Parayana [teachings]. Ramdas had no doubts to be cleared, no questions to ask. In the course of the reading, Siddharudha Swami in some connection said, "You see, we have to realize the Truth not merely for our own sake, but we must see that by our contact and influence, others also get a push towards the realization of God. It is not enough if we enjoy peace ourselves, but we must share it also with others."

At that time Ramdas was moving from place to place like one gone mad, in a state of divine intoxication. Ramnam was on his tongue ceaselessly. He had hardly any sleep in the nights. Food was reduced to the minimum so that he might not get into Tamasic [dull and lazy] mood. Then came the universal vision, when the inner illumination was complete through repetition of

Ramnam and the contact and grace of saints. Thereafter the mind ceased to trouble him because the mind itself ceased to be, and with the mind all Vasanas [mental tendencies] disappeared. When you attain universal vision, the entire individuality ceases. You see the universe as the expression of the Self or Atman. Atman is nameless and formless. The universe is with names and forms. So the universe is the manifest and the Atman is the unmanifest. Actually they are both one and the same. This is a mystery which you cannot explain in words or grasp with the mind.

We can keep Vasanas under control temporarily. We cannot entirely destroy them without the grace of saints or Guru. We attain Jnana when the mind disappears with all its desires. Thereafter there is no Sadhana necessary for self-control, because there is no mind. We live in a natural state. It is called Sahaja.

When you attain to the Sahaja state, there is nothing left for you to do. That is the end of all Sadhanas. That is the Siddha Avastha, which means the state of spiritual perfection. You have nothing more to attain. Worldly desires are replaced by desire for Jnana or liberation. When liberation is achieved, that desire also disappears. Then you are perfectly desireless. That is your normal state. When you are desiring things and running here and there in pursuit of them you are in an abnormal state.

Till we reach the Sahaja state we are, as it were, in a diseased condition. Ignorance is the disease which has made the soul bound and miserable. Health returns when we know that we are the Self. Otherwise we think we are the body. Identification with the body and the senses gives rise to duality. Then comes the dual throng and you are caught up in the Gunas and Dwandwas like praise and blame, honor and dishonor, etc. You have forgotten or ignored your real nature which is the eternal, infinite Self. You think you are a body subject to birth, decay, disease and death though you are the immortal, changeless Spirit. Instead of identifying yourself with the Atman, you identify yourself with the body and the result is pain, misery, anxiety and death. Thus runs the prayer in the Upanishads:

Lead me from the unreal to the Real.
Lead me from darkness to Light.
Lead me from death to Immortality.

Such a soul who has realized the pristine glory of his immortal Self is happy and cheerful at all times. Sorrow and death cannot touch him. He has conquered death and will bravely face it without flinching.

From *God Experience* by Swami Ramdas.

WITH THE DIVINE MOTHER

IN THE BEGINNING, there was only my Infinite beginningless and endless Papa (God). Then, in order to enjoy His own bliss, He projected forth as this vast universe and all the things in it. In the creation man alone is endowed with all such qualities as would help him to return eventually to his source—infinite Papa himself. To help him in his spiritual progress, Papa created the Rishis [sages], Vedas, Mantras and other religious practices as would help man to take his mind within. This infinite, eternal Papa also came in the form of "Ramdas" to teach the world how to attain His own Supreme Being.

When Papa first gave me the Ram mantra, he told me to practise *Bhakti* [devotion] Yoga, *Karma* [action] Yoga and *Jnana* [knowledge] Yoga simultaneously in order to attain His Supreme Being. Papa asked me to repeat the Name constantly—that became Bhakti Yoga; to bring to mind all the universal attributes of Papa such as "Papa, Thou art infinite, Papa, Thou art eternal, Thou art manifest and unmanifest and beyond both" and so on. That became Jnana Yoga. And, Papa told me that whatever work

I did with my hands I should regard as His service and this became Karma Yoga. By doing all these three simultaneously, Papa granted me three of the four *Sakshatkars* (realizations). Before I got the final experience, the fourth Sakshatkar, I had to leave the place for another town. There, bereft of Papa's company, I was afraid I might lose whatever I had gained till then.

So, I came back to Papa and, then, Papa granted me the fourth and ultimate Sakshatkar. Till that moment, the Kundalini [coiled serpent power] had come up to *Bhrukuti* or the point between the eyebrows. Papa told me that up to that point, he would guide me from outside. Thereafter, in the final journey of Kundalini from Bhrukuti to *Sahasrara* [thousand-petaled lotus], only the "Ramdas who was within me" would take me upward. By His Grace, in fact whatever I had achieved was only by His Grace—for, I had neither the strength nor the capacity to go so fast on my own—a flame of indescribable luster shot past the Bhrukuti to Sahasrara and I got lost in that *Ananda* or bliss divine.

The experience that I had at that time cannot be described because, in that supreme state, there was only one Void, none to experience and no state to be experienced. Everything was absolute stillness and vacant, like the empty space between the earth and the sky. When Papa brought me back to the plane of relativity, it was with the consciousness that I was Eternal and this perishable universe was itself my body. Before I attained the final realization, my body consciousness might have been like a whiff of breeze but, in that brilliant flame, even this faint body-idea was burnt to ashes.

After bringing me to the relative plane, Papa made me a child. And, it is now in the spirit of a child that I live and work in the world. So as a child, my *Namaskar* [salutations] to all of you who are but Papa's form.

From the *Om Sri Ram* newsletter.

SIXTEEN

PARAMAHANSA YOGANANDA

1893–1952, INDIA

P ARAMAHANSA YOGANANDA, author of the 1946 classic, *Autobiography of a Yogi*, was born in India, trained in yoga, and sent to the West by his gurus. Babaji, the youthful and immortal guru of his lineage, instructed Yogananda, "You are the one I have chosen to spread the message of Kriya Yoga in the West." Yogananda's gentle, sweet, and beautiful face led audiences to be quite surprised to hear the excitement in his bellowing voice, as deep as the ocean of consciousness in which he was so immersed. Yogananda charmed seekers in the West, most of who were new to the teachings of India, in hundreds of venues across the country. It was in Los Angeles, in 1925, that he established Self-Realization Fellowship to facilitate the dissemination of his teachings. By his death in 1952, Yogananda had initiated over 100,000 people into the path of Kriya Yoga (the practice of yoga taught by the lineage of Yogananda) during his more than thirty years in the United States.

Yogananda's autobiography, probably more than any other book of its kind, was and continues to be responsible for turning countless devotees toward the path of yoga. His descriptions of cosmic experiences, selfless saints and *sadhus* (wandering renunciates), and amazing yogic practices remain indelibly imprinted on the minds of seekers throughout the world. What were once considered attributes only of Jesus were in fact spiritual states attainable by anyone with the interest and will for spiritual practice. As it turned out, the practice was for most of us neither as easy nor as glorious as Yogananda suggested, but the inspiration he provided was invaluable nonetheless.

To those who had the fortune of knowing him, Yogananda was an awesome presence, in silk saffron-colored robes, with flowing dark hair

PARAMAHANSA YOGANANDA

and considerable girth. He taught with boundless energy, his deep booming voice giving encouragement and inspiration as well as strict discipline to all those who wished to understand and practice meditation and yoga.

Yogananda's work has been very fruitful. He was both a mystic and a practical man, developing techniques such as energization exercises, healing affirmations, and laws of success to help his disciples deal with their stressful lives in the West. His Los Angeles-based organization, Self-Realization Fellowship (SRF), and his Yoganda Satsanga Society of India are still thriving.

During his life he was most known for his great devotional love for God, his disciples, and his homeland, India. He passed away while reciting the poem, *My India,* at a banquet in honor of the Indian ambassador. Remarkable, but true to the kind of stories in his autobiography, his body was free from rigor mortis or any signs of decomposition for twenty-one days after his *mahasamadhi* (yogic death).

The selection comes from the classic *Autobiography of a Yogi,* first published in 1946, which is responsible for interesting thousands of seekers in a further exploration of spiritual life, Eastern philosophy, and yoga.

BRINGING COSMIC CONSCIOUSNESS TO THE WEST

An Experience in Cosmic Consciousness

"I AM HERE, Guruji." My shamefacedness spoke more eloquently for me.

"Let us go to the kitchen and find something to eat." Sri Yukteswar's manner was as casual as though hours and not days had separated us.

"Master, I must have disappointed you by my abrupt departure from my duties here; I thought you might be angry with me."

"No, of course not! Wrath springs only from thwarted desires. I do not expect anything from others, so their actions cannot be in opposition to wishes of mine. I would not use you for my own ends; I am happy only in your own true happiness."

"Sir, one hears of divine love in a vague way, but today I am indeed having a concrete example of it from your angelic self! In the world, even a father does not easily forgive his son if he leaves his parent's business without warning. But you show not the slightest vexation, though you must have been put to great inconvenience by the many unfinished tasks I left behind."

We looked into each other's eyes, where tears were shining. A blissful wave engulfed me; I was conscious that the Lord, in the form of my guru, was expanding the small ardors of my heart into the vast reaches of cosmic love.

A few mornings later I made my way to Master's empty sitting room. I planned to meditate, but my laudable purpose was unshared by disobedient thoughts. They scattered like birds before the hunter.

"Mukunda!" Sri Yukteswar's voice sounded from a distant balcony.

I felt as rebellious as my thoughts. "Master always urges me to meditate," I muttered to myself. "He should not disturb me when he knows why I came to his room."

He summoned me again; I remained obstinately silent. The third time his tone held rebuke.

"Sir, I am meditating," I shouted protestingly.

"I know how you are meditating," my guru called out, "with your mind distributed like leaves in a storm! Come here to me."

Thwarted and exposed, I made my way sadly to his side.

"Poor boy, mountains cannot give you what you want."

Master spoke caressingly, comfortingly. His calm gaze was unfathomable. "Your heart's desire shall be fulfilled."

Sri Yukteswar seldom indulged in riddles; I was bewildered. He struck gently on my chest above the heart.

My body became immovably rooted; breath was drawn out of my lungs as if by some huge magnet. Soul and mind instantly lost their physical bondage and streamed out like a fluid piercing light from my every pore. The flesh was as though dead, yet in my intense awareness I knew that never before had I been fully alive. My sense of identity was no longer narrowly confined to a body but embraced the circumambient atoms. People on distant streets seemed to be moving gently over my own remote periphery. The roots of plants and trees appeared through a dim transparency of the soil; I discerned the inward flow of their sap.

The whole vicinity lay bare before me. My ordinary frontal vision was now changed to a vast spherical sight, simultaneously all-perceptive. Through the back of my head I saw men strolling far down Rai Ghat Lane, and noticed also a white cow that was leisurely approaching. When she reached the open ashram gate, I observed her as though with my two physical eyes. After she had passed behind the brick wall of the courtyard, I saw her clearly still.

All objects within my panoramic gaze trembled and vibrated like quick motion pictures. My body, Master's, the pillared courtyard, the furniture and floor, the trees and sunshine, occasionally became violently agitated, until all melted into a luminescent sea; even as sugar crystals, thrown into a glass of water, dissolve after being shaken. The unifying light alternated with materializations of form, the metamorphoses revealing the law of cause and effect in creation.

An oceanic joy broke upon calm endless shores of my soul. The Spirit of God, I realized, is exhaustless Bliss; His body is countless tissues of light. A swelling glory within me began to envelop towns, continents, the earth, solar and stellar systems, tenuous nebulae, and floating universes. The entire cosmos, gently luminous, like a city seen afar at night, glimmered within the infinitude of my being. The dazzling light beyond the sharply etched global outlines faded slightly at the farthest edges; there I saw a mellow radiance, ever undiminished. It was indescribably subtle; the planetary pictures were formed of a grosser light.

The divine dispersion of rays poured from an Eternal Source, blazing into galaxies, transfigured with ineffable auras. Again and again I saw the beams condense into constellations, then re-solve into sheets of transparent flame. By rhythmic reversion, sextillion worlds passed into diaphanous luster, then fire became firmament.

I cognized the center of the empyrean as a point of intuitive perception in my heart. Irradiating splendor issued from my nu-cleus to every part of the universal structure. Blissful *amrita*, nectar of immortality, pulsated through me with a quicksilver-like fluidity. The creative voice of God I heard resounding as *Aum*, the vibration of the Cosmic Motor.

Suddenly the breath returned to my lungs. With a disap-pointment almost unbearable, I realized that my infinite immen-sity was lost. Once more I was limited to the humiliating cage of a body, not easily accommodative to the Spirit. Like a prodigal child, I had run away from my macrocosmic home and had im-prisoned myself in a narrow microcosm.

My guru was standing motionless before me; I started to prostrate myself at his holy feet in gratitude for his having be-stowed on me the experience in cosmic consciousness that I had long passionately sought. He held me upright and said quietly:

"You must not get overdrunk with ecstasy. Much work yet re-mains for you in the world. Come, let us sweep the balcony floor; then we shall walk by the Ganges."

I fetched a broom; Master, I knew, was teaching me the secret of balanced living. The soul must stretch over the cosmogonic abysses, while the body performs its daily duties.

When Sri Yukteswar and I set out later for a stroll, I was still entranced in unspeakable rapture. I saw our bodies as two astral pictures, moving over a road by the river whose essence was sheer light.

"It is the Spirit of God that actively sustains every form and force in the universe; yet He is transcendental and aloof in the blissful uncreated void beyond the worlds of vibratory phenom-ena," Master explained. "Those that attain Self-realization on earth live a similar twofold existence. Conscientiously performing their work in the world, they are yet immersed in an inward beatitude.

"The Lord has created all men from the illimitable joy of His being. Though they are painfully cramped by the body, God nevertheless expects that men made in His image shall ultimately rise above all sense identifications and reunite with Him."

The cosmic vision left many permanent lessons. By daily stilling my thoughts, I could win release from the delusive conviction that my body was a mass of flesh and bones, traversing the hard soil of matter. The breath and the restless mind, I saw, are like storms that lash the ocean of light into waves of material forms—earth, sky, human beings, animals, birds, trees. No perception of the Infinite as One Light can be had except by calming those storms.

As often as I quieted the two natural tumults, I beheld the multitudinous waves of creation melt into one lucent sea; even as the waves of the ocean, when a tempest subsides, serenely dissolve into unity.

A master bestows the divine experience of cosmic consciousness when his disciple, by meditation, has strengthened his mind to a degree where the vast vistas would not overwhelm him. Mere intellectual willingness or open-mindedness is not enough. Only adequate enlargement of consciousness by yoga practice and devotional *bhakti* can prepare one to absorb the liberating shock of omnipresence.

The divine experience comes with a natural inevitability to the sincere devotee. His intense craving begins to pull at God with an irresistible force. The Lord as the Cosmic Vision is drawn by that magnetic ardor into the seeker's range of consciousness.

I wrote, in my later years, the following poem, "Samadhi," endeavoring to convey a glimpse of its glory:

> Vanished the veils of light and shade,
> Lifted every vapor of sorrow,

Sailed away all dawns of fleeting joy,
Gone the dim sensory mirage.
Love, hate, health, disease, life, death:
Perished these false shadows on the screen of duality.
The storm of *maya* stilled
By magic wand of intuition deep.
Present, past, future, no more for me,
But ever-present, all-flowing I, I, everywhere.
Planets, stars, stardust, earth,
Volcanic bursts of doomsday cataclysms,
Creation's molding furnace,
Glaciers of silent x-rays, burning electron floods,
Thoughts of all men, past, present, to come,
Every blade of grass, myself, mankind,
Each particle of universal dust,
Anger, greed, good, bad, salvation, lust,
I swallowed, transmuted all
Into a vast ocean of blood of my own one Being!
Smoldering joy, oft-puffed by meditation
Blinding my tearful eyes,
Burst into immortal flames of bliss,
Consumed my tears, my frame, my all.
Thou art I, I am Thou,
Knowing, Knower, Known, as One!
Tranquiled, unbroken thrill, eternally living, ever-new peace.
Enjoyable beyond imagination of expectancy, *samadhi* bliss!
Not an unconscious state
Or mental chloroform without wilful return,
Samadhi but extends my conscious realm
Beyond limits of the mortal frame
To farthest boundary of eternity
Where I, the Cosmic Sea,
Watch the little ego floating in Me.
Mobile murmurs of atoms are heard,
The dark earth, mountains, vales, lo! molten liquid!

Flowing seas change into vapors of nebulae!
Aum blows upon vapors, opening wondrously their veils,
Oceans stand revealed, shining electrons,
Till, at the last sound of the cosmic drum,
Vanish the grosser lights into eternal rays
Of all-pervading bliss.
From joy I came, for joy I live, in sacred joy I melt.
Ocean of mind, I drink all creation's waves.
Four veils of solid, liquid, vapor, light,
Lift aright.
I, in everything, enter the Great Myself.
Gone forever, fitful, flickering shadows of mortal memory;
Spotless is my mental sky, below, ahead, and high above;
Eternity and I, one united ray.
A tiny bubble of laughter, I
Am become the Sea of Mirth Itself.

Sri Yukteswar taught me how to summon the blessed experience at will, and also how to transmit it to others when their intuitive channels are developed. For months, after the first time, I entered the state of ecstatic union, comprehending daily why the *Upanishads* say that God is *rasa*, "the most relishable." One morning, however, I took a problem to Master.

"I want to know, sir—when shall I find God?"

"You have found Him."

"O no, sir, I don't think so!"

My guru was smiling. "I am sure you aren't expecting a venerable Personage, adorning a throne in some antiseptic corner of the cosmos! I see, however, that you are imagining that possession of miraculous powers is proof that one has found God. No. One might gain the power to control the whole universe—yet find the Lord elusive still. Spiritual advancement is not to be measured by one's displays of outward powers, but solely by the depth of his bliss in meditation.

"*Ever-new Joy is God.* He is inexhaustible; as you continue your meditations during the years, He will beguile you with an infinite ingenuity. Devotees like yourself who have found the way to God never dream of exchanging Him for any other happiness; He is seductive beyond thought of competition.

"How quickly we weary of earthly pleasures? Desire for material things is endless; man is never satisfied completely, and pursues one goal after another. The 'something else' he seeks is the Lord, who alone can grant lasting joy.

"Outward longings drive us from the Eden within; they offer false pleasures that only impersonate soul happiness. The lost paradise is quickly regained through divine meditation. As God is unanticipatory Ever-Newness, we never tire of Him. Can we be surfeited with bliss, delightfully varied throughout eternity?"

"I understand now, sir, why saints call the Lord unfathomable. Even everlasting life could not suffice to appraise Him."

"That is true; but He is also near and dear. After the mind has been cleared by *Kriya Yoga* of sensory obstacles, meditation furnishes a twofold proof of God. Ever-new joy is evidence of His existence, convincing to our very atoms. Also, in meditation one finds His instant guidance, His adequate response to every difficulty."

"I see, Guruji; you have solved my problem." I smiled gratefully. "I do realize now that I have found God, for whenever the joy of meditation has returned subconsciously during my active hours, I have been subtly directed to adopt the right course in everything, even in minor details."

"Human life is beset with sorrow until we know how to tune in with the Divine Will, whose 'right course' is often baffling to the egoistic intelligence," Master said.

"God alone gives unerring counsel; who but Him bears the burden of the cosmos?"

From *Autobiography of a Yogi* by Paramahansa Yogananda.

❧ SEVENTEEN ❧
MEHER BABA
1894–1969, INDIA

MEHER BABA was quite certain that he was God incarnate, the *Avatar* (incarnation of God) of the Age. Who else would title his book, *God Speaks*? His overwhelming love for humanity, his selfless service and rigorous austerity, and his apparent omniscience—communicated via alphabet board, sign language, and books, despite a forty-four-year vow of silence—are convincing evidence that if not the divine Avatar, he was certainly an extraordinarily spiritual and compassionate human being. Many thousands of pilgrims sought his blessing in the latter years of his life, and thousands still attend the annual celebration of his passing in 1969. This saintly master, who owed allegiance to no religion, encouraged humanity to love God ever more. He also diligently served the poor and the uneducated, and especially the *masts,* God-intoxicated people considered by the rest of society to be hopelessly deranged.

Meher Baba is probably best known for the phrase "Don't Worry, Be Happy" long before it was popularized by singer Bobby McFerrin. His smiling, captivating, mustachioed visage graces business-sized cards and refrigerator magnets distributed by his devotees, known as Baba Lovers.

The transformation of Merwan, a college student in Poona, India, into Meher Baba, the Avatar, is a fascinating story. One day in January 1914 a wild, disheveled old woman named Hazrat Babajan, a self-realized Sufi saint in disguise, called Merwan to her beneath a neem tree as he was returning from college on his bicycle. As she kissed his forehead, Babajan catalyzed a spiritual awakening that forever changed the fate of the young man, and millions of others. Merwan was driven so mad for nearly a year that he beat his head forcefully against a sizeable rock in

MEHER BABA

order to regain his senses. During a grueling five years of spiritual transformation, Meher Baba was assisted by those he called the Five Perfect Masters, including Sai Baba of Shirdi and Upasani Maharaj, who helped him return to "normal consciousness" while maintaining awareness of his divinity.

Meher Baba had often said that the breaking of his silence would be a defining moment. "When I break my Silence, the impact of my Love will be universal and all life in creation will know, feel and receive of it. It will help every individual to break himself free from his own bondage in his own way. I am the Divine Beloved who loves you more than you can ever love yourself. The breaking of my Silence will help you to help yourself in knowing your real Self," he promised. Whether this breaking of the silence was meant to be literal or metaphorical was never revealed. Though he went to his tomb without actually speaking, his last communication to his disciples was, "Do not forget that I am God."

Meher Baba's story comes from his own biography of Hazrat Babajan, the Sufi woman saint, who, with a kiss on the forehead, began his incredible transformation from schoolboy to Avatar.

THE UNIVERSAL LOVE OF AN AVATAR

WHEN THE five Perfect Masters bring me down they draw a veil over me. Although Babajan was in the form of a woman, she was one of them (the five Perfect Masters) and she unveiled me in my present form. With just a kiss on the forehead, between the eyebrows, Babajan made me experience (May 1913) thrills of indescribable bliss which continued for about nine months. Then one night (January 1914) she made me realize in a flash the infinite bliss of self-realization (God-realization).

At the time Babajan gave me the nirvikalp (inconceptual) experience of my own reality, the illusory physical, subtle and mental bodies—mind, worlds, and one and all created things—

ceased to exist for me even as illusion. Then I began to see that only I, and nothing else, existed.

The infinite bliss of my self-realization was, is and will remain continuous. At the moment I experience both infinite bliss as well as infinite suffering. Once I drop the body, only bliss will remain.

But after I became self-conscious I could not have said all this. Nor could I say it even now if it had not been for the indescribable spiritual agonies which I passed through for another period of nine months (until October 1914) in returning to normal consciousness of the suffering of others. During those nine months I remained in a state which no one else could have tolerated for even nine days.

After physical death an ordinary man is usually dead to the world and the world is dead to him. Yet he continues to live his discarnate life beyond the sphere of gross existence. During the first three days of my superconscious state (January 1914) I was truly dead to everybody and everything other than my own infinite Reality, although my physical body continued to function more or less normally. Actually dead, though really living, I was consequently considered by others to be seriously ill. I was allowed to remain in bed, lying with wide open, vacant eyes which saw nothing.

When man (the individualized soul) enters the seventh plane, which is the one and only plane of Reality, his consciousness is fully freed once and for all from everything else. It then is wholly occupied by the Reality of the real self or God. So it is said that the individual soul becomes superconscious, or God-conscious.

To other souls who function within the illusion of duality, the God-conscious one may seem to be physically as much alive as they are. Nevertheless, regardless of the fact that the superconscious one's gross, subtle, and mental bodies may remain functioning, he is dead to illusion for all time. His consciousness has transcended the illusory limitations of births and deaths that lie within the illusion of duality.

The conscious state of God is known only to those who have achieved it. Such a state of realization on divine oneness is completely beyond the domain of mind itself. It is rare for man to become superconscious. One in millions might achieve it. It is rarer still for the God-consciousness to be able to return with God-consciousness to normal consciousness of all the illusory existence—gross, subtle, and mental—as a Perfect Master.

Usually the gross, subtle, and mental bodies of the God-conscious one automatically drop within four days if, after attaining superconsciousness, he does not begin to return to normal consciousness of the illusory world of duality. In an unusual case all three bodies of the God-conscious one continue to function indefinitely in the relative higher and lower spheres of illusion. Then, for others, such a one is truly the ever-living dead, a real *Majzoob-e Kamil,* or conscious God in the midst of illusion-conscious humanity. To touch such a one is to touch God Himself!

In my ease, I did not drop the body on the fourth day, nor did I become established in the gross sphere as a *Majzoob,* nor did I begin to regain the normal consciousness of a Perfect Master. Only such a Perfect One is capable of knowing the state in which I had to remain for nine months.

On the fourth day and after I was slightly conscious of my body and began to move about without any consciousness of my surroundings. I received no promptings from my mind as would an ordinary man. I had no knowledge of the things I did or did not do. I did not sleep and had no appetite. No one had any idea throughout this period that I sat, talked, walked, lay down, and did everything by instinct, more like an automaton than an ordinary human being.

My sleepless, staring, vacant eyes worried my mother most. She believed and told others that I had gone mad. In her anguish she could not refrain from going once to Babajan and demanding to know what she had done to me. Shirinmai did this because she knew that I used to go and sit near Babajan for a while each night during the previous nine months (May 1913–January 1914).

Babajan indicated to my mother that I was intended to shake the world into wakefullness, but that meant nothing to Shirinmai in her distress.

For a long time I was given regular medical treatment, but no amount of drugging and injections could put me to sleep. As Shirinmai used to say, "Having exhausted all available means," she sent me to Bombay to stay with Jamshed for a change.

Thinking to keep me occupied with day-to-day activities, Jamshed encouraged me to cook the food for the two of us. Sometimes I did the cooking all right, but I did it as I did other things—without knowing what I was doing. I can recall the particular bench in the Victoria Gardens on which I passed most of the time, sitting alone, entirely oblivious of the world and its affairs.

Although the infinite bliss I experienced in my superconscious state remained continuous, as it is now, I suffered agonies in returning towards normal consciousness of illusion. Occasionally, to give some sort of relief, I used to knock my head so furiously against walls and windows that some of them showed cracks.

In reality there is no suffering as such, only infinite bliss. Although suffering is illusory, still, within the real of illusion, it is suffering. In the midst of illusion, Babajan established my reality. My reality, although untouched by illusion, remained connected with illusion. That was why I suffered incalculable spiritual agonies.

Nine months after my self-realization (November 1914) I began to be somewhat conscious of my surroundings. Life returned to my vacant eyes. Although I would not sleep, I began regularly to eat small quantities of food. (It is an incredible fact that Baba did not eat for the nine months following his self-realization in January 1914.) I now knew what I was doing but I continued to do things intuitively, as impelled to do them by inner forces. I did not do things of my own accord or when asked by others. For example, when I began to teach (December 1915) Persian to Buasaheb, my mother tried to collect more pupils for me, thinking this would hasten my "recovery." But I would attend to no one else and continued to teach only Buasaheb.

Later on (April 1915) I also began to go for long distances on foot or by vehicle. Once I left Poona by rail for Raichur (more than three hundred miles south of Poona), but after travelling for only thirty-four miles I felt the urge to leave the train at Kedgaon. There for the first time I came in physical contact with Narayan Maharaj (one of the five Perfect Masters) whose *ashram* is not far from that railway station.

Similarly, from time to time I was also drawn to see Majzoobs like Banemiyan Baba at Aurangabad and Tipoo Baba at Bombay. Once in the company of Behram (Buasahib) I travelled as far north as Nagpur and saw Tajuddin Baba (another of the five Perfect Masters).

Finally (December 1915) I felt impelled to call on Sai Baba, the Perfect Master among Masters. At that time he was returning in a procession from Lendi (in Shirdi), a place to and from which he was led everyday in order to ease himself. Despite the crowds I intuitively prostrated myself before him on the road. When I arose, Sai Baba looked straight at me and exclaimed, "Parvardigar" (God-Almighty-Sustainer).

I then felt drawn to walk to the nearby temple of Khandoba in which Maharaj (Shri Upasani Maharaj) was staying in seclusion. He had been living on water there under Sai Baba's direct guidance for over three years. At that time Maharaj was reduced almost to a skeleton due to his fast on water. He was also naked and surrounded by filth.

When I came near enough to him, Maharaj greeted me, so to speak, with a stone which he threw at me with great force. It struck me on my forehead exactly where Babajan had kissed me, hitting with such force that it drew blood. The mark of that injury is still on my forehead. But that blow from Maharaj was the stroke of dnyan (*Marefat of Haqiqat*, or divine knowledge).

Figuratively, Maharaj had started to rouse me from "sound sleep." But in sound sleep man is unconscious, while I, being superconscious, was wide awake in sound sleep. With that stroke, Maharaj had begun to help me return to ordinary consciousness of the realm of illusion.

That was the beginning of my present infinite suffering in illusion which I experience simultaneously with my infinite bliss in Reality. But it took me seven years of acute struggle under Maharaj's active guidance to return completely to, and become established in, normal human consciousness of the illusion of duality, while yet experiencing continuously my superconsciousness.

The more normally conscious I became, the more acute my suffering grew. For years therefore I continued to knock my head frequently on stones. That was how I eventually lost all my teeth, for through the constant knocking they became prematurely loose. This also resulted in a wound which was constantly fresh, and therefore I always used to keep a colored handkerchief tied around my forehead.

The more I returned to worldly normality, the more impatient my mother became to see me settled into the routine of life. To satisfy her I joined the Kan (Kavasji) Khatau theatrical company as its manager (1916) and traveled with the show to Lahore.

Several years later, after becoming almost three-fourths normally conscious while retaining full superconsciousness, I went to Sakori and stayed for six months (July–December, 1921) near Maharaj. At the end of this period Maharaj made me *know* fully what I am, just as Babajan had made me feel in a flash what I am.

During those six months Maharaj and I used to sit near each other in a hut behind closed doors almost every night. On one such occasion Maharaj folded his hands to me and said, "Merwan, you are the Avatar and I salute you."

For about four months after this (January–May, 1922) I stayed in a small *jhopdi* (thatched hut). It was built for me temporarily on the edge of some fields in the very thinly populated area of what is now the Shivajinagar area of Poona. In this manner I began to live independently, surrounded by men who formed the nucleus of the *mandali*. One of these was the first to start addressing me as "Baba." (Meher Baba means literally, "Compassionate Father.") Some of the men were drawn intuitively to me long before they had any clear idea of my inner state. Others were attracted to me by hints from Babajan and Maharaj. And still others I drew directly to me.

At that time both Babajan and Maharaj began telling various people, referring to me, that "The child is now capable of moving the whole world at a sign from his finger." Once (May 1922) Maharaj addressed a large gathering of the *mandali* and said, "Listen to me most carefully. I have handed over my key (spiritual charge) now to Merwan, and henceforth you are all to stick to him and do as he instructs you. With God's grace you will soon reach the goal." Still others, Maharaj asked individually to follow me.

From *Hazrat Babajan* by Avatar Meher Baba and A. G. Munsif.

J. KRISHNAMURTI

EIGHTEEN

J. KRISHNAMURTI

1895–1986, INDIA

J IDDU KRISHNAMURTI was born in Madanapalle, a small village in South India. His parents were middle-class Brahmins. The boy's father was a District Magistrate and member of the Theosophical Society. His loving mother cared for him and his brother Nitya until her death when Krishnamurti was ten. At this time his father retired from the government and worked for the Theosophical Society in Madras. There Krishnamurti was discovered by C. W. Leadbeater and Mrs. Annie Besant, the head of the society. Believing he was to be the vehicle for the World Teacher, Lord Maitreya, Leadbeater took on the task of educating the boy, teaching him appropriate behavior and making him a fit instrument for his later work. Krishnamurti's education included nightly astral visits with Leadbeater to the feet of Master Kuthumi, Leadbeater's immortal Tibetan guru. He was soon taken under the wing of Annie Besant as well. His spiritual education and initiation into the White Brotherhood of Masters continued.

Krishnamurti's education continued to England, France, India, and Australia. Though remaining devoted to Theosophy, he grew increasingly independent of the influence of Leadbeater and Besant once he turned eighteen. In his mid-twenties, Krishnamurti began to undergo an intense process of spiritual purification and illumination, culminating in the enlightenment experience recounted here. By the time he was supposed to take over the reigns of the Order of the Eastern Star and assume the mantle of World Teacher for the Theosophists, this budding world teacher had questioned intently and become disillusioned with the idea of organizations, masters, gurus, and spiritual paths.

In one of his most famous speeches, at the age of thirty-three, Krishnamurti, instead of continuing his leadership of the Order, dissolved it. He proclaimed, "I maintain the Truth is a pathless land, and you cannot approach it by any path whatsoever, by any religion, by any sect.... Truth, being limitless, unconditioned, unapproachable by any path whatsoever, cannot be organized; nor should any organization be formed to lead or coerce people along a particular path.... The moment you follow someone you cease to follow Truth.... I am concerning myself with only one essential thing: to set man free. I desire to be free him from all cages, from all fears, and not to found religions, new sects, nor to establish new theories and new philosophies.... My only concern is to set men absolutely, unconditionally free."

Krishnamurti pursued that single aim until his death in 1986 at the age of ninety in Ojai, California, the site of many of his talks and activities. He traveled the world spreading his philosophy of understanding the nature of the mind in order to gain liberation from the limitations imposed by self and society. Krishnamurti believed that education is the key to developing a more harmonious and peaceful society, and so was influential in the founding of schools and retreat centers in England, India, and the United States. The author of more than 200 books, Krishnamurti's legacy of written and spoken philosophy is enormous and reflective of his having become a World Teacher of a different kind than that for which he had been prepared by his Theosophical mentors.

The selection is from a letter to C. W. Leadbeater and Mrs. Annie Besant recorded in the biography entitled *Krishnamurti: The Years of Awkening* by Mary Luytens, a close associate during his early years.

I AM GOD-INTOXICATED

EVER SINCE I left Australia I have been thinking and deliberating about the message which the Master K. H. gave me while I was there. I naturally wanted to achieve those orders as soon as I could, and I was to a certain extent uncertain as to the best method of attaining the ideals which were put before me. I do not think a day passed without spending some thought over it, but I am ashamed to say all this was done most casually and rather carelessly.

But at the back of my mind the message of the Master ever dwelt.

Well, since August 3rd, I meditated regularly for about thirty minutes every morning. I could, to my astonishment, concentrate with considerable ease, and within a few days I began to see clearly where I had failed and where I was failing. Immediately I set about, consciously, to annihilate the wrong accumulations of the past years. With the same deliberation I set about to find out ways and means to achieve my aim. First I realized that I had to harmonize all my other bodies with the Buddhic plane [the highest plane of consciousness] and to bring about this happy combination I had to find out what my ego wanted on the Buddhic plane. To harmonize the various bodies I had to keep them vibrating at the same rate as the Buddhic, and to do this I had to find out what was the vital interest of the Buddhic. With ease which rather astonished me I found the main interest on that high plane was to serve the Lord Maitreya and the Masters. With that idea clear in my physical mind I had to direct and control the other bodies to act and to think the same as on the noble and spiritual plane. During that period of less than three weeks, I concentrated to keep in mind the image of the Lord Maitreya throughout the entire day, and I found no difficulty in doing this. I found that I was getting calmer and more serene. My whole outlook on life was changed.

Then, on the 17th August, I felt acute pain at the nape of my neck and I had to cut down my meditation to fifteen minutes. The pain instead of getting better as I had hoped grew worse. The climax was reached on the 19th. I could not think, nor was I able to do anything, and I was forced by friends here to retire to bed. Then I became almost unconscious, though I was well aware of what was happening around me. I came to myself at about noon each day. On the first day while I was in that state and more conscious of the things around me, I had the first most extraordinary experience. There was a man mending the road; that man was myself; the pickaxe he held was myself; the very stone which he was breaking up was a part of me; the tender blade of grass was my very being, and the tree beside the man was myself. I almost could feel and think like the roadmender, and I could feel the wind passing through the tree, and the little ant on the blade of grass I could feel. The birds, the dust, and the very noise were a part of me. Just then there was a car passing by at some distance; I was the driver, the engine, and the tires; as the car went further away from me, I was going away from myself. I was in everything, or rather everything was in me, inanimate and animate, the mountain, the worm, and all breathing things. All day long I remained in this happy condition. I could not eat anything, and again at about six I began to lose my physical body, and naturally the physical elemental did what it liked; I was semi-conscious.

The morning of the next day (the 20th) was almost the same as the previous day, and I could not tolerate too many people in the room. I could feel them in rather a curious way and their vibrations got on my nerves. That evening at about the same hour of six I felt worse than ever. I wanted nobody near me nor anybody to touch me. I was feeling extremely tired and weak. I think I was weeping from mere exhaustion and lack of physical control. My head was pretty bad and the top part felt as though many needles were being driven in. While I was in this state I felt that the bed in which I was lying, the same one as on the previous day, was dirty and filthy beyond imagination and I could not lie in it. Suddenly I found myself sitting on the floor and Nitya and Rosalind asking me to get into bed. I asked them not to touch me and cried out that the bed was not clean. I went on like this for some time till eventually I wandered out on the verandah and sat a few moments exhausted and slightly calmer. I began to come to myself and finally Mr. Warrington asked me to go under the pepper tree which is near the house. There I sat crosslegged in the meditation posture. When I had sat thus for some time, I felt myself going out of my body, I saw myself sitting down with the delicate tender leaves of the tree over me. I was facing the east. In front of me was my body and over my head I saw the Star, bright and clear. Then I could feel the vibrations of the Lord Buddha; I beheld Lord Maitreya and Master K. H. I was so happy, calm and at peace. I could still see my body and I was hovering near it. There was such profound calmness both in the air and within myself, the calmness of the bottom of a deep unfathomable lake. Like the lake, I felt my physical body, with its mind and emotions, could be ruffled on the surface but nothing, nay nothing, could disturb the calmness of my soul. The Presence of the mighty Beings was with me for some time and then They were gone. I was supremely happy, for I had seen. Nothing could ever be the same. I have drunk at the clear and pure waters at the source of the fountain of life and my thirst was appeased. Never more could I be thirsty, never more could I be in utter darkness. I have seen the Light. I have touched compassion which heals all sorrow and suffering; it is not for myself, but for the world. I have stood on the mountain top and gazed at the mighty Beings. Never can I be in utter darkness; I have seen the glorious and healing Light. The fountain of Truth has been revealed to me and the darkness has been dispersed. Love in all its glory has intoxicated my heart; my heart can never be closed. I have drunk at the fountain of joy and eternal Beauty. I am God-intoxicated.

From *Krishnamurti: The Years of Awkening* by Mary Luytens.

FRANKLIN MERRELL-WOLFF

NINETEEN

FRANKLIN MERRELL-WOLFF

1897–1985, UNITED STATES

FRANKLIN MERRELL-WOLFF, a brilliant mathematician, gold miner, philosopher, and mystic, awoke spontaneously in 1936. Born in Pasadena, California, in 1887, the son of a Methodist minister, Franklin studied mathematics, philosophy, and psychology as an undergraduate at Stanford University. He pursued graduate studies in philosophy at Harvard, but returned to teach mathematics at Stanford prior to receiving his degree. His philosophical studies, influenced by Kant, eventually caused him to entirely abandon academia in a successful twenty-year quest for self-realization.

Franklin was influenced by Sufi, Theosophical, and Hindu philosophies, particularly the Advaita Vedanta of the Indian master, Shankara (the founder of Hindu monasticism), whom he considered his guru. He was also guided to clarity by an unnamed sage, who, while helpful, did not claim to be Franklin's guru. Through his own contemplation of Shankara's thoughts on spiritual liberation, Franklin understood that what was to be realized was not experiential, nor did it involve a change in the content of consciousness. Rather it was the realization of a Nothingness that was identical with his own Self. Fourteen years before his final realization, Franklin had realized, "I am Atman" (Self). The year before his complete awakening, he further recognized, "I am identical with Nirvana." Nevertheless, he had always expected that the final realization would involve some form of experiential happening. As you will read, it was not until he completely dropped any expectations of finding something that could be experienced that the transformation he had long been seeking occurred. As many masters have found, it is often necessary to abandon all seeking, so that finding may happen without interference.

Franklin's account of his enlightenment was discovered by John Lilly, M.D., a researcher in the field of consciousness and interspecies communication, who sought out Franklin in retirement at his remote retreat at Lone Pine, California, in the Sierras. The work was published in 1973 as *Pathways Through to Space*. Franklin's further description of his enlightenment, *The Philosophy of Consciousness Without an Object,* is an extraordinary philosophical companion to the original manuscript. The aphorisms in the second book are not to be missed by anyone sincerely interested in self-realization. Both works have been reprinted as *Franklin Merrell-Wolff's Experience and Philosophy* by the State University of New York Press.

A Western pioneer in the field of mysticism and transcendental awareness, though largely unsung, Franklin produced work that is still appreciated today by sincere seekers of realization. His bodhisattva vow (promise to dedicate oneself, above all else, to spiritual practice until all beings are enlightened), taken before awakening, did not permit him to remain in a state of blissful inactivity. After realization, he continued writing, lecturing, teaching, and working on his land. His close, long-term relationship with his wife and spiritual partner, Sherifa (Sarah), sustained him through the years. He passed away in Lone Pine in 1985, at the age of ninety-eight.

The following account of his 1936 awakening is reprinted from his spiritual autobiography, *Pathways Through to Space*.

PATHWAYS THROUGH TO SPACE

The Light Breaks Forth

August 17, 1936

THE INEFFABLE transition came, about ten days ago.

We had just returned to our Southern California home after a few weeks' stay in a small town in the Mother Lode country in the northern part of the State, and I was resting from the fatigue induced by the all-night driving of the automobile. At the time, I was engaged in the reading of portions of "The System of the Vedanta" by Paul Deussen, as I had been doing more or less systematically during the preceding three weeks. This work is an interpretation in western philosophic form of the Vedanta as it is developed in the commentaries of Shankara on the Brahma-sutras. I had been led to this specific program of reading through the realization that Shankara's words had peculiar power, at least in my own experience. For some time I had spontaneously looked to him as to a Guru (spiritual teacher) with whom I was in complete sympathetic accord. I had found him always clear and convincing, at least in all matters relative to the analysis of consciousness, while with the other Sages I either found obscurities or emphases with which I could not feel complete sympathy. For some months I had resolved to delve more deeply into the thought of Shankara, in so far as it was available in translated form. It was in pursuance of this purpose that I was slowly reading and meditating upon "The System of the Vedanta."

I had been following this course while completing a cross-cut in a gold-prospect near the small town of Michigan Bluff. Much of this time I was completely alone and was more than usually successful in penetrating the meaning and following the logic of what I was reading. One day, after the evening meal and while still sitting at the table, I found that, by gradual transition, I had passed into a very delightful state of contemplation. The actual content of the thought of that period is forgotten, but as I made careful note of the state I was in and submitted it to close scrutiny, the quality of the state was well impressed upon my memory. My breath had changed, but not in the sense of stopping or becoming extremely slow or rapid. It was, perhaps, just a little slower than normal. The notable change was in a subtle quality associated with the air breathed. Over and above the physical gases of the air there seemed to be an impalpable substance of indescribable sweetness which, in turn, was associated with a general sense of well-being, embracing even the physical man. It was like happiness or joy, but these words are inadequate. It was of a very gentle quality, yet far transcended the value of any of the more familiar forms of happiness. It was quite independent of the beauty or comfort of the environment. At that time the latter was, to say the least, austere and not in any sense attractive. This quality, associated with the air, I had, in a smaller measure, previously experienced at high altitudes in the mountains, but in the present instance the altitude was only 1800 feet and the air was far from invigorating, due to the period being exceptionally warm. However, introspective analysis revealed the fact that the elixirlike quality was most marked during the exhalation, thus indicating that it was not derived from the surrounding air. Further, the exhaled breath was not simply air expelled into the outer atmosphere, but seemed to penetrate down through the whole organism like a gentle caress, leaving throughout a quiet sense of delight. It seemed to me like a nectar. Since that time I have learned that it is the true Ambrosia.

It is, perhaps, pertinent to note in passing that a few days previously, as a result of thought stimulated by my readings, I had developed an interpretation of the nature of ponderable matter that seemed to me to clear away certain logical difficulties which always have seemed to persist in the efforts to reconcile Transcendent Being with the physical universe. The idea is that ponderable matter—meaning by that term all things sensed whether gross or subtle—is, in fact, a relative absence of substance, a sort of partial vacuum. At the present time I shall not develop the evidence and logic supporting this idea, though this was outlined in my consciousness during the days following the origin of it. The significant point in connection with the present record is the effect this idea had upon my own consciousness. It seems to have had a vital part in clearing the way for the Illumination that came later. This effect was produced in the following manner: Habitually we regard the material filling of sensation as being substantial. To offset this, we may have been theoretically convinced that so-called empty space is not only filled, but actually more substantial than the portions of it occupied by ponderable matter. This idea is not new to metaphysics, and much in the literature of modern physics is not incompatible with it. But I have found that ideas received from outer sources, even though in convincing form, lack the power over consciousness possessed by an original idea. *The effect of this idea with me was a far more effective acceptance of substantial reality where the senses reported emptiness, and a greater capacity to realize unreality—or merely dependent and derivative reality—in the material given through the senses.*

There are further prior pertinent factors which, it seems, should be noted. About eighteen months ago there began a series of conversations with one whom I recognized as a Sage. I checked the validity of my recognition of this One in every way that I could and proved His genuineness to my complete satisfaction. I acted on His word when I could not see clearly and found that clarity gradually unfolded. Acting upon His suggestions, Sherifa—my wife—and I undertook a phase of public work not hitherto attempted. Both of us found as we progressed in the work a gradual growth of understanding that has steadily brought Light where there had been obscurity. Among other things this Sage suggested my correlation with a previous incarnation of special importance. He advised me that He was not, and could not be, my personal Guru, as that relationship was dependent upon alignments that are not arbitrary.

In the past, two important Recognitions have come to me. First, nearly fourteen years ago, in a setting which it is not necessary to delineate, I suddenly recognized "I am Atman." This effected important changes of outlook that persisted. Second, less than one year ago, while engaged in the public work mentioned above, and while deeply interested in a book giving a report of a living Indian Sage, I also suddenly recognized that Nirvana is not a field, or space, or world which one entered and that contained one as space might contain an external object, but rather that "I am identical with Nirvana, and always have been and always will be so." This Recognition likewise had its persistent effects upon the personal consciousness.

We are now ready to return to the Recognition of ten days ago. I say "Recognition" rather than "experience" for a very definite reason. Properly it was not a case of experiential knowledge, which is knowledge from the senses whether gross or subtle, nor knowledge from deduction, though both forms, particularly the latter, have helped in a subsidiary sense. It was an Awakening to a Knowledge which I can best represent by calling it Knowledge through Identity and thus the process—in so far as we can speak of process in this connection at all—is best expressed by the word "Recognition."

I had been sitting in a porch swing, reading as previously stated. Ahead of the sequence in the book, I turned to the section devoted to "Liberation," as I seemed to feel an especial hunger for this. I covered the material quickly and it all seemed very clear and satisfactory. Then, as I sat afterward dwelling in thought upon the subject just read, suddenly it dawned upon me that a common mistake made in the higher meditation—i.e., meditation for Liberation—is the seeking for a subtle object of Recognition, in other words, something that could be experienced. Of course, I had long known the falseness of this position theoretically, yet had failed to recognize it. (Here is a subtle but very important distinction.) At once, I dropped expectation of having anything happen. Then, with eyes open and no sense stopped in functioning—hence no trance—I abstracted the subjective moment—the "I AM" or "Atman" element—from the totality of the objective consciousness manifold. Upon this I focused. Naturally, I found what, from the relative point of view, is Darkness and Emptiness. *But I Realized It as Absolute Light and Fullness and that I was That.* Of course, I cannot tell what IT was in Its own nature. The relative forms of consciousness inevitably distort nonrelative Consciousness. Not only can I not tell this to others, I cannot even contain it within my own relative consciousness, whether of sensation, feeling, or thought. Every metaphysical thinker will see this impossibility at once. I was even prepared not to have the personal consciousness share in this Recognition in any way. But in this I was happily disappointed. Presently I felt the Ambrosia-quality in the breath with the purifying benediction that it casts over the whole personality, even including the physical body. I found myself above the universe, not in the sense of leaving the physical body and being taken out in space, but in the sense of being above space, time, and causality. My karma seemed to drop away from me as an individual responsibility. I felt intangibly, yet wonderfully, free. I sustained this universe and was not bound by it. Desires and ambitions grew perceptibly more and more shadowy. All worldly honors were without power to exalt me. Physical life seemed undesirable. Repeatedly, through the days that followed, I was in a state of deep brooding, thinking thoughts that were so abstract that there were no concepts to represent them. I seemed to comprehend a veritable library of Knowledge, all less concrete than the most abstract mathematics. The personality rested in a gentle glow of happiness, but while it was very gentle, yet it was so potent as to dull the keenest sensuous delight. Likewise the sense of world-pain was absorbed. I looked, as it were, over the world, asking: "What is there of interest here? What is there worth doing?" I found but one interest: the desire that other souls should also realize this that I had realized, for in it lay the one effective key for the solving of their problems. The little tragedies of men left me indifferent. I saw one great Tragedy, the cause of all the rest, the failure of man to realize his own Divinity. I saw but one solution, the Realization of this Divinity.

From *Pathways Through to Space* by Franklin Merrell-Woolf.

Photograph by Jim Morrill, courtesy of Linda Scott

PEACE PILGRIM

I SHALL REMAIN a wanderer until mankind has learned the way of peace, walking until I am given shelter and fasting until I am given food." So bore the white letters of the tunic of this surrendered and determined soul as she traversed more than 25,000 miles on foot for peace. When questioned about her personal history, Peace Pilgrim replied that she had no other name and no home, other than a forwarding address in New Jersey, and revealed only that she came from a poor family, received little formal education, possessed no special talents, and led a guided life. Peace Pilgrim saw no purpose in discussing her age. "As long as I counted birthdays and started thinking about getting older, I did get older. Age is a state of mind, and I think of myself as ageless."

Born on a small farm on the East Coast sometime in the early 1900s, Peace Pilgrim grew from modest roots, acquired money and material positions, then realized the futility of worldly goods and a self-centered life. This led to an all-night vigil of walking through the woods culminating in "a complete willingness, without any reservations, to give my life to God and to service." Adopting a life of voluntary simplicity, she embarked on a fifteen-year period of engaging in volunteer work for peace groups and with individuals suffering from physical, emotional, and mental problems.

On the morning of January 1, 1953, Peace Pilgrim took her vow to walk for peace. She was clad in a navy blue shirt and slacks, and her pocketed tunic contained her few worldly possessions: a comb, folding toothbrush, pen, copies of her message, and her current correspondence. Over the next eleven years, this silver-haired phenomenon walked 25,000 miles, after which time she continued her mission, though she stopped counting miles, until her death in 1981. Her growing demand as an inspirational speaker led her to accept rides when necessary.

Peace Pilgrim spoke with thousands of people in all fifty states, all of the Canadian provinces, and parts of Mexico during the McCarthy era, the Korean and Vietnam wars, and afterward. Whether at a truck stop or during a national radio or television interview, on a dusty road, in a ghetto, or lecturing at a university, Peace Pilgrim's message for peace remained clear and consistent. Sleeping beside the road, in bus stations, and on beaches when no home was offered, she never considered personal danger an issue.

At the time of her death, Peace Pilgrim was crossing the United States for the seventh time. She made what she called "the glorious transition to a freer life" on July 7, 1981, dying instantly in a head-on collision as she was being driven to yet another engagement. In her final newspaper interview, she had spoken of being in radiant health. On a taped radio program the day before she died, the host remarked, "You seem to be a most happy woman." Peace Pilgrim responded, "I certainly am a happy person. How could one know God and not be joyous?"

Peace Pilgrim's enlightenment story is excerpted from her inspiring autobiography, *Peace Pilgrim: Her Life and Message*.

WALKING FOR WORLD PEACE

THESE ARE my steps toward inner peace that I wanted to share with you. There is nothing new about this. This is universal truth. I merely talked about these things in everyday words in terms of my own personal experience with them. The laws which govern this universe work for good as soon as we obey them, and anything contrary to these laws doesn't last long. It contains within itself the seeds of its own destruction. The good in every human life always makes it possible for us to obey these laws. We do have free will about all this, and therefore how soon we obey and thereby find harmony, both within ourselves and within our world, is up to us.

During this spiritual growing up period I desired to know and do God's will for me. Spiritual growth is not easily attained, but it is well worth the effort. It takes time, just as any growth takes time. One should rejoice at small gains and not be impatient, as impatience hampers growth.

The path of gradual relinquishment of things hindering spiritual progress is a difficult path, for only when relinquishment is complete do the rewards really come. The path of quick relinquishment is an easy path, for it brings immediate blessings. And when God fills your life, God's gifts overflow to bless all you touch.

To me, it was an escape from the artificiality of illusion into the richness of reality. To the world it may seem that I had given up much. I had given up burdensome possessions, spending time meaninglessly doing things I knew I should not do and not doing things I knew I should do. But to me it seemed that I had gained much—even the priceless treasures of health and happiness.

The Attainment of Inner Peace

There were hills and valleys, lots of hills and valleys, in that spiritual growing up period. Then in the midst of the struggle there came a wonderful mountaintop experience—the first glimpse of what the life of inner peace was like.

That came when I was out walking in the early morning. All of a sudden I felt very uplifted, more uplifted than I had ever been. I remember I knew *timelessness* and *spacelessness* and *lightness*. I did not seem to be walking on the earth. There were no people or even animals around, but every flower, every bush, every tree seemed to wear a halo. There was a light emanation around everything and flecks of gold fell like slanted rain through the air. This experience is sometimes called the illumination period.

The most important part of it was not the phenomena: the important part of it was the realization of the oneness of all creation. Not only all human beings—I knew before that all human beings are one. But now I knew also a oneness with the rest of creation. The creatures that walk the earth and the growing things of the earth. The air, the water, the earth itself. And, most wonderful of all, *a oneness with that which permeates all and binds all together and gives life to all.* A oneness with that which many would call God.

I have never felt separate since. I could return again and again to this wonderful mountaintop, and then I could stay there for longer and longer periods of time and just slip out occasionally.

The inspiration for the pilgrimage came at this time. I sat high upon a hill overlooking rural New England. The day before I had slipped out of harmony, and the evening before I had thought to God, "It seems to me that if I could always remain in harmony I could be of greater usefulness—for every time I slip out of harmony it impairs my usefulness."

When I awoke at dawn I was back on the spiritual mountaintop with a wonderful feeling. I knew that I would never need to descend again into the valley. I knew that for me the struggle was over, that finally I had succeeded in giving my life or finding inner peace. Again this is a point of no return. You can never go back into the struggle. The struggle is over now because you will to do the right thing and you don't need to be pushed into it.

I went out for a time alone with God. While I was out a thought struck my mind: I felt a strong inner motivation toward the pilgrimage—toward this special way of witnessing for peace.

I saw, in my mind's eye, myself walking along and wearing the garb of my mission. . . . I saw a map of the United States with the large cities marked—and it was as though someone had taken a colored crayon and marked a zigzag line across, coast to coast and border to border, from Los Angeles to New York City. I knew what I was to do. And that was a vision of my first year's pilgrimage route in 1953!

I entered a new and wonderful world. My life was blessed with a meaningful purpose.

However, progress was not over. Great progress has taken place in this third phase of my life. It's as though the central figure of the jigsaw puzzle of my life is complete and clear and unchanging, and around the edges other pieces keep fitting in. There is always a growing edge, but the progress is harmonious. There is a feeling of always being surrounded by all of the good things, like love and peace and joy. It seems like a protective surrounding, and there is an unshakeableness within which takes you through any situation you may need to face.

The world may look at you and believe that you are facing great problems, but always there are the inner resources to easily overcome the problems. Nothing seems difficult. There is a calmness and a serenity and unhurriedness—no more striving or straining about anything. That's a very important thing I've learned. If your life is in harmony with your part in the Life Pattern, and if you are obedient to the laws which govern this universe, then life is full and life is good but life is nevermore overcrowded. If it is overcrowded, then you are doing more than is right for you to do—more than is your job to do in the total scheme of things.

Now there is a living to give instead of to get. As you concentrate on the giving, you discover that just as you cannot receive without giving, so neither can you give without receiving—even the most wonderful things like health and happiness and inner peace. There is a feeling of endless energy, it just never runs out, it seems to be as endless as air. You seem to be plugged in to the source of universal energy.

You are now in control of your life. Your higher nature, which is controlled by God, controls the body, mind, and emotions. (The ego is never really in control. The ego is controlled by wishes for comfort and convenience on the part of the body, by demands of the mind, and by outbursts of the emotions.)

I can say to my body, "Lie down there on that cement floor and go to sleep," and it obeys. I can say to my mind, "Shut out everything else and concentrate on the job before you," and it is obedient. I can say to my emotions, "Be still, even in the face of this terrible situation," and they are still. A great philosopher has said, *he who seems to be out of step may be following a different drummer*. And now you are following a different drummer: the higher nature instead of the lower nature.

When you have done the spiritual growing up you realize that every human being is of equal importance, has work to do in this world, and has equal potential. We are in many varied stages of growth; this is true because we have free will. You have free will as to whether you will finish the mental and emotional growing up. Many choose not to. You have free will as to whether you will begin the spiritual growing up. The beginning of it is the time when you feel completely willing, without any reservations, to leave the self-centered life. And most choose not to. But it was doing that growth and finding inner peace that prepared me for the pilgrimage that I walk today.

Looking through the eyes of the divine nature you see the essence within the manifestation, the creator within the creation, and it is a wonderful, wonderful world!

I realized in 1952 that it was the proper time for a pilgrim to step forth. The war in Korea was raging and the McCarthy era was at its height. It was a time when congressional committees considered people guilty until they could prove their innocence. There was great fear at that time and it was safest to be apathetic. Yes, it was most certainly a time for a pilgrim to step forward, because a pilgrim's job is to rouse people from apathy and make them think.

With the last bit of money I had left, I bought not only paper and stencil for my first messages but material for my first tunic. Although I designed it, the sewing was done by a lady in California, and the lettering was painted by a man who was a sign painter. My initial reaction when I first put it on was a wonderful 'rightness' about it, and I immediately accepted it.

From *Peace Pilgrim* by Peace Pilgrim.

GOPI KRISHNA

TWENTY-ONE

GOPI KRISHNA

1908–1984, INDIA

Gopi Krishna was born in a small village not far from Srinigar in Northern India, his parents were Kashmiri Brahmins. His mother became quite alarmed when, as an infant, Gopi Krishna developed such a severe inflammation of the throat that he was unable to nurse. In one of her dreams, there appeared a well-respected adept who was reputed to perform miracles. The holy man gently stroked the inside of Gopi Krishna's throat, signaled his mother to give him food, then vanished. When she awoke, the infant was suddenly cured. Several years later, the family ventured forth on horseback to visit the saint. As they entered his dwelling, he casually inquired whether Gopi Krishna was able to take milk after the dream.

A second remarkable occurrence took place when Gopi Krishna was eight. Spontaneously overtaken by the question, "What am I?" he fell to ground in a faint. Days later, an extraordinarily vivid dream came to him in which he was surrounded by ethereal beings and found himself transformed in an atmosphere of luminous serenity. This image, he concluded, was the answer to his inquiry.

Spiritual questioning was in Gopi Krishna's blood. His father, a man known for his integrity and compassion, found himself called to pursue the life of a spiritual aspirant and no longer engaged in conversation with his three children. His retirement from career and worldly responsibilities proved challenging for the family. After completing his education, Gopi Krishna secured a government position in Kashmir, married, and raised a family. He subsequently initiated an organization dedicated to social reforms, such as the abolition of the dowry system and the prohibition of the remarriage of widows.

In 1937, at the age of thirty-four, Gopi Krishna experienced a powerful awakening of the *kundalini* (coiled spiritual energy resembling a serpent, emanating from the base of the spine). Employed as a government clerk at the time, he found the "radical alteration" of his nervous system bewildering and even horrifying. From the sensation of "a jet of molten copper" ascending his spine and dashed against his crown to brilliant showers of incandescent light to a variety of distortions of size and shape, Gopi Krishna enjoyed no respite. Utterly exhausted, his torturous days gave way to even worse torment at night. Fearing for his sanity over the extended period of his kundalini awakening, Gopi Krishna ultimately attained permanent awakening.

Kundalini: The Evolutionary Energy in Man, published in 1967, is his phenomenal account of his inner journey. This clear, meticulously well-documented description of the kundalini experience was a first. Soon published in the United States and the United Kingdom and subsequently translated into eleven languages, this book has served as an invaluable guidebook to many on the spiritual path. This work and Gopi Krishna's other books catalyzed a steadily growing interest in the field of consciousness. He spent the last seventeen years of his life enthusiastically introducing this information to the scientific world. The mission of Gopi Krishna was not only the evolution of the human brain and consciousness, but its direct application to establishing and maintaining world peace. Following his death in 1984, various individuals and organizations have dedicated themselves to carrying on his noble mission.

Gopi Krishna's enlightenment story is excerpted from his autobiography, *Living with Kundalini.* His wealth of experiences in this and his other books are well worth reading.

THE AWAKENING OF THE KUNDALINI

DURING THOSE days, an ardent member of our small band of zealous workers in Kashmir was on a visit to Jammu. She often came to my place, usually to have news of our work at Srinagar, about which I received regular reports from our treasurer or our secretary. One day I offered to accompany her home when she rose to depart, intending by the long stroll to rid myself of a slight depression I felt at tbe time.

We walked leisurely, discussing our work, when suddenly while crossing the Tawi Bridge I felt a mood of deep absorption settling upon me until I almost lost touch with my surroundings. I no longer heard the voice of my companion; she seemed to have receded into the distance, though walking by my side. Near me, in a blaze of brilliant light, I suddenly felt what seemed to be a mighty conscious presence, sprung from nowhere, encompassing me and overshadowing all the objects around, from which two lines of a beautiful verse in Kashmiri poured out to float before my vision, like luminous writing in the air, disappearing as suddenly as they had come.

When I came to myself, I found the girl looking at me in blank amazement, bewildered by my abrupt silence and the expression of utter detachment on my face. Without revealing to her all that had happened, I repeated the verse, saying that it had all of a sudden taken form in my mind in spite of myself, and that it accounted for the break in our conversation.

She listened in surprise, struck by the beauty of the rhyme, weighing every word, and then said that it was indeed nothing short of miraculous for one who had never been favored by the muse before to compose so exquisite a verse on the very first attempt with such lightning rapidity. I heard her in silence, carried away by the profundity of the experience I had just gone through. Until that hour, all I had experienced of the superconscious was purely subjective, neither demonstrable to nor verifiable by others. But now for the first time I had before me a tangible proof of the change that had occurred in me, unintelligible to and independently of my surface consciousness.

After escorting my companion to her destination I returned to my residence in time for dinner. All the way back, in the stillness of a pleasant evening and the welcome solitude of an unfrequented path, I remained deeply engrossed in the enigma presented by the vision and the sudden leap taken by my mind in a new direction. The more intently I examined the problem the more surprised I became at the deep meaning of the production, the exquisite formation, and the highly appealing language of the lines. On no account could I claim the artistic composition as mine, the voluntary creation of my own deliberate thought.

I reached my place while still deeply absorbed in the same train of thought and, still engrossed, sat down for dinner. I took the first few morsels mechanically, in silence, oblivious to my surroundings and unappreciative of the food in front of me, unable to bring myself out of the state of intense absorption into which I had fallen, retaining only a slender link with my environment, like a sleepwalker instinctively restrained from colliding with the objects in his path without consciously being aware of them.

In the middle of the meal, while still in the same condition of semi-entrancement, I stopped abruptly, contemplating with awe and amazement, which made the hair on my skin stand on end, a marvelous phenomenon in progress in the depths of my being. Without any effort on my part, and while seated comfortably on a chair, I had gradually passed off, without becoming aware of it, into a condition of exaltation and self-expansion similar to that which I had experienced on the very first occasion, in December 1937, with the modification that in place of a roaring noise in my ears there was now a cadence like the humming of a swarm of bees, enchanting and melodious, and the encircling glow was replaced by a penetrating silvery radiance, already a feature of my being within and without.

The marvelous aspect of the condition lay in the sudden realization that, although linked to the body and surroundings, I had expanded in an indescribable manner into a titanic personality, conscious from within of an immediate and direct contact with an intensely conscious universe, a wonderful inexpressible immanence all around me. My body, the chair I was sitting on, the table in front of me, the room enclosed by walls, the lawn outside and the space beyond, including the earth and sky, appeared to be most amazingly mere phantoms in this real, interpenetrating, and all-pervasive ocean of existence which, to explain the most incredible part of it as best I can, seemed to be simultaneously unbounded, stretching out immeasurably in all directions, and yet no bigger than an infinitely small point.

From this marvelous point the entire existence, of which my body and its surroundings were a part, poured out like radiation, as if a reflection as vast as my conception of the cosmos were thrown out upon infinity by a projector no bigger than a pinpoint, the entire intensely active and gigantic world picture dependent on the beams issuing from it. The shoreless ocean of consciousness in which I was now immersed appeared infinitely large and infinitely small at the same time—large when considered in relation to the world picture floating in it and small when considered in itself, measureless, without form or size—nothing and yet everything.

It was an amazing and staggering experience for which I can cite no parallel and no simile, an experience beyond all and everything belonging to this world conceivable by the mind or perceptible to the senses. I was intensely aware internally of a marvelous being so concentratedly and massively conscious as to outluster and outstature infinitely the cosmic image present before me, not only in point of extent and brightness, but in point of reality and substance as well. The phenomenal world, ceaselessly in motion, characterized by creation, incessant change, and dissolution, receded into the background and assumed the appearance of an extremely thin, rapidly melting layer of foam upon a substantial rolling ocean of life, a veil of exceedingly fine vapor before an infinitely large conscious sun, constituting a complete reversal of the relationship between the world and the limited human consciousness. It showed the previously all-dominating cosmos reduced to the state of a transitory appearance, and the formerly care-ridden point of awareness, circumscribed by the body, grown to the spacious dimensions of a mighty universe and the exalted stature of a majestic immanence before which the material cosmos shrank to the subordinate position of an evanescent and illusive appendage.

I awoke from the semi-trance condition after about half an hour affected to the roots of my being by the majesty and marvel of the vision, entirely oblivious to the passage of time, having in the intensity of the experience lived a life of ordinary existence. During this period, probably due to fluctuations in the state of my body and mind caused by internal and external stimuli, there were intervals of deeper and lesser penetration not distinguishable by the flow of time but by the state of immanence, which, at the point of the deepest penetration, assumed such an awe-inspiring, almighty, all-knowing, blissful, and at the same time absolutely motionless, intangible, and formless character that the invisible line demarcating the material world and the boundless, all-conscious Reality ceased to exist, the two fusing into one; the mighty ocean sucked up by a drop, the enormous three-dimensional universe swallowed by a grain of sand, the entire creation, the knower and the known, the seer and the seen, reduced to an inexpressible sizeless void which no ordinary mind could conceive nor any language describe.

Before coming out completely from this condition and before the glory in which I found myself had completely faded, I found, floating in the luminous glow of my mind, the rhymes following the couplet that had suddenly taken shape in me near the Tawi Bridge that day. The lines occurred one after the other, as if dropped into the three dimensional field of my consciousness by another source of condensed knowledge within me. They started from the glowing recesses of my being, developing suddenly into fully formed couplets like falling snowflakes which, from tiny specks high up, become clear-cut, regularly shaped crystals when nearing the eye, and vanished so suddenly as to leave me hardly any time to retain them in my memory. They came fully formed, complete with language, rhyme, and meter, finished products originating, as it seemed, from the surrounding intelligence, to pass before my internal eye for expression.

I was still in an elevated state when I rose from the table and went to my room. The first thing I did was to write down the lines as far as I could remember them. It was not an easy task. I found that during the short interval that had elapsed I had forgotten not only the order in which the rhymes had occurred but also whole portions of the matter, which it was extremely difficult for me to recollect or supply. It took me more than two hours to supply the omissions.

I went to bed that night in an excited and happy frame of mind. After years of acute suffering I had at last been given a glimpse into the supersensible and at the same time made the fortunate recipient of divine grace, which all fitted admirably with the traditional concepts of kundalini. I could not believe in my good luck; I felt it was too astounding to be true. But when I looked within myself to find out what I had done to deserve it, I felt extremely humbled. I had to my credit no achievement remarkable enough to entitle me to the honor bestowed on me. I had lived an ordinary life, never done anything exceptionally meritorious and never achieved a complete subdual of desires and appetites.

I reviewed all the noteworthy incidents of the last twelve years in my mind, studying them in the light of the latest development, and found that much of what had been dark and obscure so far was now assuming a deep and startling significance. In the intensity of joy which I felt at the revelation I forgot the terrible ordeal I had passed through, as also the grueling suspense and anxiety that had been my companions for all that period. I had drunk the cup of suffering to the dregs to come upon a resplendent, never-ending source of unutterable joy and peace lying hidden in my interior, waiting for a favorable opportunity to reveal itself, affording me in one instant a deeper insight into the essence of things than a whole life devoted to study could do.

From *Living with Kundalini* by Gopi Krishna.

LESTER LEVENSON

TWENTY-TWO

LESTER LEVENSON

1909–1994, UNITED STATES

LESTER LEVENSON is relatively unknown to most spiritual seekers, unless they have come upon what is called the "Sedona Method" Lester's own method of achieving enlightenment, which has been systematized for his students. A self-made man, Lester was not particularly spiritual in his early years. A physicist and engineer, he also achieved financial success in restaurant, lumber, building, oil, and real estate businesses. He lived in New York City, and his life revolved mainly around his relationships with women and his business endeavors, although he was also an avid patron of the arts.

By 1952, however, at the age of forty-two, after his second heart attack, Lester found himself on the brink of death. Suffering also from chronic jaundice, kidney stones, migraine headaches, and a perforated ulcer, Lester was abandoned by his doctor and sent home to die.

Not eager to succumb to his physician's death sentence, Lester began seriously to question and reevaluate the very purpose of his life. Over a three-month period, he not only succeeded at releasing each and every obstacle to his happiness, but all of his health problems spontaneously disappeared! Lester found a way to become enormously happy and to develop yogic powers he had never even known existed. All this without any spiritual instruction whatsoever.

Realizing that his problems were self-caused by his own erroneous thinking, Lester found freedom. When he was able to release negative thoughts and feelings, he felt tremendous relief and inner peace. Lester became acutely aware that the only time he had been really happy was not when he was loved, but when he was loving others, particularly the women in his life. He resolved to love not only women, but everyone he met, and to release any feelings that interfered with that loving. Such an attitude served to enhance his happiness even more.

Soon Lester noticed that his life changed dramatically for the better. Having discovered the secrets of happiness and freedom, he found himself identified with every being and every atom in the universe. Lester saw God in everyone and everything and was in a state of complete harmony. His delight knew no bounds.

Following his realization, Lester relinquished his businesses and moved to the desert outside Sedona, Arizona. He taught small groups of students, whoever found him out of their own search for ultimate freedom. Eventually a center grew around him, though Lester never sought fame. For nearly twenty years, he and his students shared the Sedona Method with people from all walks of life, including Hollywood celebrities. Lester Levenson's sole desire was to share with others what he had been so fortunate to realize: permanent happiness.

The selection is from unpublished autobiographical material by Lester Levenson, made available by Hale Dwoskin, a student of Lester's for eighteen years, who carries on his work.

RELEASING FOR ULTIMATE FREEDOM

I WAS at the end of my rope. I was told not to take a step unless I absolutely had to because there was a possibility that I could drop dead at any moment. This was a terrible, shocking thing to suddenly be told that I couldn't be active anymore, having been so active all my life. It was a horrible thing.

An intense fear of dying overwhelmed me, the fear that I might drop dead any minute. This stayed with me for days. I went through a real, horrible, low, spinning period there, in the grip of intense fear of dying or of being a cripple for the rest of my life in that I wouldn't be able to be active. How could I take care of all that, and me. I felt that life would not be worthwhile any more.

This caused me to conclude with determination, "Either I get the answers, or I'll take me off this earth. No heart attack will do it!" I had a nice easy way to do it, too. I had morphine the doctors gave me for my kidney stone attacks.

After several days of this intense fear of dying, I suddenly realized, "Well, I'm still alive. As long as I'm alive there's hope. As long as I'm alive, maybe I can get out of this. What do I do?"

Well, I was always a smart boy, always made the honor roll. Even got myself a four-year scholarship to Rutgers University at a time when scholarships were very rare through competitive examinations. But what does this avail me? Nothing! Here I am with all this brilliance, as miserable and scared as can be.

Then I said, "Lester, you were not only not smart, you were dumb! Dumb! Dumb! There's something wrong in your intellect. With all your knowledge, you've come to this bottom end! Drop all this knowledge you've so studiously picked up on philosophy, psychology, social science, and economics! It is of no avail! Start from scratch. Begin all over again your search for the answers."

And with an extreme desperation and intense wanting out—not wanting to die, I began to question, "What am I? What is this world? What is my relationship to it? What do I want from it?"

"Happiness."

"Well, what is happiness?"

"Being loved."

"But I am loved. I know several very desirable girls with beauty, charm, and intellect who want me. And I have the esteem of my friends. Yet, I'm miserable!"

I sensed that the closest thing related to happiness was love. So I began reviewing and reliving my past love affairs, looking at the points where the little happiness that I had were. I began to pull up and dissect all my high moments of loving. Suddenly, I got an inkling that it was when I was loving that I had the highest feeling!

I remembered one evening, a beautiful balmy evening, in the mountains when I was camping with Virginia. We were both lying on the grass, both looking up at the sky, and I had my arm around her. The nirvana, the perfection of the height of happiness was right there. I was feeling how great is love for Virginia! How wonderful is knowing all this nature! How perfect a setting!

Then I saw that it was my loving her that was the cause of this happiness! Not the beauty of the setting, or being with Virginia.

Then I immediately turned to the other side. Boy it was great when she loved me! I remembered the moment when publicly this beautiful, charming girl told the world that she approved of Lester, she loved Lester—and I could feel that nice feeling of approval. But I sensed that it was not as great as what I had just discovered. It was not a lasting feeling. It was just for the moment. In order for me to have that feeling continuously, she had to continue saying that.

So, this momentary ego approval was not as great as the feeling of loving her! As long as I was loving her, I felt so happy. But when she loved me, there were only moments of happiness when she gave me approval.

Days of further cogitation gradually revealed to me that this was correct! I was happier when I loved her than I was when I got that momentary ego-satisfaction when she loved me. Her loving me was a momentary pleasure that needed constant showing and proving on her part, while my loving her was a constant happiness, as long as I was loving her.

I concluded that my happiness equated to my loving! If I could increase my loving, then I could increase my happiness! This was the first inkling I had as to what brings about happiness. And it was a tremendous thing because I hadn't had happiness. And I said, "Gee, if this is the key to happiness, I've got the greatest!" Even the hope of getting more and more happiness was a tremendous thing, because this was the number one thing I wanted—happiness.

That started me on weeks and weeks of reviewing my past love affairs. I dug up from the past, incident after incident when I thought I was loving, and I discovered that I was being nice to my girlfriends, trying to get them to love me, and that that was selfish. That was not really love. That was just wanting my ego bolstered!

I kept reviewing incidents from the past, and where I saw that I was not loving, I would change that feeling to loving that person. Instead of wanting them to do something for me, I would change it to my wanting to do something for them. I kept this up until I couldn't find any more incidents to work on.

This insight on love, seeing that happiness was determined by my capacity to love, was a tremendous insight. It began to free me, and any bit of freedom when you're plagued feels so good. I knew that I was in the right direction. I had gotten hold of a link of the chain of happiness and was determined not to let go until I had the entire chain.

I felt a greater freedom. There was an easier concentration of my mind because of it. And I began to look better at my mind. What is my mind? What is intelligence?

Suddenly, a picture flashed of amusement park bumper-cars that are difficult to steer so that they continually bump into each other. They all get their electrical energy from the wire screen above the cars through a pole coming down to every car.

The power above was symbolic of the overall intelligence and energy of the universe coming down the pole to me and everyone else, and to the degree we step on the gas do we use it. Each driver of the cars is taking the amount of energy and intelligence that he wants from that wire, but he steers his car blindly and bumps into other cars, and bumps and bumps.

I saw that if I chose to, I could take more and more of that overall intelligence. And so I dug into that. I began to examine thinking and its relationship to what was happening. And it was revealed that everything that was happening had a prior thought behind it and that I never before related the thought and the happening because of the element of time between the two.

When I saw that everything that was happening to me had a thought of it before it happened, I realized that if I could grab hold of this, I could consciously determine everything that was happening to me!

And above all, I saw that I was responsible for everything that had happened to me, formerly thinking that the world was abusing me! I saw that my whole past life, and all that tremendous effort to make money and in the end, failing, was due only to my thinking!

This was a tremendous piece of freedom, to think that I was not a victim of this world, that it lay within my power to arrange the world the way I wanted it to be, that rather than being an effect of it, I could now be at cause over it and arrange it the way I would like it to be!

That was a tremendous realization, a tremendous feeling of freedom!

I was so ill when I started my searching; I had one foot in the grave. And when I saw that my thinking was cause for what was happening to me, I immediately saw my body from my chin down to my toes as perfect. And instantly, I knew it was perfect! I knew the lesions and adhesions of my intestine due to perforated ulcers were undone. I knew everything within me was in perfect running order. And it was.

Discovering that my happiness equated to my loving, discovering that my thinking was the cause of things happening to me in my life gave me more and more freedom. Freedom from unconscious compulsions that I had to work, I had to make money, I had to have girls. Freedom in the feeling that I was now able to determine my destiny, I was now able to control my world, I was now able to arrange my environment to suit me. This new freedom lightened my internal burden so greatly that I felt that I had no need to do anything.

Plus, the new happiness I was experiencing was so great! I was experiencing a joy that I had never known existed. I had never dreamed happiness could be so great.

I determined "If this is so great, I'm not going to let go of it until I carry it all the way!" I had no idea how joyous a person could be. So, I began digging further on how to extend this joy. I began further changing my attitudes on love. I would imagine the girl I wanted most marrying one of my friends, or the boy I would want her to marry least, and then enjoy their enjoying each other. To me, this was the extreme in loving, and if I could achieve it, it would give me more of this wonderful thing that I was experiencing.

And so I worked on it. I took a particular fellow, Burl, and a particular girl, and I wouldn't let go until I could really feel the joy of their enjoying each other.

Then I knew I had it—or almost had it.

Then later on, I had further tests of this in talking to people who were opposing me no end when I was trying to help them. I would consciously feel the greatest love for them when they were attacking me. And the joy of loving them was so wonderful, I would, without any thought, thank them so profusely for having given me the opportunity of talking with them, that it threw them into a dither.

But I really felt that. I thanked them from the bottom of my heart for having given me the opportunity of loving them when they were making it as difficult as they possibly could. I didn't express that to them. I just thanked them for the opportunity of having been able to talk with them.

That I was able to do this was good news to me because, like other things, I was able to carry loving to the extreme. I could love people who were opposing me. And I would not stop until I could see the end of the line of this happiness I was getting. I would go higher and higher and higher and say, "Oh, my gosh, there can be nothing higher than this!" But I would try. And, I would go higher. Then I would say, "Oh, there can't be anything higher than this!" But I would try, and go higher! And then say, "Oh, there can't be anything happier than this!" until I realized there was no limit to happiness!

I would get incapacitated. I could look at my body, and I couldn't move it I was so top-heavy with ecstasy and joy. I was actually incapacitated. I would do this for hours, going higher and higher and then I would have to work for hours to keep coming down and down and down until I could start being the body again in order to operate it.

Contemplating the source of intelligence and energy, I discovered that energy, as well as intelligence, was available in unlimited amounts, and that it came simply by my freeing myself from all compulsions, inhibitions, entanglements, hang-ups. I saw that I had dammed up this energy, this power, and all I had to do was pry loose the logs of the dam which were my compulsions and hang-ups—and that was what I did. As I let go of these things, I was removing logs and allowing this infinite energy to flow, just like a water dam flows if you pull the logs out, one by one. The more logs you pull out, the greater the flow. All I needed to do was to remove these logs and let the infinite power and energy flow.

Seeing this, the power that was right behind my mind was allowed to flow through like it had never flowed before. There were times when I'd get this realization of what I am that would put so much energy into me, I would just jump up in the air from my chair. I would go right straight out the front door, and I would start walking and walking and walking, for hours at a time—sometimes for days at a time! I just felt as though my body would not contain it, that I had to walk or run some of it off. I remember walking the streets of New York City in the wee hours of the morning, just walking at a very good pace, and not being able to do anything otherwise! I had to expend some of that energy. It was so tremendous.

I saw that the source of all this energy, of all intelligence was basically harmonious, and that harmony was the rule of the universe. And that was why the planets were not colliding, and that was why the sun rose every day, and that was why everything went.

When I started my search, I was a very convinced and absolute materialist. The only thing that was real was that which you could feel and touch. My understanding of the world was as solid as concrete. And when some of these revelations came to me that the world was just a result of my mind, that thinking determined all matter, that matter had no intelligence, and that our intelligence determined all matter and everything about it. When I saw that the solidity that I formerly had was only a thought itself, my nice, solid, concrete foundations began to crack. Twenty years of buildup began to tumble.

And my body shook, and shook so much; I just shook for days. I shook just like a nervous old person. I knew that the concrete view I had had of the world was never going to be again. But it didn't drop away gracefully, with ease. For days, I actually shook, until I think I shook the whole thing loose.

Then, my view was just the opposite of what it had been months previously, that the real solid thing was not the physical world, was not my mind, but something, which was much greater. The very essence, the very Beingness of me was the reality. It had no limits, it was eternal and all the things that I saw before were the least of me, rather than the all of me. The all of me was my Beingness.

I saw that the only limitations I had were the ones that I accepted. So, wanting to know what am I? And looking for this unlimited Being that I had had an inkling of, I got insight of this tremendous unlimited Being that I am.

And on seeing that, I right there and then realized, "Well, I'm not this limited body and I thought I was! I am not this mind with its limitations that I thought I was!" And I undid all body limitation, and almost all mind limitation, just by saying, "I am not it! Finished! Done! Period! That's it!," I so declared.

It was obvious to me that I wasn't that body and mind that I had thought I was. I just saw—that's all! It's simple when you see it. I let go of identifying with this body. And when I did that, I saw that my Beingness was all Beingness. That Beingness is like one grand ocean. It's not chopped up into parts called drops of bodies. It's all one ocean.

This caused me to identify with every being, every person and even every item in this universe. Then you are finished forever with separation and all the hellishness that's caused only by separation. Then you can no more be fooled by the apparent limitations of the world. You see them as a dream, as an appearancy, because you know that your very own Beingness has no limits.

In reality, the only thing that is, is Beingness. That is the real, changeless substance behind everything.

Everything of life itself was open to me—the total understanding of it. It is simply that we are infinite beings, over which we have superimposed concepts of limitation (the logs of the dam). And we are smarting under these limitations that we accept for ourselves as though they are real, because they are opposed to our basic nature of total freedom.

Life before and after my realization was at two different extremes. Before, it was just extreme depression, intense misery, and sickness. After, it was a happiness and serenity that's indescribable. Life became so beautiful and so harmonious that all day, every day, everything would fall perfectly into line.

As I would drive through New York City, I would rarely hit a red light. When I would go to park my car, people sometimes two or three people would stop and even step into the street to help direct me into a parking space. There were times when taxi cab drivers would see me looking for a parking space and would give up their space for me. And after they did, they couldn't understand why they had done it. There they were, double-parked!

Even policemen who were parked would move out and give me their parking place. And again, after they did, they couldn't understand why. But I knew they felt good in doing so. And they would continue to help me.

If I went into a store, the salesman would happily go out of his way to help me. Or, if I would order something in a restaurant and then change my mind, the waitress would bring what I wanted, even though I hadn't told her.

Actually everyone moves to serve you as you just float around. When you are in tune and you have a thought, every atom in the universe moves to fulfill your thought. And this is true.

Being in harmony is such a delightful, delectable state, not because things are coming your way, but because of the feeling of God-in-operation. It's a tremendous feeling; you just can't imagine how great it is. It is such a delight when you're in tune, in harmony—you see God everywhere! You're watching God in operation. And that is what you enjoy, rather than the time, the incident, the happening. His operation is the ultimate.

When we get in tune, our capacity to love is so extreme that we love everyone with an extreme intensity which makes living the most delightful it could ever be.

From an unpublished autobiographical manuscript by Lester Levenson.

JEAN KLEIN

TWENTY-THREE

JEAN KLEIN

CIRCA 1916–1998, CZECHOSLOVAKIA

I
T IS DIFFICULT to discover the birth date of Jean Klein, because for
him such temporal data was of little importance. Nor is it possible
to elucidate much information about his childhood, except that
it was spent in Czechoslovakia and Austria and that he descended from
a family of musicians. A student of violin at age seven, Jean later became a musicologist. He was drawn by his love of freedom to study intensively, at the age of sixteen, the works of great writers such as
Nietzsche, Dostoyevsky, Gandhi, Sri Aurobindo, Krishnamurti, Lao Tzu,
Tagore, and Rene Guenon, and to become a vegetarian. At seventeen he
enjoyed his first experience of what he called "my own silence." Jean
pursued a lifelong practice of yoga and a study of the subtle energy
body or aura, which led him to later assert that the yoga postures could
be performed independently of the physical body.

After completing training as a medical doctor in Austria and Germany, Jean spent World War II in France, where he secretly assisted
thousands of people to escape from Germany. After the war, in 1950, he
followed his soul's call to India. There Dr. Klein shared a "sacred relationship" with his Advaitist (nondualistic) teacher, Pandiji, a Sanskrit profes-
sor in Bangalore, who directed him to the question, "Who Am I?" One
morning, in a state between deep sleep and awakening, his individual
identity disappeared and was replaced by an all-pervading light, which
he recognized as the one reality.

Dr. Klein's urge to share his experience with others in the West, encouraged by Pandiji, was fulfilled in 1960 when he began teaching. Just
as he refrained from answering personal questions, explaining that, in
truth, there is no person to respond, never did he promote himself as a
teacher. The teacher appears, according to Dr. Klein, only because there
are students searching for the teaching.

For the next thirty-eight years, Dr. Klein traveled all over the world transmitting the teaching of the nature of reality and truth. His teaching was impersonal, in the knowledge that there is indeed no such thing as an individual. Dr. Klein spoke of life as awareness itself, existing between thoughts, concepts, and perceptions. It was only in silence, he instructed, that truth would reveal itself. Self-inquiry would inevitably lead to the realization that there was no inquirer and nothing to attain. Though his teaching was strongly influenced by Advaita, Dr. Klein's transmission was direct and unencumbered even by the unassuming trappings of his predecessors such as Ramana Maharshi. Dr. Klein authored various books, including *I Am, Be Who You Are,* and *Transmission of the Flame.* He died in 1998 in Santa Barbara, California, and his foundation is in the process of publishing his unpublished works and dialogues.

FROM INDIVIDUAL TO IMPERSONAL

HOW THEN did you meet your "unknown teacher"?

Some of the friends I met, and with whom I spoke of peace, freedom and joy, had a spiritual guide. One day I met their teacher and on this and several other meetings, I asked him many questions, questions that expressed all my earnestness to find my real center.

It seems that you trusted him at once.

I was open to him. I was struck by his lack of striving, his humility. He never tried to impress or convince. There was simply no personality. All his answers came from nowhere, no one, and yet his gentle openness was apparent. I was struck too by his argument that potentially you are, it only needs actualizing. He never saw anyone as not knowing. He gave no hold to my personality.

He gave me many answers, but during the several weeks that I didn't see him I became aware that all my questions had been an escape, an evasion of the real question. The existential crisis I had always lived in became acute. I lived with this feeling that I had missed the real question, a question I was not able to formulate. Then I had the opportunity to visit him where he lived in a little room in the Sanskrit College at Bangalore where he was a teacher. Two other young Indians were present and they were talking about the *Karikas* of Gaudapada and the *Mandukya Upanishad* [sacred Hindu texts]. The talk was of the four states, waking, sleeping, dreaming and *turiya* (the absence of objects). He said that *turiya* is not properly speaking a state which one enters and leaves. It becomes a non-state *(turiyacitta)* when you are awake in it. It is the absence of ourself which is our total presence. Then there was a silence, the other students left and he suddenly looked at me and asked, "Do you know yourself?" I was a bit disturbed by this question because I didn't really know what he meant. I couldn't find a way to look at it. I said hesitatingly, "Yes," because I was thinking I knew my body, senses and mind very well. He said to me, "You are the knower of your body, senses and mind, but the knower can never be known, because you are it and there's nobody to know it. It can never become an object of observation because it is your totality." This saying had a very strong impact on me. I had a glimpse of reality in this moment because it stopped all intellectual faculties. We were silent and I left.

And did this impact remain with you when you got home?

It left a very strong echo in me of freedom from old beliefs. I went home and lived with it free from all conceptualization and felt myself awake in this not-knowing. It was completely new, there was no absence of knowing.

Did life change or go on as usual?

Life went on, eating, meeting people. But there was now a feeling that I was behind all daily activities. I saw Pandiji many times afterwards and realized that he was my guru because this profound impact could only come from a guru. So you see he found me when I was not looking for him!

Were you at any point in the quest convinced that you would one day know your real nature?

Yes. After the first meeting with him in Bangalore. I never formulated it. It was never a goal. The word "enlightenment" never entered my thoughts. Pandiji certainly didn't use the term. It was simply a lively feeling, without formulation, of being free from myself, free from all restrictions, all ideas, free from the knowing of freedom.

How did you spend the time together?

He was teaching at the college all day. Sometimes we ate together and every morning he knocked on my door very early and we sat together in silence. Sometimes we spoke about the scriptures, because, being a man of tradition, he very often referred his sayings to the scriptures. But he never did so arbitrarily. Each time he spoke this way, it was exactly the moment when I needed to know it. There was really a feeling of oneness. I was not aware of a "me" and a "he" in our being together. There was real love, not in the way we are accustomed to mean it. It was the most exalted being in love. His presence was continually drenched with warm feeling.

Did he ever transmit to you through touch?

That was not his way with me. We communicated mostly through the eyes. Sometimes he touched my shoulder or hand, but our closeness was closer than all touching.

We also walked together. He was an admirer and this appealed to my artistic nature. He loved music and singing and could imitate the sound of any bird.

Were there any disciplines or exercises that he taught you during this time?

Only to be aware of when conditioning comes in in daily life. He emphasized the problem of day-dreaming and strategy-building. He also emphasized that one should never push away conditioning but only see it clearly, and he reminded me to constantly refer to the first insight, the first non-experience.

You mean, to remember it?

Go knowingly in it, not remember it intellectually. It is presence, not a memory.

Was he in your thoughts very often?

I did not think of him because I could not personify, objectify him. There was a deep feeling of oneness. I was not at all attached to his physical being. Everything he gave was a pearl. I took it as a pearl and lived with it.

There were many moments when we were just happy to be together, not talking, not thinking. His presence was my presence and my presence was his presence. His being was the transmission. In a real teacher this is all transmission is. Any intentional transmission is sentimentality, romanticism.

Would you say your approach was more jnani *than* bhakti, *more the way of knowledge than devotion?*

Yes. Not so much *bhakti,* of course. But all my questions were carried by love. It was never a dry, mental exercise. He also had a great intellect. Traditionally, when you are a pandit there is nothing you must not know. [laughs]

But you can only come to knowledge when there is love, unconditional adoration.

And how did you meet Dibianandapuri?

On a bus in Bangalore. He was in a state of *mauna* (not speaking). We got out at the same station and he took a little blackboard out of his dhoti and wrote asking me where I came from and that he felt I was his brother. I said, "How can it be otherwise?" Then he wrote, "If you have the time, let us go for a walk." So we walked and talked (he with his blackboard). He was living in a little Siva temple outside Bangalore and we met often. He was originally from Puri and had lived a long time in Kashmir. We talked about the Kashmir teachings, how they emphasize the energy body not the physical body. This was my main concern. I was already aware of the energy body and regarded it, and not the bone-muscle structure, as the real body. Dibianandapuri confirmed and expanded my intuition and experience. He gave the energy body priority and showed me how all postures could be done independently of the physical body.

Did you see other teachers on the level of Pandiji while you were in India?

I saw Krishna Menon four or five times later on, and found him highly able in *vidya vritti*, the formulation of what cannot be formulated. Absolutely a beautiful being.

And Ramana Maharshi?

Unfortunately I never met him because he passed away a few months before I arrived in India.

So while you were a disciple of Pandiji's you were never drawn to other teachers for clarification?

There was no desire at all in me for that. I didn't go to India to find a teacher. The teacher found me. There's only one teacher. I quickly came to the conviction that there is nothing to teach and that what you are looking for doesn't belong to any teaching or "teacher." So why look for anyone? It is the presence of the guru that shows there is nothing to teach because the teacher is established in the "I am." So I realized that only the "I am," not a mind or a body, can bring you to the "I am."

How long did you live in this way, seeing Pandiji?

For about three years.

And then you left Bangalore and went to Bombay?

Yes, I went sightseeing.

And during this stay there was the moment of enlightenment?

Yes, it was a total switch-over from the residual conditioned state to the unconditioned state. Awareness expanded completely and I felt myself in globality.

Had this happened before?

No. There had been glimpses, but this was more than a glimpse. There was no going back. I had found my real ground.

Did you know in the moment itself that it would be permanent or did you discover this in the days that followed?

Because of the quality of the switch-over there was no doubt that I could be again taken by duality, and this was confirmed in the days and weeks that followed. I felt a rectification in my body and in my brain, as if all the parts had found their right place, their most comfortable position. I saw all daily events spontaneously appearing in the non-state, in my total absence, real presence.

Could you say what were the exact conditions, physical and mental, before this moment: The Threshold?

There had been, for two years, a retreat of all the energy commonly used in becoming, so that when some flying birds crossed my horizon, instead of becoming lost in them, they were lost in me and I found myself in awareness free from all objects. This time what I admired, the birds, dissolved in my admiring, in presence. And admiring dissolved in the Admired. Before the birds appeared, I had been in a profound and prolonged state of being open to openness. Now I found myself as the openness, identical with openness. Openness was my being. There was no more duality.

Was there any other difference between this time and other times when you had looked at birds?

Before, there was still a looker looking at something. This was a moment when there was simply looking without a looker. Previously, it had become my nature to live in pure perception with objects, not living in the divided mind. I had for a long time ignored the arising of all qualifications.

Ignored?

It belongs to the traditional approach, and so that of my teacher, never to refuse or indulge the coming up of qualifications, but simply to ignore, and eventually forget them. Neither to look for freedom nor avoid non-freedom. The mind simply ceased to play a role except in a purely functional way.

So in a certain way you were ripe for the moment?

In other words the moment was waiting for me!

How is life different now?

There is no more identification with time and space, body, senses and mind. All events happen in awareness.

Did your relationships change?

There was no more relationship. As there's no longer an "I," there is not another.

Can this non-state be described at all?

It is love where the mind is dissolved in love. [long pause]

Were you in a hurry to return to Bangalore to see Pandiji?

No. I enjoyed my total freedom, freedom from all doing. I postponed all projects and stayed in Bombay another week or so.

How was your next meeting with Pandiji? Was it full of tears of joy and gratitude?

He was never absent, so there was no hurry to see him. He never acknowledged or mentioned anything, though he recognized a change. I could tell from his way of speaking. He would never talk about it and risk making a state of it. Quite frankly, tears and emotion after an insight show that it is a state. As for gratitude, there was from the beginning gratitude to him. There was no emotivity in our meeting, only joyful togetherness, and an unvoiced laughter that the seeker is the sought and is always so very, very near.

From the introduction to *Transmission of the Flame* by Jean Klein.

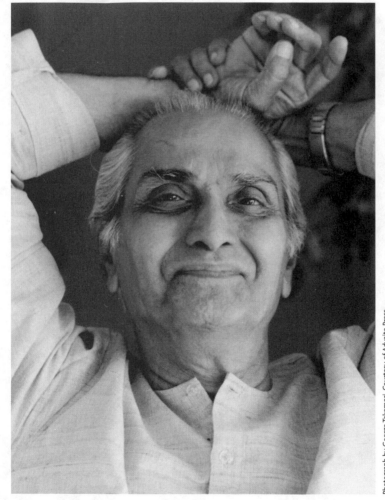

RAMESH BALSEKAR

┌─────────────────────────────────┐
│   ∽ TWENTY-FOUR ∾   │
├─────────────────────────────────┤
│   RAMESH BALSEKAR   │
├─────────────────────────────────┤
│   1919–PRESENT, INDIA   │
└─────────────────────────────────┘

R AMESH IS anything but flashy. Kind, intellectual, patient, perhaps grandfatherly, and even ordinary are the words that you may use when you first sit with him. In fact, what Ramesh offers is anything but ordinary and, at the same time, he has nothing whatsoever new to say. Yet he is approachable, has a very keen mind, and is always ripe for a lively discussion about the nature of consciousness, quantum physics, or whatever else may be on your mind.

Eighty-one years old, radiant and remarkably relaxed, Ramesh was no *sadhu* (wandering ascetic monk). A highly successful Indian businessman and avid golfer, he worked his way up from clerk to C.E.O. of the Bank of India. Married in 1940, Ramesh is the father of three children, one of whom died in the late 1980s. During the ten years in which Ramesh headed India's most influential bank, he guided it through a period of tremendous expansion. He demonstrated the entrepreneurial and interpersonal skills to oversee the hiring of thousands of employees and the opening of several hundred new branches of the bank within India and abroad.

Upon his mandatory retirement in 1977 at the age of sixty, Ramesh happened upon a magazine article about a master named Nisargadatta Maharaj, a teacher of Advaita (nondualism). Recognizing his guru immediately, Ramesh soon began translating for Nisargadatta, and continued to sit with his teacher for a number of years. Ramesh attained the state of nondual consciousness described by Maharaj and, upon his guru's death, found himself, somewhat reluctantly, in the role of the teacher.

Ramesh's teaching, based on the tradition of Advaita, is plain and simple. Consciousness is all that exists. All the events in this choiceless universe occur naturally and inevitably due to prior programming. Analyzing, conceptualizing, and introspecting are a waste of time because events will unfold as they will. All that happens must happen due to our conditioning. Period. Enlightenment is nothing more or less than an empty mind. It will occur in time and there is nothing we can do to speed the process, except to do what we are guided by our natures to do and to wake up to the truth that we just are. Then we find that we have already reached where we are trying to go. This may explain why Ramesh, both in pictures and in the flesh, appears so uncannily relaxed. For he has reached an understanding that self-realization requires no effort, that seeking is unnecessary, that we are both everything and nothing, and that problems, in and of themselves, do not actually exist. The notion of ourselves as individuals will dissolve when we are ready and, at that time and at that time only, we will simply surrender.

If you hold the conviction that realization is attained only through years or lifetimes of disciplined *sadhana* (spiritual practice), you may find yourself in cognitive dissonance with the teachings of Ramesh. Or you may find your previously held notions and concepts shattered, left only with the inevitable reality of consciousness itself.

The account of Ramesh Balsekar's enlightenment is from a book entitled *Consciousness Speaks,* a collection of transcribed talks to his students.

IT HAD TO HAPPEN

Ramesh's Enlightenment

PERHAPS YOU *could tell us something about your enlightenment and how it came to you.*

Well, you see, enlightenment is an extremely obtuse word. The word enlightenment somehow seems to suggest a sort of occurrence where there are lights blazing and bliss coming out of the ears, you see. But it isn't, at least not in my case.

I've heard that it can be a very mild but distinctive occurrence and particularly when I read a story about Lao Tzu and his disciple, it struck me that that was so. Some of you perhaps know it, but I don't suppose there is any harm in repeating it.

One of Lao Tzu's disciples went to him one morning with his eyes blazing and his face glowing with a sense of achievement, and he said, "Master, I have arrived." And Lao Tzu with great compassion put his hands on his shoulders and said, "Son, you have not arrived anywhere." So the disciple went away. He came back after some time and then, with great quiet composure, said, "Master, it has happened." So Lao Tzu looked in his eyes, embraced him and said, "Now tell me what happened."

He said, "I accepted your word that nothing had happened. But I also knew that I could not have possibly put in any more effort. So I gave up thinking of enlightenment, I gave up all effort towards enlightenment and went about my normal business. Then it suddenly occurred to me that there was nothing to be achieved. It was there all the time!"

The understanding had dawned that there is no individual to want anything. The state is already there. The ultimate state, before it can happen, is the absence of the "me" wanting something to happen.

What you are saying then is, the arrival at that place will happen when it is time to happen.

Yes! When it is His Will. When it is time for it to happen, is correct.

In the meantime there is nothing we can do to encourage it?

Correct again. [laughter] So, in my case I know the specific date when it happened. There is one day in the year which is called the Divali Day, the festival of light, which is a common festival throughout India. This festival of light is supposed to signify the victory of right over wrong, of good over evil, the victory of Rama over Ravana.

Normally in Maharaj's place that used to be the day of cleaning up his loft, sort of a "spring cleaning," and no talks were held on that day. This happened on the year I first went to visit him. That was in 1978. The following year, on the day previous to Divali, when the announcement was being made that there would be no talks the following day for this reason, a colleague of mine suggested that if Maharaj agreed he could hold the talks at his own place which was very close to Maharaj's place, and known to most people who used to attend. The result was that the next day we had the talk at this residence of the colleague. This colleague used to be one of the translators. So on that day he said he would look after the people coming in, would I translate? I agreed.

The moment Maharaj started to talk, something peculiar happened. Maharaj's voice seemed to come to me from a distance, very, very clear. In fact, clearer than it used to be normally. Maharaj didn't have any teeth, so I needed some time to get used to his words. But that morning his voice seemed to come from a distance, yet much much clearer than it ever was before, needing no concentration on my part. I found that the translation began to come so spontaneously that in actual fact I was not translating, I was merely witnessing the translation taking place. It was as if Maharaj was translating into English and I was merely sitting there, a witness.

At the end of the translation I felt quite ill. I didn't know what was happening and the body had reacted in a certain way for the simple reason that it was not used to that experience. My colleague later said, "Ramesh, you were in great form today!"

"How so?"

He said, "You were talking louder than you normally do, you spoke with great authority and you were making gestures that you never did before." So I just accepted that. It was confirmation that something had happened. But the something that had happened was internally a complete change, a total change. Outside, the only change that I could find was that my body felt a peculiar kind of weightlessness. I couldn't name it and I think that was noticed for a day or two before it settled down. But if you ask me when it happened, this is how and when it happened. As I say, it was a very quiet event, sudden of course, as sudden as anything could be . . . totally unexpected . . . totally spontaneous.

After that, the translations were always that way and Maharaj noticed it, too. Maharaj didn't understand English, but he could sense when the translation was not strictly accurate. When the translations were taking place, Maharaj would often ask whoever was translating, "What did you tell them?" He would make him repeat and then he would confirm it or he would say, "No, that is not what I meant. You see you have got it wrong. You often get it wrong." [laughter] But after that day I noticed I was no longer paying attention to what was being said, so the translations came out smoothly and spontaneously.

One morning when I was waiting for Maharaj to get ready for me to take him out for the usual car ride, he was in a particularly calm mood and he said, "I'm glad it's happened." He also knew at that time the book, *Pointers* was coming out, so he said, "I'm glad it's happened. It's not just one book. Several books will come out. And what the books will say will not be a parroting of what I have said. How it will come about, I won't know. Even you won't know."

Ramesh, you had said when the awakening happened that there was a peculiar sense of the body, some sense of discomfort and disorientation. Is that because Consciousness is no longer identified with the body?

Yes.

When you were talking about the experience of enlightenment, you spoke about Maharaj and that particular moment when he said, "So it's happened." Was there a particular moment when you made that comment to yourself, "So it's happened"?

After a day or two, when I came back to normal, physically, then I knew it had happened, and there was no doubt at all. Quite frankly I did not feel any need for certification from Maharaj, but when it did come it was welcome. But the basic fact is that I did not need any certificate from anybody.

It sounds like that moment for you came at the end of this two or three day period.

The feeling that something had happened, yes. The awareness of what had happened, the consciousness of what had happened.

From *Consciousness Speaks* by Ramesh S. Balsekar.

TWENTY-FIVE

ROBERT ADAMS

1928–1997, UNITED STATES

R OBERT ADAMS is known to only a few fortunate souls, yet his realizations and teachings are among the highest expressions of spiritual liberation we have heard of or read. His earliest memories were of a two-foot tall, white bearded man standing at the end of his crib, who would talk "gibberish" to him. The little man stayed with [Robert] until he was seven. Then [he] developed a Siddhi (spiritual power). Whenever he wanted anything—a candy bar, a musical instrument, answers to test questions at school, he would repeat God's name three times, and whatever he wished for would come to him. One day, while preparing for a math test, when he was 14, he repeated God's name as usual. Instead of the test answers, he had a complete enlightenment experience, a great Satori, which left him stunned and transformed. . . . (From the Introduction to *Silence of the Heart*)

After this experience, Robert lost all interest in worldly life. He left home at sixteen and became a disciple of Paramahansa Yogananda, who, despite Robert's requests, refused to allow him to join his order of monks. Instead, Yogananda sent him on to find his guru in the little known (at that time) village of Tiruvannamalai, at the base of the holy mountain Arunachala, in Southern India. When Robert first saw his guru descending the path from the mountain, a frail looking man with a fringe of white beard and a remarkably compassionate face, he recognized that this was the one who had spoken nonsense to him for years as a child. He realized that he was home at last. This was Ramana Maharshi, later to be known as one of the greatest sages of the twentieth century. In giving credit to the Maharshi's clarifying influence, Robert said, "It was with Ramana that my eyes were opened to the meaning of my experience." (*Silence of the Heart*, Introduction)

After Ramana's death, Robert continued to travel for seventeen years, meeting many masters and teachers, verifying his enlightenment, and completing his understanding. Robert was a *Jnani* (knower of Truth), and he openly shared his wisdom with seekers who came to him. Never desiring to be a guru in the traditional sense, he nonetheless attracted students wherever he briefly settled. His last years were spent in Sedona, Arizona. He never sought publicity or a large following. In fact, he has never even allowed his picture to be published.

Robert's teachings, simple, direct, clear and profound, are from the tradition of Advaita, or nondualism. Like his guru, Ramana, he emphasized the transcendence of the individual "I" through the process of self-enquiry, realizing the one Self in all. The essence of Robert's philosophy was, "You are neither the body nor the doer. All is consciousness. All is well."

From the recorded *satsangs* (gatherings of seekers of truth) held in Sedona, Arizona—published in his only book, *Silence of the Heart*—his story comes to us.

THE SILENCE OF THE HEART

THERE IS the Pure Awareness that is with you all the time, just awaiting your recognition, awaiting your understanding that you are not the body, that you are a spirit, called the Atman, Brahman, Absolute Reality. This is who you really are. This is your real nature.

You've heard me talk on many occasions on the subject of love, compassion, and humility. These three things are very important to understand. They have to be nurtured and developed. When you understand what love, compassion, and humility really are, at that time, you become a living embodiment of the truth, and the Self will pull your ego into the heart center, and you will become liberated and free.

When I speak to you of all these things, I'm referring to my own experiences. Therefore, do not take these things I say lightly, even though I tell you many times to not believe a word I say. It sounds like a contradiction, but it isn't. You are not to believe anything I say, yet you are to reflect and ponder on the things I say at the same time. Try to become a living embodiment of the highest truth.

When I had my spiritual awakening, I was fourteen years old. This body was sitting in a classroom taking a math test. And all of a sudden I felt myself expanding. I never left my body, which proves that the body never existed to begin with. I felt the body expanding, and a brilliant light began to come out of my heart. I happened to see this light in all directions. I had peripheral vision, and this light was really my Self. It was not my body and the light. There were not two. There was this light that became brighter and brighter and brighter, the light of a thousand suns. I thought I would be burnt to a crisp, but alas, I wasn't.

But this brilliant light, which I was the center and also the circumference, expanded throughout the universe, and I was able to feel the planets, the stars, the galaxies, as myself. And this light shone so bright, yet it was beautiful, it was bliss, it was ineffable, indescribable.

After a while the light began to fade away, and there was no darkness. There was just a place between light and darkness, the place beyond the light. You can call it the void, but it wasn't just a void. It was this pure awareness I always talk about. I was aware that I AM THAT I AM. I was aware of the whole universe at the same time. There was no time, there was no space, there was just the I AM.

Then everything began to return to normal, so to speak. I was able to feel, and understand, that all of the planets, the galaxies, the people, the trees, the flowers on this earth, everything, were myriads of energy, and I was in everything. I was the flower. I was the sky. I was the people. The I was everything. Everything was the I. The word "I" encompassed the whole universe.

Now, here's the point I'm trying to make: I felt a love, a compassion, a humility, all at the same time. That was truly indescribable. It wasn't a love that you're aware of. Think of something that you really love, or someone that you really love with all your heart. Multiply this by a jillion million trillion, and you'll understand what I'm talking about. This particular love is like no thing that ever existed on this earth, consciously. There is nothing you can compare it with. It is beyond duality, beyond concepts, beyond words and thoughts. And since the "I" which I was, was all pervading, there was no other place for anything else to be. There was no room for anything, because there was no space, and no time. There was just the I AM, ever present, self-existent. The love of everything was the love of the Self. This is why, in scripture, it tells you to love your brother, and your sister, to love everyone and everything under all circumstances.

This love couldn't differentiate. It couldn't say, "You're good, so I love you. You're bad, so I don't love you." Everything was going on as myself. I realized I am the murderer, I am the saint, I am the so called evil on this earth, I am the so called goodness of this earth. Everything was the Self. And it was all a game. All of the energy particles changed from one thing to another thing. But the love never changed.

Another word for this love was compassion. There was this fabulous, fantastic compassion. For everything! For everything was the Self, the I AM. There was no differentiation. There was not me, what you call "me," and those things. There was only one expression, and that was Consciousness.

Of course, I didn't understand all these words at that time. There were no words like I'm talking about now. I'm trying my best to speak intelligently and try to use words to explain what happened, but you can't. All the games that people are playing, on all the planets, throughout the universe, is really the Self. It was all the Self, and I realized that nothing else existed but the Self. Yet all of these things, the multiplicities of planets, of galaxies, of people, of animals, were really the Self. Again, there are no words to describe this. I felt and knew that these multiplicities do not exist. Things do not exist. Only the Self existed, only Consciousness, Pure Awareness.

Yet, at the same time, creation came into existence. And there's no creation. We cannot understand this in human form. As long as we're thinking with our brains it's incomprehensible. For how can they both be simultaneously creating each other? There was creation going on, and yet there was no creation at all! There was no creation taking place, and creation was taking place. Sounds like the thoughts of a mad man. And it seemed normal. There's absolutely nothing strange about this at all, being nothing and everything at the same time.

So this great compassion was there. Since I was everything, the compassion was for everything. No thing was excluded, for the things were really the Self. And then there was this fantastic humility. The love, compassion, and humility are all synonymous. I'm trying to break it down to make you understand, to an extent, what was going on. The humility was there not to change anything. Everything was right just the way it was. Planets were exploding, new planets were being born. Suns were evaporating, new suns were being born. From the suns the planets came, and then life began on the planets. All this was taking place instantaneously, at the same time. And yet nothing was taking place at all.

Therefore the humility is that everything was alright. There was nothing I had to change. There was nothing I had to correct. The people dying of cancer were in their right place, and nobody dies, and there is no cancer. Wars, man's inhumanity to man, was all part of it! There cannot be a creation if there is not an opposite to good. In order to have a creation there has to be opposites. There has to be the bad guy and the good guy. I was able to understand all these things.

The next thing I remember is, my teacher was shaking me. I was the only one left in the class, everybody had gone, the bell rang, and I had not even started the mathematics test. Of course I got a great big zero. But those feelings and the understanding never left me. From that time on, my whole life changed. I was no longer interested in school. I was no longer interested in the friends I had. I won't go on any more than that for now, as far as that's concerned.

The point I'm trying to make is this: If the end result of realization is love, compassion, and humility, what if we were able to develop these qualities now? Do you see what I'm getting at? If we are able to develop this love, this beautiful joyous love, for everything, without exception, without being judgmental, and we had a great compassion, for everything, without being judgmental, you can't have a compassion for one thing and not for another thing. Then, of course, there's humility. Humility means we don't have to try to straighten things out, to get even, to stick up for our rights. For there is no one really left to do that. If some of us were to work on those aspects, it would lift us up and make us free.

This is something for you to think about. We have to learn to leave the world alone. We become so involved in politics, in family life, in work, and the rest of these things we're involved in, that we forget that we only have so many years left on this earth in the body. And what are we doing with all of the time we have? We're spending the time on things that do not really exist, things that make no sense.

Confession of the Jnani [Knower of Truth]

by Bhagavan Sri Robert

For the Jnani who has realized the identity
of his inner being
with the infinite Brahman,
there is no rebirth, no migration and no liberation.
He is beyond all this.
He is firmly established in his own Absolute,
Existence-Knowledge-Bliss true nature.

The further existence of his body and the world
appears to the Jnani as an illusion,
which he cannot remove,
but which no longer deceives him.
After the death of this body, as in life,
he remains where and what he eternally is,
the first principle of all beings and things:
formless, nameless, unsoiled, timeless, dimensionless
and utterly free.
Death cannot touch him, cravings cannot torture him,
sins do not stain him; he is free from all
desire and suffering.
He sees the Infinite Self in all, and all in the Infinite Self,
which is his Being.

The Jnani confesses his experience thus:
I am infinite, imperishable, self-luminous, self-existent.
I am without beginning or end.
I am birthless, deathless, without change or decay.
I permeate and interpenetrate all things.
In the myriad universes of thought and creation,
I ALONE AM.

From *Silence of the Heart* by Robert Adams.

AUTHORS' NOTE: The work of Robert Adams is being carried on according to his wishes by *The Infinity Institute*, 2370 West Highway 89A, Box 11-182, Sedona, Arizona 86336.

TWENTY-SIX

BERNADETTE ROBERTS

1931–PRESENT, UNITED STATES

THE CHILD of a devout Catholic family, Bernadette Roberts had her first contemplative experiences at an early age. It was at fifteen that the experiences began to fit into a frame of reference within her Christian tradition. Ten years of seclusion in a monastery followed, during which Bernadette realized an abiding state of oneness with God. According to the Christian mystical tradition, this egoless, unitive state is as far as one can progress in this life—the ultimate state, of course, being the glorious estate of heaven.

After leaving the monastery, Bernadette's contemplative life continued with many years of teaching as well as raising four children. At the age of forty-seven, she was surprised to encounter the possibility of not only an abiding loss of all self-consciousness, but equally a loss of God-consciousness. In the unitive state, consciousness of God and self make up a kind of "we-consciousness." Thus to be without self-awareness is also to be without awareness of God. In short, no-self implies the absence of the unitive state.

In her first book, *The Experience of No-Self,* Bernadette describes this falling away of self and the two years immediately following. She affirms that only God can take away self, the requirement being perfect trust in God such that the slightest movement of fear will make it impossible. She is refreshingly willing to admit her own puzzlement and initial fear at the prospect of losing self—having no idea of how her life would subsequently unfold.

The burning question for Bernadette, following the no-self event, was, "What is the true nature of this that remains?" Although she searched for the answer in the Christian, Buddhist, and Hindu literature, her quest was not satisfied. This was a journey Bernadette had to make alone. The answers could be revealed by God alone.

Bernadette describes her experiences as a process of "acclimating" to a new dimension of existence, which took a full ten years. It could not be aptly described as a "transforming" process because there was no such being as the self left to be transformed. Looking back over the entire journey, Bernadette learned that, after many years of living out the "egoless, unitive condition," this state comes to an end. Her three books affirm the culmination in the falling away of all self. *What Is Self,* Bernadette's third book, explores the true nature of the self, its gradual transformation, and its final transcendence.

Such a journey, explains Bernadette, is not for the faint of heart or those seeking only love and bliss. This is a path for the hardy who possess unshakeable trust in "that which lies beyond the known, beyond the self, beyond union, and even beyond love and trust itself." Bernadette invites us to fix our "uninterrupted gaze upon the Unknown" and to fall outside of ourselves permanently as we "journey into the silent and still regions of the Unknown." For this journey is not for Bernadette alone. Sooner or later, she assures, each one of us will do so, too.

The selection is from Bernadette Robert's first book, *The Experience of No-Self.*

THE JOURNEY TO NO-SELF

Compendium of the Journey

I

THE MOMENT was unheralded, unrecognized, and unknown; it was the moment "I" entered a great silence and never returned. Beyond the threshold of the known, the door upon self was closed, but the door upon the Unknown was opened in a fixed gaze that could not look away. Impossible to see the self, to re-

---

AUTHOR'S NOTE: This biography was largely written for us by Bernadette Roberts herself.

member the self, or to be self-conscious, the mind was restricted to the present moment. The more it tried to reflect back on itself, the more overpowering the silence.

II

By steadily gazing outward upon the Unknown, the silence abated and the emptiness of self became a joy. But the search for the still-point—God within—revealed not one emptiness, but two, for when there is no self, there is no Other; without a personal self there is no personal God—without a subject, there is no object. The still-point had vanished, and with its disappearance it took every sense of life the self possessed—a self which could no longer be felt to exist. What remained was not known. There was no life, no will, no energy, no feelings, no experiences, no within, no spiritual or psychic life. Yet, life was somewhere because all was as usual.

III

Though it could not be localized or found within any object of sight or mind, somewhere out-of-doors, life was flowing peacefully, assuredly. On a bluff above the sea, it revealed itself: life is not in anything; rather, all things are in life. The many are immersed in the One, even that which remains when there is no self, this too, is absorbed in the One. No longer a distance between self and the other, all is now known in the immediacy of this identity. Particulars dissolve into the One; individual objects give way to reveal that which is the same throughout all variety and multiplicity. To see this new dimension of life is the gift of amazing glasses through which God may be seen everywhere. Truly, God is all that exists—all, of course, but the self.

IV

But what sees this Oneness and knows that it sees? The eye that looks is not within, it is not of mind or body, it is not of the self. Unknown and outside—at first like glasses, then later, above the head—the eye was known to exist, but it could neither be seen nor looked at. It did not dissolve into Oneness—the seer and seen were not identical. But a greater mystery still: what remained in the absence of self? What is this that walks, thinks, and talks? What is this that is aware of the eye upon Oneness? Among them—no-self, the eye, the Oneness—no identity could be found.

V

At one time, the Oneness grew to an overpowering intensity, as if drawing itself together from all parts, drawing inward and obliterating all that existed, including the eye that saw it and that which remained. At the threshold of extinction, the eye flickered and grew dim; instantly, that which remained, turned away. To bear the vision, to enter in, the light of the eye must not go out. Somehow it must become stronger, but what kind of strength is this and how could it be acquired? There was something still to be done, but what? No-self is helpless; it has no strength; it is not the light of the eye nor the eye itself.

VI

Nine months passed before the eye upon Oneness became the eye upon nothingness. Without warning or reason, all particulars dissolved into emptiness. At one point, the mind came upon the hideous void of life, the insidious nothingness of death and decay strangling life from every object of sight. Only self can escape such a vision because only self knows fear, and only fear can generate the weapons of defense. Without a self, the only escape is no escape; the void must be faced—come what may. On the hillside, the epitome of all that is dreadful and insane was confronted—but who, or what beheld this terror? And who or what could endure it? In the absence of self, all that remained was an immovable stillness, an unbreakable, unfeeling silence. Would it move—crack open? Or would it hold? This could not be known, surmised, or even hoped for. What would be, would be.

VII

The stillness held fast because nothingness and emptiness cannot know fear or dread. Yet the wildflower yielded, gave way, expanded infinitely, to reveal a great intensity that could now be seen without the eye growing dim or the light going out. The body dissolves and melts into the stillness of what remains. Afterwards, the eye no longer sees anything at all. Instead, it presses downward on the mind like a terrible taskmaster demanding that it "See!" The mind can no longer focus on anything in particular or in general; it can see nothing within or without. It is in a state of complete unknowing, a dire state and a Passageway wherein, for months, the mind is fixed in a rigid now-moment out of which it cannot move, and in which there is nothing to see.

VIII

In this Passageway, true life, unlocalized and nowhere, reveals itself as that which remains and knows no death. It is this life that continues despite unseeing and unknowing, an eternal life that, strangely, has no God as the object of vision. But how can ordinary life go on without the energies of self, and when true life has no such energies? How is it possible to stay in the flesh and in the ordinary mind when no life seems to lie therein? The only answer is time—time to grow accustomed, to acclimate, to learn all over again how to live with this new life. To do so, the self is nowhere to help, the mind does not know how, and the body keeps melting away.

IX

When the adjustment is made—but barely—the journey appears to be over. At first, the nothingness of existence becomes endurable; later, it is an ordinary sight; and finally, it is so taken for granted it is never noticed or seen again. When nothing moves in to take its place, nothingness becomes all that is; and this had, finally, to be accepted as the most obvious of ultimate truths. Here it could be clearly seen that all the searching, speculating, and experiencing of a lifetime had been a gigantic waste—a head-trip of such proportions that only the infant mentality can bare such a truth: the end is like the beginning, and everything in between is pure deception. The state of un-knowing is permanent; since the mind can hold on to no con-tent, there is nothing more that can be learned. There will be no more journeys; this is the last, the end—an end that is absolute nothingness.

X

As the river flows, a smile emerges, and out of nothingness arises the greatest of great realities, more real than anything that can be seen or known—yet, explicable only in such terms. *The smile it-self, "that" which smiled, and that at which it smiled were identi-cal.* This was the great reality. The relative mind cannot hold, grasp, convey, see, or even believe, that which has revealed itself. This identity can never be communicated because it is the one existent that is Pure Subjectivity, and can never be objectified. This is the Eye seeing itself, and wherever it looks it sees nothing but itself.

XI

Later, after its four-month absence, the Oneness reappeared, but no longer through a medium (the particular); it was "there"— everywhere. But its return was too late; something had now been seen and known, compared to which, all else was but a decep-tion. Still, the mind wanted to look at it, it had to look, and when it did, the Oneness vanished and instantly the mind understood why. It understood what it meant, how it worked, and what still remained to be done. After a long passage, the mind had finally come to rest and rejoice in its own understanding. Now it was ready, prepared, to take its rightful place in the immediacy and practicality of the now-moment. No more searching, looking, retaining; no need to know that which it understands it can never know. And in this state of unknowing, the mind is content to dwell forever. The Eye—which is not of the mind—alone sees and knows itself as all that exists; it is Oneness, and it is itself all that remains when there is no self.

XII

Yet another period of acclimating, of adjusting to the non-relative life beyond the Passageway. Then, just as the self had once faded into silence, so too, the silence and stillness of no-self faded beyond recognition. The journey—its experiences, insights, and learning devices—had only been the means of transition from the old to the new life, from a relative to a non-relative way of knowing and seeing. It was over now; the gap between subject and object had been irrevocably closed. Beyond the relational there is only the Eye seeing itself, which is not static; rather, it sees itself as so continuously new, that the now-moment is never the same. Since the movement into the new is of its essence, the journey moves on, endlessly onward into the Unknown.

From *The Experience of No-Self* by Bernadette Roberts.

DEEPA KODIKAL

GRACIOUS and articulate, Deepa Kodikal is remarkable in many ways. In addition to being a scientist and accomplished in Indian cuisine and oil painting, Deepa plays the sitar, has performed Indian classical dance, written and directed plays, designed ceramic murals, and taken training in glider-flying. Aside from her amazing spiritual journey, Deepa is delightful.

Perhaps the most extraordinary of all is that Deepa was not seeking enlightenment. As a timid child, she became aware that she could direct her own dreams. She was haunted by vivid images of ghosts or wild cats pursuing her, and her mother assured her that the creatures could bring no harm. From that point on, "I concluded that I could do all sorts of impossible things in a dream." A mischievous, playful girl in her outer life, Deepa remained immersed in her dream world. "A trio of deities, Lord Krishna, Shri Ram, and Maha-Vishnu, held me captive day and night."

Educated in the best of schools and colleges in New Delhi, Deepa was quite content with "a charmed circle" of her husband, three daughters, relatives, and friends. Married and fully engaged in a busy social life, Deepa found that each of her four pregnancies brought to her periods of ethereal serenity in which she was free of thoughts and desires. She later recognized these to be *samadhi*-like states of absorption beyond the mind.

> I had not read any scriptures prior to my experiences outlined here nor had I any yearning at all for Knowledge of the Divine. Life was perfect for me. I needed no change. Desire for this or hankering for that was unknown to me. Then, one day, I began perceiving a new dimension to life, stark and spread everywhere. I began to wonder how I had

been blind to it when it was all-pervasive and so obvious. How could I have been so insensitive to all this divine grandeur?

I began writing down every thought, every feeling, every event, as it occurred to me, as it was revealed to me. It was an urge I could not suppress. Impelled by an inner force, I put my pen to the paper. . . . Words which had no meaning to me, profundities which I had not grasped before, presented themselves with a clarity that only an inner experience can give. . . . The diary covers a period of my life starting when I was forty-three years of age.

Her fourth daughter was under three when Deepa began her narrative.

Deepa ultimately chose to be a householder rather than an ascetic. After her spiritual awakening, though, her life would never be the same. Now she is often called upon to assure professional men that their wives' spiritual experiences are genuine, rather than forays into madness.

Deepa Kodikal's story is from her marvelous spiritual diary, *A Journey Within the Self.*

BECOMING THE COSMOS
WITHOUT LEAVING HOME

THROUGHOUT the night, I was in deep meditation. I was in meditation in spite of myself. Henceforth, my sleep would be my meditation, and my meditation my sleep. In deep meditation I was again told I was in "turyavastha" and I was being led to "Parabrahma (Supreme God)." And then I saw the "vishwarupa" as is described in the *Gita.* That is a visualization in anthropomorphological terms. What I saw was the universe as it is. In its entirety and in its universality. The "vishwarupa" (universal form) as it is.

I saw the entire span of the sky as seen from the earth. I was shown countless luminous stars scattered across the sky. Some of these were twinkling, some were static. Each was an independent star, each spinning round its axis as also swirling in its orbit. Some were moving as constellations, in groups. There was enough room between the stars to steer comfortably without colliding with each other. Each star knew its path, took enjoyment in its movement, was aware of the grand spectacle, the cosmic picture, obeyed the laws of the giant and the tiny star-systems of the universe and accepted its being part of the whole.

I saw that these myriad stars, seen and unseen, receding into the unknown, together formed a galaxy, girdling the heavens; and I saw this mighty galaxy receding to tiny star structure, then appearing as a single star among another group of a mightier galaxy, where each star was a galaxy itself. Each galaxy and each star within it was spinning around itself and in its own orbit, and, this super-galaxy itself, as a whole, was swirling around in an orbit of awesome dimensions.

This mighty ocean of star-clusters, composed of galaxies within a galaxy, was now but a lone star amidst yet another giant star-system wheeling in the depths of space. The stars, the star-groups, the star-systems, maintained their own axial and orbital flights, tiny and mighty, resembling interwoven galactic wheels. It was a galactic tapestry, in motion.

This went on, each galactic super-system eventually forming only a part of a bigger group. Revolving, gyrating, vista upon vista unfolded, unfurling giant star-systems, each composed of hundreds of millions of stars and galaxies wheeling in the depths of space. The span of the cosmodrama, the immense orbits, the stupendous speeds, the immensity of the universe, the stars compassing it, was awesome and beautiful.

This went on endlessly into infinity. Suddenly, I found I was not on the earth watching this busy, hurling universe. I was at a point beyond the endless complex of galaxies, beyond the outer lonely galaxies girdling the fathomless depths of inter-galactic spaces. I was at a point where I found this entire endlessness and infinity as a single star, and, this endlessness and infinity, now compressed and comprehended as a tiny star, was but a single star in a sky full of such stars in countless numbers...!

Each star-universe was in itself an endlessness, infinity, and was composed of stars and galaxies of a different kind. The space beyond the galaxies was composed of such star-universes of various sizes and colors, some barely moving, some oscillating, some vibrating, some hurtling across the sky, some huge, some like decorative lanterns, some like discus. Stars mighty and small, all in motion and twinkling like diamonds, of various hues. Each star was endlessness and infinity.

Slowly, I perceived this sky acquiring depth. Deeper and deeper, further and further it went, and, I saw this deep space studded with deep-sunk star-universes, all endlessness in themselves, of various colors, of various shapes and hues, and of various movements.

As I beheld this magnificence, I found the grand vista was not only to my front but also behind me, and, in fact, all around me. I was now the center of a circle whose frontiers were simply not there.

All this time, I was huge enough compared to the stars to have a span of vision encompassing the entire field of the firmament. My proportion to the stars was as is man's in relation to a gnat. Huge! The stars too were distant. But as I observed the star-studded sky, the distance between me and the sky suddenly dwindled and the star-universes were all around me, encircling me, floating by me.

I found myself becoming smaller and smaller till finally I became non-existent. I was snuffed out.

Now I was everywhere! I was everywhere at the same time! All-pervading. Any point and every point was a center. There was now nobody excepting these heavenly bodies floating gently by and me—all-pervading and all-seeing.

Every point was the center of this vastness, and, the frontiers from any point were fathomless. Each point was in itself an endlessness and all around was endlessness.

The sky was chock-a-block full of stars but with adequate room for them to move with no panic of collision. And I was everywhere.

The star-universe systems in their movements were passing through other star-universe systems, effortlessly, as one slips through compartment after crowded compartment in a moving train. What's more, these star trains were moving not only horizontally, but also vertically, radially, in all possible directions much the same way as would a sky full of divine bursting fireworks.

Each star-universe system was slipping through many star-universe systems at a time, and, in turn allowing many other such systems to pass through in larger groups, yet managed to retain its own size, identity, movement and rhythm. That is, each system was moving from and through system to system yet was in its allotted place in relation to other systems, moving or oscillating within its own span of movement.

Now, the entire process was reversed as if a powerful lens had been inserted, and, I saw that these star-universe systems, each an endlessness in size, was not like a tiny star but was a construct of super-galaxies; each part of this construct in turn splitting into the galaxies of which it was composed. And this entire complex inter-mingled with other complexes, yet retained its size, shape, identity and form.

Each super-galaxy again broke up into a system of galaxies, each one passing through the others; and so on and on.

It was endless.

Thus each star or star-cluster appeared to be merging in or forming a part of other clusters flung in different directions, all at the same time, yet retaining its place in its own cluster.

Each star, each galaxy, each super-galaxy, moved around its axis and around its orbit, yet managed the above merging. Thus each star, each system, whizzing through the other, formed a part of a bigger whole, inseparable from the other groups and the even bigger grand pattern, yet retaining its own identity.

As each star or star-system spun on, retaining its place, its relative distance, its perfect placement in relation to the bigger groups, it appeared to be hardly moving. The firmament appeared to be in an equipoise, and, each of its components in perfect equilibrium. And yet I knew the firmament moved.

The lens was now removed: The stars regained their forms, concealing their complexities of galaxies, floating gently in endless emptiness and endless time. . . .

This was only one aspect of the universe. There were universes within universes, invisible universes, visible ones, universes lying side by side, in one place, "existing" through each other simultaneously in "different" dimensions of time, in different spatial dimensions; it went on endlessly. . . .

These were the manifest universes. Then there were the unmanifest ones. Only in their potential. . . .

This was a glimpse of the universe!

I began by seeing the universe as one sees the sky from earth. Slowly, my individual identity was broken down, and, when my limiting individuality was totally demolished, I assumed the universal form. I was everywhere at one time, seeing everything, the micro, the macro, from the closest quarters, from the furthest range. I was everywhere, all-pervading, formless, omnipresent, all-knowing and all-enjoying.

I was omnipresent, all-knowing and all-enjoying. But I was not the universe. I was totally free of it, independent of it and uninvolved in it. I spread everywhere, but formlessly and unencumbered by attachments, an eternal witness not bound by the universe. I was pure and intelligent consciousness, seeing all and knowing all but not depending upon the universe for sustenance.

I felt light, free and unmoving, yet I was at all points, all at the same time. Witness to everything.

Uninvolved, free of emotions, free of thought, pure, and vast, I remained poised in eternity and in infinity, in quiet enjoyment; still, composed, calm, and in repose!

From *A Journey Within the Self* by Deepa Kodikal.

GANGAJI

⤳ TWENTY-EIGHT ⤳

GANGAJI

1942–PRESENT, UNITED STATES

ORN IN Texas in 1942, Gangaji grew up in Mississippi. A member of a noncommunicative, alcoholic family, she did not have a joyful childhood. Even after she married and gave birth to a daughter, the South did not feel like home to her. Upon moving to San Francisco in 1972, Gangaji immersed herself in a search for spirit. Following a divorce and a period of political activism, she took Buddhist vows, practiced Zen and Vipassana meditation, and helped run a Tibetan Buddhist center. For five years Gangaji, an acupuncturist, and her partner (later to become her husband) Eli, a neurolinguistic programmer, ran a clinic in San Francisco and lived well in Marin County. Material success and an enormous mortgage became a burden rather than a blessing. One day they took an honest look at their lives and wondered what had happened to them. In search of a simpler lifestyle, they sold their home and moved to Hawaii.

Gangaji continued to experience a persistent longing for truth and fulfillment and prayed that she might find her teacher. This prayer was answered in 1990 when she met Poonjaji (affectionately known as Papaji), a disciple of Ramana Marharshi, in India. Upon meeting Poonjaji, Gangaji experienced a profound release and a sense of having found that which she was seeking. Simply and directly, Poonjaji pointed out, "You are freedom. You are truth." This realization penetrated Gangaji to the very core, and her life was never the same.

Following in the Advaita (nondualistic) lineage, Gangaji directs her students to ask again and again and again, "Who Am I?" To be quiet, still, and fully present. To be 100 percent willing to surrender the sense of personal identification, acquisition, and doership. To cease searching and

215

stop trying. The very secret of going deeper, explains Gangaji, is not to go anywhere. For there is nothing to accomplish or attain. All that is asked of us is to be, and that is no secret.

Gangaji reminds us that we are immensely "lucky" to receive the gift of Ramana's and Papaji's realization. And even more so to receive the invitation or grace to discover the truth of what we really are through direct experience. She enjoins us to give up our personal stories, which inevitably bring with them endless attachments and the pain and suffering of separation. In order to plunge into the limitless depths of our own hearts, we must face our deepest fears and allow the world as we know it to disappear.

The simplicity and directness of the truth that Gangaji shares appeals to thousands of people from diverse backgrounds, professions, and nationalities. She offers satsangs (to be in the company of truth) and retreats worldwide to inspire all to honor and live the truth willingly, openly, and joyfully.

The following words of Gangaji were shared specially for readers of this book.

WHO ARE YOU? YOU ARE THAT!

THERE IS no formula for discovering the truth of who you are. When I first was on the path of seeking truth, I was quite certain that I could make this discovery on my own. Besides, I had seen the horrors of the guru scene, and I thought that I was certainly above that.

Finally, I recognized that I could not; that my mental process continued to spin in circles, always just missing the revelation of truth. There had been experiences of oneness, experiences of bliss, but I always just missed the eternal ground of truth.

By the standards of our culture, I was successful in life, but I remained disillusioned. Disillusioned with myself and disillusioned with the constant, everyday attention I had on fixing myself. I had come to realize that there was a certain cycle to my self-involvement. On one end of the cycle was a sense of satisfaction of the rightness of things, a belief that all is exactly as it should be. In opposition to that, on the other end of the cycle, were feelings of impending doom, the experience of misery, and a belief in the hopelessness of the plight of the entire universe. I sought out, actually craved, the experience of oneness, and with my arsenal of techniques and strategies worked to avoid the possibility of despair.

After a cycle goes around for many millions of times, it begins to get very familiar. The thoughts, the images, and the conclusions that would appear had appeared before. They weren't creative or fresh. Still I know what to do. I had tried everything I knew to unravel this psychological knot of suffering. I tried pleasure, and I tried pain. I tried a husband. I tried a child. I tried lovers. I tried certain mind-expanding substances. I tried meditation. I tried getting *shakti* [spiritual energy transmission] from certain teachers. I tried retreats. I tried empowerments. And there were tastes, glimpses, and moments of peace. But every path I traveled led once again to the arising of suffering. Whatever taste I experienced was somehow inadvertently pushed aside in the attempt to keep hold of a psychological me. Finally I realized that I needed a teacher. I needed help.

So I prayed for a true teacher, a real teacher, a final teacher, having no idea of what a true teacher meant, what a true teaching was, or what the result would be. I simply knew that I wanted to be free of the struggle. I wanted to recognize the truth. And I know how to do that. I do it. I gave up.

Within a very short time, within just six months of praying for a true teacher, I found myself in India at the feet of my teacher, H. W. L. Poonja (Papaji). I was greeted in an extraordinary way. He welcomed me with the most open invitation to come in and take whatever he could give me. He did not check my credentials. He did not check my karma. He did not tally up any merits. He simply asked me if I wanted freedom. When he saw that I did, he invited me to come in and receive.

The moment I looked into Papaji's eyes, I recognized the whole cosmos existed there. There was a force and clarity that literally and metaphorically stopped me in my tracks. He took me by the shoulders, and he gently shook me and said, "Don't miss this chance. Who knows when it will come again."

Through mysterious grace I recognized that whatever the results, truth could be found here with him. His warmth and love melted any emotional resistance. His humor and mental sharpness opened the gates of my mental defenses. Remarkably, I was able to give all attention to him, to what he was showing me in his be-ing and what he was inviting me to investigate with my full being.

When I questioned him regarding how to attain eternal truth, Papaji replied, "Lay aside every technique, every tool, every concept. Just be still, just be quiet, and see."

After a moment of fearing what would be lost (all the ground I had gained!) if I were to truly give up all strategies and techniques, I stopped. And in that stopping, I was simply able to hear what he had to say. What he said, and how he said it, and how he invited me to investigate for myself what he was pointing to, was exactly what I had been praying for.

I knew he was speaking the truth. In meeting with him I saw that there was something huge, something more vast and more mysterious than the capacity of any thought process to own, to conquer, or to process.

To be able to hear it sounds like a simple thing. But with the complexity of our personalities, and our ideas and beliefs, there is usually much complication covering simple hearing. If one is preoccupied with past techniques and definitions and paths and defeats and victories, one is too busy to really hear the truth. The truth so simple, it is usually overlooked.

Finally I realized that whatever I thought, it was always just a thought, subject to disappearance, and therefore, impossible to be eternal. To discover eternal truth, I could no longer rely on thought. Thought was no longer the master. The previous fear of not knowing was transformed to the joy of not knowing. To not know was the opening of my mind to what cannot be known by mind! What relief, what profound release.

When you don't know who you are, there is an opening; there is a crack in the structure of the mind. In that moment the mind isn't filled with the latest definition of identity, or the battle between the latest and the habitual definition. In that moment there is silence. There is no generation of definition and no agreement or disagreement with that definition. There is just silence.

And Papaji said, "That, right there. That's who you are."

What followed cannot truly be put into constraints of time. Although time did pass, time passed through (continues to pass through) what is revealed to be eternal.

Past, present, and future, all phenomena of mind, exquisite, mysterious and deeply entertaining, but not real.

Reality indefinable, unprocessable, unholdable, yet undeniably here. Eternity here. Regardless of thought, regardless of event, regardless of experience (even regardless of experience of appearance of 'me' or disappearance of "me").

Unspeakable moment that neither began when I think it did, nor ends. Now happening, while really not happening at all.

Impossible to understand because it is always closer than understanding. Alive with the energy that gives rise to the entire cosmos as well as every speck of dust; every cathedral as well as every mundane thought.

All.

All is here. Here is eternal God, eternal Truth. Here I am. All.

After some passage of time, with the challenges of released latent tendencies, he saw that I had recognized the boundless indefinability of true Self. He then asked me to go "door to door" and speak with others of my experience. At the time I said to him, "I truly don't know how to do that."

And he said, "Good. Speak from your experience only."

"But Papaji," I said, "I don't know how. I don't know if it is possible."

He directed me again to trust not knowing. In this trust, knowing is present and alive. The appearance of mind is then the vehicle rather than the director. He directed me to invite you to recognize yourself without knowing yourself, to see yourself without any image of yourself, to be yourself without any definition of yourself.

So I appear to knock on your door in the dream of "you and me" and I have something very wonderful to tell you. You are free to hear and you are free to turn away. Your response is not my business. I welcome you to the possibility of really hearing. In true hearing all secrets are transmitted, and the truth of hearing is that what is heard already exists within your own heart. The heart of consciousness is here now. It knows no other time. The heart of consciousness recognizes Itself, finally, in all, as all. You.

Consciousness is free. You are freedom itself. You have only imagined yourself to be separate from consciousness, imagined yourself limited to a body you imagine yourself to be. Consciousness is free already. You have always been free. When this is realized, there may be great laughter, and there may be many tears, there may be shouts, and there may be dancing. The recognition of who you truly are, of your natural state, is beginning the adventure of what is before beginning. It is the ending of the preoccupation with the cycle of self-involvement, and the beginning of true self-discovery, which knows no limits, knows no other.

When Papaji died, an interviewer asked me what Papaji has meant to my life. I answered, "Before Papaji I didn't have a life. I had a story of suffering. There were moments of pleasure, even moments of bliss, but still a story of suffering. In the meeting of Papaji, that story was discarded. When I met him, I saw I only have life. I am only Life."

From the unpublished words of Gangaji.

ECKHART TOLLE

TWENTY-NINE

ECKHART TOLLE

1948–PRESENT, GERMANY

ONCE YOU have met Eckhart, you realize the paradox of discussing his background and personal particulars. For Eckhart is quite understated, and, of any teacher you will find, one of the least attached to persona. Born in Germany, even as a child he experienced intense despair and contemplated ending his life. Eckhart discontinued his formal studies at age thirteen upon moving to Spain. After graduation from the University of London, he became a research scholar and supervisor at Cambridge University, however his academic success was driven by fear. Overcome by a sense of purposeless and on the verge of suicide, Eckhart saw no reason for his existence. His subsequent profound spiritual transformation radically changed the course of his life and the lives of many others.

During the few years following Eckhart's transformation, he dedicated himself to integrating and deepening his understanding. Aligned with no particular religion or tradition, Eckhart's message is uncomplicated: The path from suffering to peace is readily available.

The Power of Now, written by Eckhart in 1997, was so practical yet profound that it attracted the attention of seekers worldwide, including Oprah Winfrey. Residing in Vancouver, Canada, since 1996, Eckhart conveyed his message to small groups of spiritual seekers in North America and Europe. He now teaches and travels extensively throughout the world, and his seminars are filled within days of their announcement. That such an unassuming teacher, in this age of media glitz and hype, can spread to so many a message so simple and universal is an inspiration.

Eckhart confines his attention and awareness to the present moment, aspiring to nothing more than residing in *it* alone. He cautions us not to take the mind too seriously—to dwell neither in past or future.

To sit with Eckhart is to immerse oneself in a profound atmosphere of timeless Presence. When around Eckhart's delightful humor and gestures, one cannot help but laugh at the absurdity of the mind forms we call reality. A highlight of the conclusion of Eckhart's retreats are his hugs, during which time one can gaze into the deep ocean of stillness and vastness reflected in his clear, blue eyes.

As he has done himself, Eckhart encourages us to dissolve emotional suffering, which he terms "the pain body," to let go of our concepts of "psychological time," and to reside in the present, which is all that exists anyway. Freeing ourselves from our mental constructs, ego identification, and time-bound reality opens us to "the joy of being." Beyond the dramas of our lives, the illusion of happiness and unhappiness, and our addiction to suffering lies the realization for which so many of us yearn. It is through surrendering to the present and relinquishing our burdens of fear, conflict, and pain that we become free. A phrase we heard at one of Eckhart's seminars remains indelible in our minds: "There will never be a moment more perfect than this one." Such is the power of now.

Eckhart Tolle's selection comes from the introduction to his best-selling book, *The Power of Now*.

THE POWER OF NOW

I HAVE little use for the past and rarely think about it; however, I would briefly like to tell you how I came to be a spiritual teacher and how this book *(The Power of Now)* came into existence.

Until my thirtieth year, I lived in a state of almost continuous anxiety interspersed with periods of suicidal depression. It feels now as if I am talking about some past lifetime or somebody else's life.

One night not long after my twenty-ninth birthday, I woke up in the early hours with a feeling of absolute dread. I had woken up with such a feeling many times before, but this time it was more intense than it had ever been. The silence of the night, the vague outlines of the furniture in the dark room, the distant noise of a passing train—everything felt so alien, so hostile, and so utterly meaningless that it created in me a deep loathing of the world. The most loathsome thing of all, however, was my own existence. What was the point in continuing to live with this burden of misery? Why carry on with this continuous struggle? I could feel that a deep longing for annihilation, for nonexistence, was now becoming much stronger than the instinctive desire to continue to live.

"I cannot live with myself any longer." This was the thought that kept repeating itself in my mind. Then suddenly I became aware of what a peculiar thought it was. "Am I one or two? If I cannot live with myself, there must be two of me: the 'I' and the 'self' that 'I' cannot live with." "Maybe," I thought, "only one of them is real." I was so stunned by this strange realization that my mind stopped. I was fully conscious, but there were no more thoughts. Then I felt drawn into what seemed like a vortex of energy. It was a slow movement at first and then accelerated. I was gripped by an intense fear, and my body started to shake. I heard the words "resist nothing," as if spoken inside my chest. I could feel myself being sucked into a void. It felt as if the void was inside myself rather than outside. Suddenly, there was no more fear, and I let myself fall into that void. I have no recollection of what happened after that.

I was awakened by the chirping of a bird outside the window. I had never heard such a sound before. My eyes were still closed, and I saw the image of a precious diamond. Yes, if a diamond could make a sound, this is what it would be like. I opened my eyes. The first light of dawn was filtering through the curtains. Without any thought, I felt, I knew, that there is infinitely more to light than we realize. That soft luminosity filtering through the curtains was love itself. Tears came into my eyes. I got up and walked around the room. I recognized the room, and yet I knew that I had never truly seen it before. Everything was fresh and pristine, as if it had just come into existence. I picked up things, a pencil, an empty bottle, marveling at the beauty and aliveness of it all.

That day I walked around the city in utter amazement at the miracle of life on earth, as if I had just been born into this world.

For the next five months, I lived in a state of uninterrupted deep peace and bliss. After that, it diminished somewhat in intensity, or perhaps it just seemed to because it became my natural state. I could still function in the world, although I realized that nothing I ever did could possibly add anything to what I already had.

I knew, of course, that something profoundly significant had happened to me, but I didn't understand it at all. It wasn't until several years later, after I had read spiritual texts and spent time with spiritual teachers, that I realized that what everybody was looking for had already happened to me. I understood that the intense pressure of suffering that night must have forced my consciousness to withdraw from its identification with the unhappy and deeply fearful self, which is ultimately a fiction of the mind. This withdrawal must have been so complete that this false, suffering self immediately collapsed, just as if a plug had been pulled out of an inflatable toy. What was left then was my true nature as the ever-present I am: consciousness in its pure state prior to identification with form. Later I also learned to go into that inner timeless and deathless realm that I had originally perceived as a void and remain fully conscious. I dwelt in states of such indescribable bliss and sacredness that even the original experience I just described pales in comparison. A time came when, for a while, I was left with nothing on the physical plane. I had no relationships, no job, no home, no socially defined identity. I spent almost two years sitting on park benches in a state of the most intense joy.

But even the most beautiful experiences come and go. More fundamental, perhaps, than any experience is the undercurrent of peace that has never left me since then. Sometimes it is very strong, almost palpable, and others can feel it too. At other times, it is somewhere in the background, like a distant melody.

Later, people would occasionally come up to me and say: "I want what you have. Can you give it to me, or show me how to get it?" And I would say: "You have it already. You just can't feel it because your mind is making too much noise." That answer later grew into the book that you are holding in your hands.

Before I knew it, I had an external identity again. I had become a spiritual teacher.

From *The Power of Now* by Eckhart Tolle.

A. H. ALMAAS

A. H. ALMAAS is the pen name of A. Hameed Ali, a contemporary Kuwaiti-born spiritual teacher, author, and founder of the Ridhwan School and the Diamond Approach to spiritual development. Ali's Diamond Approach, popularized in his own numerous books and in a new guide written by John Davis, is a combination of spirituality and psychology. Ali received training in physics, mathematics, and psychology. Just prior to receiving his doctorate in physics, he left the scientific world to seek answers to the deeper questions of life, where science had failed him. Ali founded the Ridhwan School in 1975, in Berkeley, California, and Boulder, Colorado, to make his teachings available to students, who currently number nearly a thousand worldwide.

Ali brings together an intellectual appreciation of psychology and depth psychotherapy and his own mystical experiences to provide a theoretical and practical framework for practices leading to the transcendence of the ego, or personality, and the realization of one's Essence or inner self. His "autobiographical fragment" *Luminous Night's Journey,* from which our selection is excerpted, reveals a deep and profound journey into his own Essence. In reading his experiences, it is easy to recognize that he is not speaking merely intellectually, but from the deep inner knowing of a genuine mystic. Ali and his students believe that the aspects of one's Essence are available through examining the ego and personality in a path of rediscovery.

The Diamond Approach employs a number of methods. Students, guided by Ali or one of the teachers he has trained, explore their feelings, thoughts, and actions in small groups or individually. They work with intuitive, emotional, and rational processes, breathwork, and subtle energies in a spiritual context. The object of this method is to open, purify, and clarify the soul in order to more fully experience one's unconditioned essential nature, or pure Being. Emphasis is placed on direct spiritual experience, opening the soul to Essence, and experiencing Being through direct contact with the qualities of awareness, emptiness, and presence. Although the Diamond Approach is unique, it parallels and enhances other spiritual approaches by examining the psychology of the obstacles and problems that occur during the spiritual search and offering innovative ways of overcoming spiritual barriers.

Ali's enthusiasm for understanding and explaining both philosophical and psychological concepts is evident in his many books, tapes, and videos. He and his students teach well-received courses and hold retreats throughout North America and Europe.

The selection comes from Almaas' book, *Luminous Night's Journey: An Autobiographical Fragment*.

FINDING ESSENCE THROUGH
THE DIAMOND APPROACH

A few days later . . .

I wake up in the morning with a slight tension at the left shoulder. There is discomfort with the tension. Simply being aware of the tension seems to influence it by making it expand. It becomes a line of tension along the left side of the chest, enfolded by a soft cushiony sensation.

This line is a manifestation of the ego-self that I call the "ego-line." It usually accompanies a specific psychic contraction that corresponds to the presence of the individuality of ego. In other words, the ego-line is the physical manifestation of the ego structure that gives the personality or ego-self the sense of being a separate individual, an autonomous person. The line of tension is a direct indication that the sense of being an individual on the ego level is a contraction of consciousness. This separate individuality of ego is formed or defined mostly by the separating boundaries, both bodily and psychological.

The soft cushiony sensation around the line of tension turns out to be a manifestation of consciousness that relates to a false sense of being a person. This makes sense, for the ego-line represents the person of ego, which is not an essential form, but imitates the essential form of the personal essence. As I recognize its falseness, it begins slowly to flake off, falling off the line of tension like dead skin falling off a mummy. This process goes on for most of the day.

Later in the day, the line of tension becomes a tube of a plastic-like substance, an empty plastic tube, which extends all the way to the top of the head. As I go about the business of the day, I do not lose touch with this contraction, but remain continuously aware of it as part of my conscious experience. At some point, this contemplation opens the way for a very subtle insight: my concern about the contraction is inseparable from the contraction. The concern involves a desire for the contraction not to be there, which I now recognize as my hope to go beyond it. The plastic tube contraction is the presence of the individual of ego in the posture of hoping to go beyond itself. The hope is inseparable from the contraction, because it is the future-oriented attitude of the personality, which is the contraction. As I see this, the contraction begins to dissolve. The tube of contraction first dissolves in the head, which eliminates the mental concern. A beautiful sky-blue quality of consciousness appears in the head, bringing a sense of mental rest and relaxation. Poignant settledness of all agitation in the head. The head feels filled by a delicious sensation that seems to smoothly dissolve any form in this part of the body.

As this happens, and as the totality of the tube of contraction disappears, I lose the sense of being a person, and become an awareness that recedes indefinitely, as if backward, from the familiar sense of being a person, until I recognize myself as a new kind of witnessing. I become an immaterial witness, not located within a personal consciousness. I find myself to be a witnessing of all phenomena.

A new obstacle arises at this point, a belief that constitutes a resistance against this new manifestation. This belief interferes with the sense of witnessing, without totally eliminating it. The belief is that there will be no personal life, no personal living, if there is no enmeshment in life. This exposes the belief as part of the inertia of being the separate individual of ego.

Being responds to this concern by manifesting the aspect of the personal essence, the pearl beyond price, the person of Being. The experience transforms into knowing myself as a full presence, rounded as a pearl, but transparent and sweet. I feel personal, even though I am a pure presence of transparent consciousness. This transparent fullness has a subtle sweetness, making it feel slightly sticky, or gummy. There is pure presence, with clarity and spaciousness all around. The cognitive aspect of the experience is that I am a person with no qualities, only a personal presence, devoid of images or psychological boundaries. Since I can be a person without being the product of memory, I can live a personal life without getting lost in it.

That night, during dinner, the leaden heaviness appears again, scattering the attention and presence for about an hour. The leaden heaviness becomes so dense that it disintegrates most of my capacity for attention and presence. Strong resistances arise, feelings of rubbery thickness, wooden dryness, amorphous states of consciousness, and many other confused and chaotic sensations. I feel the leaden rounded heaviness pushing from inside, scattering whatever consciousness it meets in its way. At this point I realize that the power of this heaviness arises from the transformation of the leaden consciousness into something much more substantial and powerful. The lead pearl has transformed into the shiny gray existence pearl, like a large pearl of hematite.

I feel personal but immense, a person of Being so dense that my substantiality eclipses the physical substantiality of the body. The most definite feeling is a sense of personal existence. I feel intensely real, existing so fundamentally that the mind cannot conceive of this reality. I experience myself as a person, and this person is composed of pure existence. Existence of Being, essential and fundamental, and independent of the mind, forms the very atoms of what I am. I am existence, beyond all thought of existence. The sense of truth and reality is immensely profound; it feels deeper than the universe itself. And this unimaginably real sense of existence has a very subtle sense of being a person— a person not defined by history or mind, not confined by character traits or relationships, but a person who exists, and that is all. The sense of existence has an unquestionable sense of certainty, independent of any content of mind or experience. I recognize at this point that there is no basis for the concern that there will be no personal life if I am not enmeshed in it.

This experience of being so real and certain as a person continues throughout dinner. I continue to converse with my dinner companions, while I am spontaneously attending to the inner transformation. The unusually substantial sense of presence affects the atmosphere at dinner in a subtle way not recognized by my companions. The conversation merely turns towards basic things in life, less abstract and more personal. My body feels as if all of its atoms are pulled downward, as if gravity has increased, but there is no physical discomfort. In fact, the body relaxes; the muscles let go and condense downward.

I realize that there is no real basis for believing that in order to have a personal life I need to be enmeshed in it. This is true for the person of ego, who is formed by images and psychological patterns. Now, however, I have the certainty that my personal existence is beyond any of that. My personal existence is beyond mind and history, for it is an essential manifestation of the fundamental existence of Being. I can be a person, and live a personal life in a truly involved way, without being enmeshed in any of its particulars. This is certain.

I have experienced my presence in the essential form of the pearl innumerable times. This essential form manifests mostly as a luminous white pearl, but can manifest in the color of any essential aspect, like the deep sky blue of direct knowing, the emerald green of loving kindness, or the shiny gold of truth. In each of these manifestations, the particular aspect, with all its alchemical characteristics, is experienced along with the characteristic of personalness. The presence of the pearl signifies authentic personalness, which reveals the possibility of living a personal life from the view of Being.

The existence pearl is the new development of the personal aspect of Being. It is quite amazing to see how Being resolves a particular issue, or answers a real question, not by an insight or idea but by the presentation of an essential form of its own truth. The resolution is an experience of Being, in one of its pure and universal forms, and not merely the dissolution of an obstacle or the end of a conflict. The beautiful thing about such a resolution is how exact and precise it is. Being responds with the precise state needed for the resolution, a state not anticipated by the mind, arising as an unexpected discovery. Such experiences demonstrate the awesome intelligence that Being possesses, which can only fill us with awe, and heart-felt gratitude and trust.

The concern that I started with involved the belief that there would be no personal life if there were no enmeshment in it. I believed I would not exist as a person if I were not enmeshed in the particulars of my life. Being revealed, through its messenger, the nous, that my personal existence is an essential manifestation of Being, independent of mind and situations, and hence stands on its own, independent of mental reactions. In other words, I can live a personal life by merely being, for my personal existence is a part of Being. There is no real threat to my personal existence. Before this point, I had not experienced existence of Being, itself, as a personal presence. The response of Being to my concern is exquisitely precise, beyond all expectations.

By the time dinner is over, the density and substantiality suddenly evaporate, revealing a vastness beyond comprehension. I do not perceive this vastness, but I recognize it as my very identity. I experience myself as the vast silent dark emptiness. As I experience this new identity, I learn a great deal of what I truly am when I am not trapped in the particulars of personal life and history. I can be present as personal existence, or I can transcend all personal experience. I am then the unchanging background witnessing, which has been revealing itself in the midst of personal experience, in glimpses and intimations, flashes and intuitions. Now this awareness reveals itself fully, as the universal witness.

I experience myself as beyond everything, literally everything, and not just everything in my personal life. I am a silent witness, vast and unchanging, beyond time and all space. I am absolutely still, totally uninvolved, but completely aware. This demonstrates directly that I do not need to be freed or enlightened. I am always free, always have been and always will be. Also, I cannot be trapped, for my very identity is totally detached awareness. I can see my personal life as a drama that I do not have to be involved in. It is like a movie that has a beginning and an end, but it is not me. I feel distant from everything, but acutely aware of everything.

I am a silent space, totally empty but containing everything. The recognition, which is a direct perception, is that everything is in me. The body, the universe, essence, personality, everything that can become an object of perception, is not me, but is in me. I am pure awareness, mere witnessing, where everything arises and passes away.

Four days later . . .

I wake up with the black space of intimacy, feeling pervaded by and enfolded in a sweet deliciousness. At the center of this deep intimacy, I sense the solid and dense presence of a diamond-like inner support. This brings a sense of grounded solid reality. At the same time there is spaciousness and depth. The body-mind is functioning mostly as a location for the consciousness. The spacious depth continues during the day, expanding gradually into the vastness of the silent witness. The experience of the universal witness unfolds more than it did few days ago, revealing further implications of recognizing my identity as this unchanging background of awareness. The insights, which arise as perceptions, roll effortlessly, the more I am this witnessing:

"I am not the body, not the personality, not the essence, not the mind, not God. I am nothing that is a content of experience. Yet, all experience happens within me. Everything, at all levels, from the spiritual to the physical, happens within me.

I am not touched by any of it. I am untouched and untouchable. I am unchanging. I am deathless. I am unborn. I am uncaused, unoriginated. I was never born, will never die. The concepts of life and death do not apply to me. Life and death are nothing but a process of constant transformation within me. All existence, from the lowest to the highest, is always in a state of flux, but I am the background against which this flux is seen. I am static, unchanging, nonreactive, and nonresponsive. I am beyond space and time; both space and time are within me. All of time is a movement within me. Personality, or more accurately, the personal consciousness or soul, is time. Time is the flux of this personal consciousness. Essence is timelessness. I see time as the movement of the timeless in me. All of time, the time of the body and of all of physical existence, is a small process within me. I am beyond time and timelessness. I am the beyond, beyond all and everything. Mind is within me, small and always trying to grasp me."

The silence is vast and eerie. There is a sense of ultimacy, of end. It seems that there is nothing beyond it. It is not that the universal witness is the highest. It is beyond high and low. From this silence, the revelation of all essential manifestations of Being arises in a hierarchy within the background of this the vast witnessing awareness. It contains all the levels of Being, so it exists at all the levels. Experiencing the universal witness is not a matter of ascending grades; it is rather an exit, getting out of the whole thing. It is truly the beyond, the unchanging silent background.

Its main characteristic is that it is aware. In this way it is similar to the personal witness, where the personal witness seems now to have been a limited and personal manifestation of it. The personal witness is aware of the immediate environment of the location of consciousness, while the universal witness is aware, in addition, of the totality of the universe, as if from above or from afar. This perception does not include all of the details of manifestation, but rather a general perception, as if awareness has receded backward until all that exists is in front of it. Phenomenologically, the perception is of being an endless emptiness, so vast that the whole of existence is a small manifestation within it, seen in general outline as a river of images in constant flux. The awareness is aware of itself as a witnessing of everything without being involved in anything. A dark awareness, but not exactly black. It is more dark gray, the color of the aspect of existence, but it is sheer voidness. It is not no-mind space, for although it is beyond thought and mind, mind can exist within it.

The strangest thing about this awareness is its relation to time. It is beyond time. This is different from the sense of timelessness that arises when the essential manifestation of Being outshines everything else, where it seems that time has stopped. It is beyond time. It seems to be what is there before time begins, and after time ends, and at all times.

It clearly is a space with more than five dimensions, for it includes the three dimensions of space, the dimension of time, and the dimension of essence that is the presence of Being. It also feels undefinable, in the sense that no concept can contain it. The more one perceives that it is undefinable, the more there is insight about it. The knowing of it arises by being it, as if it is known only by itself. Looking at it from outside it, or more accurately, when it looks at itself, it simply looks like space. Its relation to time, change and awareness is not seen except through its self-knowledge.

The state of the universal witness continues for a few days. I see everything, the house, friends, family, students, and situations all existing and happening within my vastness. There is a sense of utter impersonality, totally transcendent impersonalness.

Understanding and realizing the universal witness allows me to see and understand the totality of the personal life. At this point the activity at the forehead intensifies, and insights start pouring out about the connection between the personal and impersonal. This begins as curiosity about the relation between the intimacy space, which feels very personal, and the witness space, which feels utterly impersonal.

Here the diamond-like presence of support reappears as a big lead diamond in the belly. The understanding radiates out from a lead diamond between the eyes. A flow of insights pours out of this awareness, completing itself as the objective understanding of lead, of inertia, of the conditioning of the personal, and of the ego-line.

Lead is the will that supports the conditioning of consciousness. But further, the lead pearl is the unconscious will, the support and determination that has always been supporting the ego-line, the ego sense of being a person. Nevertheless, the ego-line contraction, even though it is the personality, is also a role. The role is the personal function or work, developed throughout one's personal history, as the individual capacity to function in a particular way. In other words, one is born with a work to develop and do on earth. It is the personal consciousness—which, for most individuals, is the ego-structured personality—that develops it. The witnessing space cannot do it, because it does not do. This means that one has a particular personal role, which develops mostly through the personality developing along certain lines. The personality is conditioned to be a certain way, which in time will manifest the role and its work. An unchanging and inflexible will supports this conditioned personality. The will is inertia, lead itself.

Usually one gets trapped in the personality, in the role, and takes it to be oneself. In fact, one takes the line of contraction to be oneself. However, the conditioning of the personal consciousness is a program that can develop in such a manner that it will self-destruct when the role, its attendant capacities and its work, have developed. It seems this will inevitably happen if the program leads to the impersonal, the silent witness.

Developing one's personal role and work is the same thing as the maturation and individuation of the personal consciousness. This development coincides with the realization of the personal essence, the pearl that Being develops through the friction of the life process.

Few days later . . .

An insight reveals a further relationship between the personal development and the unchanging and undeveloping universal witness. The personal needs to realize the universal impersonal in order to be free. Otherwise life becomes enmeshment in the particulars of daily life. The realization of the impersonal is not only for its own sake, it is also for the personal to complete its development in freedom. Life is then the personal consciousness experiencing itself as the flow of the realization of Being.

From *Luminous Night's Journey: An Autobiographical Fragment* by A. H. Almaas.

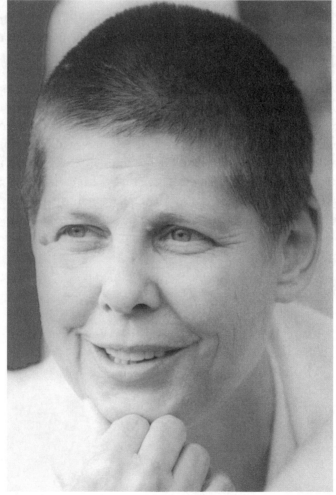

SHANTIMAYI

·: THIRTY-ONE :·

SHANTIMAYI

1950–PRESENT, UNITED STATES

B ENEATH a massive banyan tree on a plateau above the sacred Ganges, Shantimayi sits, with shaved head (formerly long, flowing blonde hair), imparting her teachings to a hundred or so, mostly European, devotees. Her teaching is a blend of Hinduism and Buddhism. An English-speaking woman, wife, mother of three, and grandmother of four, she is a spiritual teacher to whom many find it easy to relate. A woman of humble beginnings, Shantimayi's manner is sincere, direct, and available. One-pointed (holding only one thought, concentrated) yet lighthearted, fully present yet remarkably flexible, a householder yet a yogi, Shantimayi holds steadfast to her goal of guiding her devotees to ultimate peace and surrender. Welcoming of questions, she is quick to admit when she has no answer. Embracing of all aspects of human and Divine, her style allows students to be themselves as they seek to better themselves.

Shantimayi narrates her story quite descriptively:

> I am told that I was born in Akron, Ohio, in 1950 and was given the name Mary. I lived with my grandparents when I was little, back in the mountains of West Virginia. There, in the town of Jody, population two hundred, the air was fresh and filled with the scent of honeysuckle. The rhythm of a porch swing and the music of crickets provided my evening lullaby. The nights were black, tranquil, and sprinkled with zillions of stars. We lived in a tiny house on a dirt road nestled between two mountains. On Sundays, I faithfully attended the town church service with Grandma, where the Southern Baptists testified about their relationship with Jesus. Three years old and innocent and open-eyed, I loved it.

In that poor coal mining town, men came home each evening pitch black, covered with coal dust from head to toe. And every evening my grandfather came home from work and called for me. He always carried a surprise for me in his metal lunch box. I could count on it. Perhaps it was his way of teaching me about the joy of giving and receiving.

One of my starkest memories from childhood was the town well. Our town only had one. All day long folks trekked to or from that well. A bucket or two of water at a time to wash, cook, and quench their thirst. In its silent way, that well taught me a great deal. The well was deep and so was the understanding that it conveyed. Now, by the Grace of my Master, my life is an exact replica of that well.

Shantimayi's autiobiographical story was written specially for our readers.

THE CANNERY ENLIGHTENMENT

November 1988

When I arrived at my Guru's door I was ripe for him and receptive to what he had to give. Hungry and willing, I had no idea what was going to happen but I did know from the first moment that I would never leave him. I did know, however, that whatever spiritual maturity would occur in my life would now be intensified and deeply nurtured by him. Within a very short time of knowing Maharajji, he told me, "One day you will wear my shoes." I tucked that away into my heart and did nothing with it at all. Every moment I spent with Maharajji was profound and surrendered to whatever we were together for.

October 1992

One day I found myself standing outside of his door in such an empty clarity. Spontaneously I went and spoke to him, telling him how I saw and understood what he had shown me. I guess that I must have been asking him if I was finished. He said, "Wait." Not yes, not no, but wait. I said O.K., bowed to him and left his room. I could not recall exactly what we had spoken about five minutes later. I had poured my heart into his and asked for his approval and he said, "Wait." I felt the energy of our conversation for a long time. He said, "Wait," therefore . . . I would wait. The next year a very similar situation arose and I found myself there in his presence, telling him how I understood what he had shown me. He said, "Wait." Not yes, not no, but wait. Therefore I knew I would wait, I bowed low to him, and left his room, satisfied that I must wait.

A year later I was in Eugene Oregon. While working in a canning factory, in the back of the factory in a room alone, there in early October a satori of indescribable subtlety, a sensation ever so slight, ever so delicate, consumed what I thought was me. The entire satori was like a needle piercing a soap bubble in slow motion. The universe, as I knew it, disappeared, with a very subtle pop of that delicate tiny bubble. It was as though all experience washed away and what was left could not be considered at all. I could only look into the emptiness. There was no I, no looking, and no emptiness, no nothingness as well. There was no moment in time and doubt could not enter. Here nothing could enter, there was no language for doubt or validity. I could see somehow all that my Guru had ever transmitted to me in silence. In that moment, enlightenment removed that which could be enlightened. There I stood (not knowing I was standing until later) breathless for an hour peering into emptiness as emptiness. Ever so delicate and ever so subtle. It seemed as though, if there was the slightest movement the entire universe might break like silence is broken by a glass falling on cement. This is how I perceived that hour, after that hour, not during that hour. What emerged out of that time was the beginning of a way of "seeing." From that moment when I started to leave the factory at the end of that work shift, until now, the ability to see things for what they are has never failed. The totality was so over-whelming and the wordless message that was conveyed was so powerful in its subtlety that the appearance of multiplicity in existence has not ever taken predominance since that time. The satori was like an infinitesimal particle of mist falling into a shoreless ocean. Ocean, only ocean. And of course, it is much deeper than that. Nothing could be said about it and nothing could be brought out of it. There is no language for it at all. Yet, that moment changed my life forever and continues to mature. As far as the void reaches, so too does this enlightenment stretch far and near, revealing everything in utter simplicity.

Still, the beauty is that nothing had changed. What a relief. No one would guess that the lady walking out of the factory that day, wearing the yellow raingear, a hard hat, and boots had just been crowned by a line of Perfected Masters. No one would care. At 2:45, I clocked out. I went home only to return the next day. Now that "I"-dentity had awakened to the immutable perfection unruffled by perception. Since that day, change has no grip. In the same way that a day never passes in a dream.

As for mastery, my Guru entrusted his work to me. A long time ago I promised my life to him, and this is part of it. It is by his grace that my life has come to this. It is by his grace that I have realized my True nature, it is by his grace that I grace others to awaken. The Master bestows grace, transmitting the Truth in silence and inspiring a deep commitment to realize the Truth. It is by the grace of a cliff that the river becomes a waterfall. It is by the grace of the water that the basin fills. The Master is a water-fall, the disciple is the basin, grace is the flowing of a higher power which opens the way beyond consciousness here and now.

From the unpublished words of Shantimayi.

MATA AMRITANANDAMAYI

1953–PRESENT, INDIA

MATA AMRITANANDAMAYI, or Ammachi, as she is known by her devotees, arose from extremely humble beginnings in a tiny village sandwiched between the backwaters of Kerala and the Indian Ocean, near the southern tip of India. Her resemblance to the Lord Krishna from birth due to the blueness of her skin was, to some, an indication of her great affinity to him later in her life. Disparaged and mistreated by her parents, Ammachi was put in the role of the family servant. Even at a young age, she was unable to contain her bliss and her adoration of Krishna. Her embodiment of the playful Krishna amazed the local villagers. Her fame spread rapidly to the nearby communities, and soon devotees were coming by the hundreds for her blessings.

As time evolved, Ammachi developed an ever-greater identification with the Divine Mother. A small, dark, round, smiling woman, garbed in a white sari, Ammachi is now known throughout the world as the epitome of motherly love. She is loved and worshiped for her compassion, passionate singing to God, and for tirelessly enfolding in her motherly arms, one by one, as many as thousands of devotees for up to eight hours at a time.

Ammachi demonstrates apparently limitless endurance and spiritual ecstasy. One New Year's Eve, at a new temple she was consecrating at a holy site in Kerala, she presided over a special *puja* (spiritual ceremony of offering) to the Divine Mother. Each participant in the large group ceremony prayed, chanted, and lit a butter lamp over a small individual clay waterpot as an offering to the Mother of the karma of each who attended. While lamps were waved and bells clanged loudly, Ammachi, in spiritual bliss, danced, sang, prayed, and poured the water from each

MATA AMRITANANDAMAYI (AMMACHI)

of more than a thousand personal pots over the statue of the deity for hours. The air literally crackled with the spiritual power of blessing unleashed by the saint. This energy that emanates from Ammachi is the *shakti,* or Divine Feminine force.

Whether devotees have the most loving parents in the world or were raised devoid of nurturing and care, they are sure to feel profoundly loved after being blessed by Ammachi. A murmured blessing and a Hershey's Kiss enhance the feeling of a personal relationship with the Divine Mother. She also offers a remarkable *darshan* (seeing the master) called Devi Bhava, in which she dresses like a Maharani (Indian queen) and incarnates a kind of regal, Divine-Mother presence that is quite palpable. While devotees chant *bhajans,* Indian spiritual songs, she blesses visitors throughout the night until everyone has received the grace of the Divine.

Now, a large ashram has grown up amid the sea of palm trees and the collection of small huts where she was born. Ammachi has also established an orphanage, hospital, and other service projects to serve the poor throughout India. Wherever she is, whether in the ashram or while traveling the world, people come to Ammachi to enhance that love connection to the Infinite Mother in human form.

EMBRACED BY
THE DIVINE MOTHER

SUDHAMANI'S (Mata Amritanandamayi's) anguish reached a pinnacle. Her prayers had been said. In her own words,

> Each and every pore of my body was wide-open with yearning, each atom of my body was vibrating with the sacred mantra, my entire being was rushing towards the Divine Mother in a torrential stream. . . .

In unspeakable agony she cried out,

O Mother . . . here is Your child about to die drowning in unfathomable distress. . . . This heart is breaking. . . . These limbs
are faltering. . . . I am convulsing like a fish thrown on shore. . . .
O Mother. You have no kindness towards me. . . . I have nothing
left to offer You except the last breath of my life. . . .

Her voice became choked. Her breathing completely stopped.
Sudhamani fell unconscious. The Will of the Mother designates
the moment. The Divine Enchantress of the Universe, the Omniscient, the Omnipresent, the Omnipotent Being, the Ancient,
Primal Creatrix, the Divine Mother, appeared before Sudhamani
in a living form dazzling like a million suns. Sudhamani's heart
overflowed in a tidal wave of unspeakable Love and Bliss. The
Divine Mother benignly smiled and, becoming a Pure Effulgence, merged in Sudhamani.

What followed is best described in Sudhamani's own composition "Ananda Veethi" or "The Path of Bliss," wherein she has
tried to make intelligible that mystical union which is beyond
mind or intellect.

> Once upon a time, my soul was dancing
> In delight through the Path of Bliss.
> At that time, all the inner foes such as
> Attraction and aversion ran away hiding
> Themselves in the innermost recesses of my mind.
>
> Forgetting myself, I merged in a golden dream
> Which arose within me. As noble aspirations
> Clearly manifested themselves in my mind,
> The Divine Mother, with bright, gentle hands,
> Caressed my head. With bowed head, I told
> Mother that my life is dedicated to Her.
>
> Smiling, She became a Divine Effulgence
> And merged in me. My mind blossomed,

Bathed in the many-hued Light of Divinity
And the events of millions of years gone by
Rose up within me. Thenceforth,
Seeing nothing as apart from my own Self
A single Unity, and merging in the Divine Mother,
I renounced all sense of enjoyment.

Mother told me to ask the people
To fulfill their human birth.
Therefore, I proclaim to the whole world
The sublime Truth that She uttered,
"Oh man, merge in your Self!"

Thousands and thousands of yogis
Have taken birth in India and
Lived the principles visualized by the
Great Sages of the unknown past.
To remove the sorrow of humanity,
How many naked truths are there!

Today I tremble with bliss
Recollecting Mother's words,
"Oh my darling, come to Me
Leaving all other works.
You are always Mine."

O Pure Consciousness,
O Embodiment of Truth,
I will heed Your words

O Mother, why are You late in coming?
Why did You give this birth?
I know nothing, O Mother,
Please forgive my mistakes.

At this point Sudhamani developed a strong aversion toward
everything. She would dig big holes to hide herself in so as to escape from the diverse world and sensuous-minded people. She

spent her days and nights enjoying the perennial Bliss of God-realization and avoided all human company. If anyone had considered her mad before, they would stand firmly convinced of her insanity now. Who among these fisherfolk could conceive of the plane of consciousness in which the little one was established? Though internally, Sudhamani had crossed the threshold into the Absolute, externally she was the same crazy Sudhamani who was possessed three nights a week by Krishna as far as the family and villagers were concerned. The only recent change, if they had noticed any at all, was that instead of rolling in the sand she was now digging big holes.

One day Sudhamani heard a voice from within her say,

"My child, I dwell in the heart of all beings and have no fixed abode. Your birth is not for merely enjoying the unalloyed Bliss of the Self but for comforting suffering humanity. Henceforth worship Me in the hearts of all beings and relieve them of the sufferings of worldly existence. . . ."

It was after this inner call that Sudhamani started manifesting Devi Bhava, the Mood of the Divine Mother, in addition to the Krishna Bhava. At these times she revealed her incessant oneness with the Divine Mother. . . .

"From that day onwards I could see nothing as different from my own Formless Self wherein the entire universe exists as a tiny bubble. . . ."

From *Mata Amritanandamayi* by Swami Amritatma Chaitanya.

THIRTY-THREE

SUZANNE SEGAL

1955–1997, UNITED STATES

ONE DAY at a bus stop in Paris, Suzanne Segal, twenty-seven years old and pregnant, lost her sense of personal identity. "I lifted my right foot to step up into the bus and collided head-on with an invisible force that entered my awareness like a silently exploding stick of dynamite, blowing the door of my usual consciousness open and off its hinges, splitting me in two. In the gaping space that appeared, what I had previously called 'me' was forcefully pushed out of its usual location inside me into a new location that was approximately a foot behind and to the left of my head. 'I' was now behind my body looking out at the world without using the body's eyes."

This was Suzanne's "collision with the infinite." Terrified, she was amazed to find that her body kept on living and functioning relatively normally. Initially she witnessed its actions. Eventually even the sense of witnessing was lost, and she could no longer locate any sense of a personal self inside. Despite her previous spiritual training, the loss terrified her for ten years. Eventually Suzanne sought help through correspondence and personal contact from a number of therapists and spiritual teachers from the Buddhist and Hindu traditions, as well as from the written teachings of Ramana Maharshi. A number of well-respected spiritual adepts assured Suzanne that her experience was genuine and that she had attained liberation. Once she was able to perceive the fear as no different from the emptiness, it disappeared.

At this time, Suzanne published her book, *Collision with the Infinite,* and became a spiritual teacher and therapist in the San Francisco Bay Area. This new career was to be short-lived. Suzanne's realization became unstable and she plunged into self-doubt. She began to experience disorientation, vertigo, and deteriorating health, and at the age of

SUZANNE SEGAL

forty-two was diagnosed with a rapidly progressive brain tumor. Within two months she was dead.

The process of enlightenment is not always pure bliss. Suzanne's life is a demonstration of the agony and ecstasy, terror and tenuousness, vacillation and vastness that may be a part of the experience of awakening.

Many found Suzanne's death unsettling, as if her life had ended before her journey was complete. Some attributed her enlightenment experiences to the organic changes within her brain, yet the fast-growing tumor was discovered a good twelve years after her profound transformation began. For those that believe in the purposefulness of life and death, the timing was not in error. Even if her realization were lost at the very end of her life, it does not minimize the depth of her search, unfoldment, and realization. Suzanne Segal's "collision with the infinite" remains a valuable and educational experience of a modern woman growing past her fear into bliss, alternately struggling with and discovering an answer to the ancient question, "Who am I? "

Suzanne Segal's selection comes from her account of her spiritual experiences, *Collision with the Infinite*.

COLLISION WITH THE INFINITE

IT WAS IN the springtime that it happened. I was returning home to my apartment on the Left Bank after attending a class for pregnant women at the clinic across town where I would be having my baby six months from then. It was the first week of my fourth month of pregnancy, and I had just begun to feel the faintest stirring of my daughter's tiny movements, like being brushed by a feather from the inside. The month was May, and the sun felt warm on my head and face as I stood at the bus stop on the Avenue de la Grande Armee. I was in no hurry and had decided to take a bus instead of the metro in order to enjoy the lovely weather.

Several buses came and went before I finally saw the number 37 approaching down the wide avenue. Six or seven of us were waiting together at the stop, exchanging pleasantries about the weather and comments about the new advertising campaign that had been appearing on all the billboards. As the bus approached, we congregated expectantly near the curb. The bus lumbered to a halt, expelling the acrid odor of exhaust fumes and hot rubber into the warm spring air.

As I took my place in line. I suddenly felt my ears stop up like they do when the pressure changes inside an airplane as it makes its descent. I felt cut off from the scene before me, as if I were enclosed in a bubble, unable to act in any but the most mechanical manner. I lifted my right foot to step up into the bus and collided head-on with an invisible force that entered my awareness like a silently exploding stick of dynamite, blowing the door of my usual consciousness open and off its hinges, splitting me in two. In the gaping space that appeared, what I had previously called "me" was forcefully pushed out of its usual location inside me into a new location that was approximately a foot behind and to the left of my head. "I" was now behind my body looking out at the world without using the body's eyes.

From a non-localized position somewhere behind and to the left, I could see my body in front and very far away. All the body's signals seemed to take a long time to be picked up in this non-localized place, as if they were light coming from a distant star. Terrified, I looked around, wondering if anyone else had noticed something. All the other passengers were calmly taking their seats, and the bus driver was motioning me to put my yellow ticket into the machine so we could be off.

I shook my head a few times, hoping to rattle my consciousness back into place, but nothing changed. I felt from afar as my fingers fumbled to insert the ticket into the slot and I walked down the aisle to find a seat. I sat down next to an older woman I had been chatting with at the bus stop, and I tried to continue our conversation. My mind had completely ground to a halt in the shock of the abrupt collision with whatever had dislodged my previous reality.

Although my voice continued speaking coherently, I felt completely disconnected from it. The face of the woman next to me seemed far away, and the air between us seemed foggy, as if filled with a thick, luminous soup. She turned to gaze out the window for a moment, then reached up to pull the cord to signal the driver to let her off at the next stop. When she rose, I slid over into her seat by the window and bid her goodbye with a smile. I could feel sweat rolling down my arms and beading up on my face. I was terrified.

The bus arrived at my stop on the rue Lecourbe, and I got off. As I walked the three blocks home, I attempted to pull myself back into one piece by focusing on my body and willing myself back into it where I thought I belonged in order to regain the previously normal sensation of seeing through the body's eyes, speaking through the body's mouth, and hearing through the body's ears. The force of will failed miserably. Instead of experiencing through the physical senses, I was now bobbing behind the body like a buoy on the sea. Cut loose from sensory solidity, separated from and witnessing the body from a vast distance, I moved down the street like a cloud of awareness following a body that seemed simultaneously familiar and foreign. There was an incomprehensible attachment to that body, although it no longer felt like "mine." It continued to send out signals of its sensory perceptions, yet how or where those signals were being received was beyond comprehension.

Incapable of making sense of this state, the mind alternated between racing wildly in an attempt to put "me" back together and shutting down completely, leaving only the empty humming of space reverberating in the ears. The witness was absolutely distinct from the mind, the body, and the emotions, and the position it held, behind and to the left of the head, remained constant. The profound distance between the witness and the mind, body, and emotions seemed to elicit panic in and of itself, due to the sensation of being so tenuously tethered to physical existence. In this witnessing state, physical existence was experienced to be on the verge of dissolution, and it (the physical) responded by summoning an annihilation fear of monumental proportions.

As I walked into my apartment, Claude looked up from his book to greet me and ask how my day had been. The terror was not immediately apparent to him, which seemed oddly reassuring. I greeted him calmly as if nothing were wrong, telling him about the class at the clinic and showing him the new book I had purchased at the American bookstore on my way home. There was no conceivable way to explain any of this to him, so I didn't even try. The terror was escalating rapidly, and the body was panic stricken, sweat pouring in rivulets down its sides, hands cold and trembling, heart pumping furiously. The mind clicked into survival mode and started looking for distractions. Maybe if I took a bath or a nap, or ate some food, or read a book or called someone on the phone.

The whole thing was nightmarish beyond belief. The mind (I could no longer even call it "my" mind) was trying to come up with some explanation for this clearly inexplicable occurrence. The body moved beyond terror into a frenzied horror, giving rise to such utter physical exhaustion that sleep became the only possible option. After telling Claude that I didn't want to be disturbed, I lay down in bed and fell into what I thought would be the welcome oblivion of sleep. Sleep came, but the witness continued, witnessing sleep from its position behind the body. This was the oddest experience. The mind was definitely asleep, but something was simultaneously awake.

The moment the eyes opened the next morning, the mind exploded in worry. Is this insanity? Psychosis? Schizophrenia? Is this what people call a nervous breakdown? Depression? What had happened? And would it ever stop? Claude had started to notice my agitation and was apparently waiting for an explanation. I attempted to tell him what had taken place the day before, but I was just too far away to speak. The witness appeared to be where "I" was located, which left the body, mind, and emotions empty of a person. It was amazing that all those functions continued to operate at all. There was no explaining this one to Claude, and for once I was glad he was the kind of person who didn't persist in pursuing a subject I didn't want to pursue.

The mind was so overwhelmed by its inability to comprehend the current state of existence that it could not be distracted. It remained riveted to the incomprehensible, unanswerable quandaries that were generated in an unbroken stream out of this witnessing state of awareness. There was the sense of being on an edge of sorts, a boundary between existing and not existing, and the mind believed that if it did not maintain the thought of existence, existence itself would cease. Charged with this apparently life-or-death directive, the mind struggled to hold that thought, only to exhaust itself after several fitful hours. The mind was in agony as it tried valiantly to make sense of something it could never comprehend, and the body responded to the anguish of the mind by locking itself into survival mode, adrenaline pumping, senses fine-tuned, finding and responding to the threat of annihilation in every moment.

The thought did arise that perhaps this experience of witnessing was the state of Cosmic Consciousness Maharishi had described long before as the first stage of awakened awareness. But the mind instantly discarded this possibility because it seemed impossible that the hell realm I was inhabiting could have anything to do with Cosmic Consciousness.

(Twelve years later.)

Although I had received a great deal of reassurance from the people I had contacted about my experience, the wintertime of no-self was still not yielding much joy. As it turned out, the joy was to arrive all at once, crashing onto the shores of awareness suddenly and irrevocably, just as the first wave of the dropping away of self had occurred twelve years before.

From the clear experience of emptiness of self, my state of consciousness was about to transition abruptly into the next season—the experience that not only is there no personal self there is also no other. In other words, I was about to shift permanently into unity awareness, in which the emptiness that dominated my consciousness was seen to be the very substance of all creation. Once the secret of emptiness was revealed in this way, I began to describe it as the "vastness."

In the midst of a particularly eventful week, I was driving north to meet some friends when I suddenly became aware that I was driving through myself. For years there had been no self at all, yet here on this road everything was myself, and I was driving through me to arrive where I already was. In essence, I was going nowhere because I was everywhere already. The infinite emptiness I knew myself to be was now apparent as the infinite substance of everything I saw.

In the wake of this transition to the vastness of emptiness, I began to meditate intensively. I spent hours each morning and hours again each night just sitting in the vastness, as blossoms began appearing on the tree of emptiness. A strong pull arose to do a solitary retreat, so I arranged to stay for a long mid-January weekend at a Buddhist retreat center in the Santa Cruz mountains.

As I drove through the wintry landscape on my way there, everything seemed more fluid. The mountains, trees, rocks, birds, sky were all losing their differences. As I gazed about, what I saw first was how they were one; then, as a second wave of perception, I saw the distinctions. But the perception of the substance they were all made of did not occur through the physical body. Rather, the vastness was perceiving itself out of itself at every point in itself. A lovely calm pervaded everything—no ecstasy, no bliss, just calm.

At the same time, something else began emerging which continues to this day—something I can only describe as a "thickening into unity" that was both experiential and perceptual. From that day forth I have had the constant experience of both moving through and being made of the "substance" of everything. This is what is experienced first—the stuff of unity, its texture, its flavor, its substance. This non-localized, infinite substance can be perceived not with the eyes or ears or nose, but by the substance itself, out of itself. When the substance of unity encounters itself, it knows itself through its own sense organ. Form is like a drawing in the sand of oneness, where the drawing, the sand, and the finger that draws it are all one.

On my own with the vastness, I had encountered the very insight that did the work of exposing the fear and releasing its hold. I realized that the mind had been clinging tenaciously to the erroneous notion that the presence of fear meant something about the validity of the experience of no-self. Fear had tricked the mind into taking its presence to mean something that it did not. Fear was present, yes, but that was it! The presence of fear in no way invalidated the experience that no personal self existed. It meant only that fear was present.

Fear didn't need to go anywhere for the personal self to be seen to be nonexistent. After all, where could it possibly go? It had never existed. Nothing needed to change or be eradicated; nothing needed to do anything at all but to be. Everything occurs simultaneously—form and emptiness, pain and enlightenment, fear and awakening. Once seen, it seemed so incredibly simple.

Fear's grip now broke, and joy arose at once. The experience of emptiness had given up its secret. The emptiness was seen to be nothing but the very substance of everything. I finally saw what had been in front of me the whole time but had been obscured by fear: There is not only no individual self, but also no other. No self, no other. Everything is made of the same substance of vastness.

Arriving at the retreat center in the late afternoon, I unloaded my bags at the cabin and went for a walk in the surrounding woods. I knew myself to be made of nothing and everything, just like all of creation. How could I have missed it before? It was right there in front of me the whole time, as close as the emptiness, as empty as the emptiness, and as full.

All the Zen stories Richard had told me came flooding back, and I began laughing and crying uproariously, unable to stop. Finally I fell to the ground, weak with the vision of it all. For twelve years I had known, seen, breathed emptiness, and now it extended throughout the universe in great tidal waves of empty fullness. That everything was unified in the emptiness now seemed like the most obvious thing in the world, but it had taken so long for me to stumble on it. I guess it had stumbled on itself.

Needless to say, nothing has ever been the same since. The fact that "I" no longer existed, that there was no person anymore, gave way finally and completely to the realization that there is nothing that is not myself. What remains when there is no self is all that is.

From *Collision with the Infinite* by Suzanne Segal.

BIBLIOGRAPHY AND SUGGESTED READINGS

* Indicates the source of the selection for each chapter.

Gautama the Buddha
Dalai Lama, H. H. *The Heart of the Buddha's Path*. New York: Thorsons, 2000.

Hahn, Thich Nhat. *The Heart of the Buddha's Teaching*. New York: Broadway Books, 1999.

*Kohn, Sherab Chodzin. *The Awakened One*. Boston: Shambhala Publications, 2000.

Kornfield, Jack, and Gil Fronsdal, editors. *Teachings of the Buddha*. Boston: Shambhala Publications, 1993.

Hui-Neng
*Cleary, Thomas, translator. *The Sutra of Hui-neng*. Boston: Shambhala Publications, 1998.

Price, A. F. F., and Wong Mou-Lam, translators. *The Diamond Sutra and the Sutra of Hui-Neng*. Boston: Shambhala Publications, 1990.

Suzuki, D. T. and Christmas Humphreys. *The Zen Doctrine of No Mind*. York Beach, ME: Samuel Weiser, 1991.

Yeshe Tsogyal
*Changchub, Gyalwa, and Namkhai Lingpo of the Padma Translation Group. *Lady of the Lotus-Born*. Boston: Shambhala Publications, 2000.

Dowman, Keith, translator. *Sky Dancer*. Ithaca, NY: Snow Lion Publications, 1997

Jalaluddin Rumi
*Barks, Coleman, and Michael Green. *The Illuminated Rumi*. New York: Broadway Books, 1997.

Barks, Coleman, with John Moyne, A. J. Arberry, and Reynold Nicholson, translators. *The Essential Rumi.* , Edison, NJ: Castle Books, 1997.

*Harvey, Andrew, editor. *The Teaching of Rumi.* Boston: Shambhala Publications, 1999.

Disciple of Abulafia

Idel, Moshe, and Jonathan Chipman, translators. *The Mystical Experience in Abraham Abulafia.* Albany: State University of New York Press, 1987.

*Jacobs, Louis. *The Schocken Book of Jewish Mystical Testimonies.* New York: Schocken Books, 1997.

Saint Catherine of Siena

St. Catherine of Siena. *Catherine of Siena: Purgation and Purgatory, the Spiritual Dialogue.* Mahwah, NJ: Paulist Press, 1994

*Lamb, George. *The Life of Catherine of Siena.* New York: P. J. Kenedy and Sons, 1946.

Kabir

Kabir. *The Kabir Book: Forty-Four of the Ecstatic Poems of Kabir.* Robert Bly, editor. Boston: Beacon Press, 1976.

*Tagore, Rabindranath. *Songs of Kabir.* New York: Samuel Weiser, 1991.

Gendun Gyatso Palzangpo

*Mullin, Glenn H. *Mystical Verses of a Mad Dalai Lama.* Wheaton, IL: The Theosophical Publishing House, 1994.

Saint John of the Cross

St. John of the Cross. *St. John of the Cross: Alchemist of the Soul.* De Nicolas, Antonio T., translator. New York: Paragon Books, 1989.

St. John of the Cross. *The Dark Night of the Soul.* E. Allison Peers, editor. New York: Doubleday, 1990.

Matthew, Iain. *The Impact of God: Soundings from St. John of the Cross.* London: Hodder-Headline, 1999.

Hakuin

Waddell, Norman. *The Essential Teachings of Zen Master Hakuin.* Boston: Shambhala Publications, 1994.

*Waddell, Norman, translator. *Wild Ivy: The Spiritual Autobiography of Zen Master Hakuin.* Boston: Shambhala Publications, 1999.

Yampolsky, Philip B., translator. *The Zen Master Hakuin: Selected Writings.* New York: Columbia University Press, 1985.

Baal Shem Tov

Buber, Martin. *The Legend of the Baal Shem.* New York: Schocken Books, 1969.

*Jacobs, Louis. *The Schocken Book of Jewish Mystical Testimonies.* New York: Schocken Books, 1997.

Singer, Isaac B. *Reaches of Heaven.* New York: Farrar, Straus and Giroux, 1980.

Bahá'u'lláh

*Effendi, Shoghi. *God Passes By.* Wilmette, IL: National Spiritual Assembly of the Bahais of the United States, 1944, 1971, 1974.

*Nabil. *The Dawn Breakers.* Wilmette, IL: National Spiritual Assembly of the Bahais of the United States, 1932.

Sours, Michael W. *Ali's Dream: The Story of Bahaullah.* Wilmette, IL: Bahai Distribution Service, 1998.

Ramakrishna Paramahamsa

Chetananda, Swami. *Ramakrishna as We Saw Him.* St. Louis: Vedanta Society of St. Louis, 1990.

Isherwood, Christopher. *Ramakrishna and His Disciples.* Hollywood, CA: Vedanta Press, 1980.

*Ramakrishna, Paramahamsa. *Sayings of Ramakrishna.* Madras: Sri Ramakrishna Math, 1963.

Schiffman, Richard. *Sri Ramakrishna: A Prophet for the New Age.* New York: Paragon Books, 1990.

Ramana Maharshi

Maharshi, Ramana, and David Godman. *Be as You Are.* New York: Viking Penguin, 1991.

Maharshi, Ramana, and Arthur Osborne. *Teachings of Ramana Maharshi*. York Beach, ME: Samuel Weiser, 1996.
*V. S. Raman, *Sri Bhagavan Ramana: A Pictoral Biography*. Tiruvannamalai, India: Sri Ramanasramam, 1995.

Swami (Papa) Ramdas

*Ramdas, Swami. *God-Experience*. Bombay: Bharatiya Vidya Bhavan, 1969.
Ramdas, Swami. *In the Vision of God*. Bombay: Bharatiya Vidya Bhavan, 1974.

Mother Krishnabai

Ram Das, Swami. *Krishnabhai*. Enlarged 5th Edition. Kanhangad, Kerala, India: Anandashram Publications, 1994.
*Sriram (Swami Shuddhananda). *With the Divine Mother*. 3 volumes. Kerala, India: Anandashram Publications, 1996, 1998, 2001.

Paramahansa Yogananda

Ghosh, Sananda L. *Mejda: The Family and Early Life of Paramahansa Yogananda*. Los Angeles: Self-Realization Fellowship, 1980.
*Yogananda, Paramahansa. *Autobiography of a Yogi*. Los Angeles: Self-Realization Fellowship, 1959.
Yogananda, Paramahansa. *The Divine Romance*. Los Angeles: Self-Realization Fellowship, 1967.
Yogananda, Paramahansa. *Journey to Self-Realization*. Los Angeles: Self-Realization Fellowship, 1997.

Meher Baba

Anzar, Naosherwan. *Beloved: The Life and Work of Meher Baba*. Myrtle Beach, SC: Sheriar Press, 1983.
Baba, Meher. *God Speaks*. Myrtle Beach, SC: Sufism Reoriented, 1997.
Baba, Meher. *The Everything and the Nothing*. Myrtle Beach, SC: Sheriar Foundation, 1995.
*Baba, Avatar Meher, and A. G. Munsif. *Hazrat Babajan*. Ahmednagar, India: Avatar Meher Baba Trust, 1981.
Schloss, Malcom, and Charles Purdom. *Three Incredible Weeks with Meher Baba*. Myrtle Beach, SC: Sheriar Press, 1979.

J. Krishnamurti

Krishnamurti, J. *The Awakening of Intelligence.* San Francisco: Harper-SanFrancisco, 1987.

Krishnamurti, J. *Total Freedom: The Essential Krishnamurti.* New York: HarperCollins, 1996.

Krishamurti, J., John Van der Stuijf, and Cathy Van der Stuijf, editors. *The Concise Guide to Krishnamurti.* Ojai, CA: Krishnamurti Publications of America, 1999.

* Luytens, Mary. *Krishnamurti: The Years of Awakening.* Boston: Shambhala Publications, 1997.

Franklin Merrell-Wolff

Leonard, Ron. *The Transcendental Philosophy of Franklin Merrell-Wolff.* Albany: State University of New York Press, 1999.

*Merrell-Wolff, Franklin. *Experience and Philosophy.* Albany: State University of New York Press, 1994.

*Merrell-Wolff, Franklin. *Transformations in Consciousness.* Albany: State University of New York Press, 1994.

Peace Pilgrim

*Peace Pilgrim. *Peace Pilgrim.* Santa Fe, NM: Ocean Tree Books, 1991.

Peace Pilgrim. *Peace Pilgrim's Wisdom.* San Diego, CA: Blue Dove Press, 1996.

Peace Pilgrim. *Steps Toward Inner Peace.* Santa Fe, NM: Ocean Tree Books, 1992.

Gopi Krishna

Krishna, Gopi. *Kundalini: The Evolutionary Energy in Man.* Boston: Shambhala Publications, 1997.

*Krishna, Gopi. *Living with Kundalini.* Boston: Shambhala Publications, 1993.

Kieffer, Gene, editor, and Gopi Krishna. *Kundalini: Empowering Human Evolution.* New York: Paragon House, 1995.

Irving, Darrell, Gene Keiffer, and Gopi Krishna. *Serpent of Fire: A Modern View of Kundalini.* York Beach, ME: Samuel Weiser. 1996.

Lester Levenson

*Levenson, Lester. *Keys to the Ultimate Freedom*. Sedona: Sedona Institute, 1993.

Klein, Jean. *I Am*. St. Peter Port, Cayman Islands: Third Millennium Publications, 1989.

Klein, Jean. *Living Truth*. St. Peter Port, Cayman Islands: Third Millennium Publications, 1994.

*Klein, Jean. *Transmission of the Flame*. St. Peter Port, Cayman Islands: Third Millennium Publications, 1990.

Ramesh Balsekar

*Balsekar, Ramesh. *Consciousness Speaks*. Redondo Beach, CA: Advaita Press, 1992.

Balsekar, Ramesh. *Net of Jewels*. Redondo Beach, CA: Advaita Press, 1997.

Balsekar, Ramesh, and Blayne Bardo. *Your Head in the Tiger's Mouth*. Redondo Beach, CA: Advaita Press, 1998.

Robert Adams

*Adams, Robert. *Silence of the Heart*. Sedona: Infinity Institute, 1997.

Bernadette Roberts

*Roberts, Bernadette. *The Experience of No-Self: A Contemplative Journey*. Albany: State University of New York Press, 1993.

Roberts, Bernadette. *The Path to No-Self: Life at the Center*. Albany: State University of New York Press, 1991.

Roberts, Bernadette. *What Is Self? A Study of the Spiritual Journey in Terms of Consciousness*. Marina del Ray, CA: DeVorss and Co., 1989.

Deepa Kodikal

*Kodikal, Deepa. *A Journey Within the Self*. Bombay: Bharatiya Vidya Bhavan, 1992.

Gangaji

Gangaji, *You Are That!* Vols. 1-2. Novato, CA: Gangagi Foundation and Satsang Press, 1995, 1996.

Eckhart Tolle

*Tolle, Eckhart. *The Power of Now.* Vancouver, B.C.: Namaste Books, 1997.

A. H. Almaas

Almaas, A. H. *Essence with the Elixir of Enlightenment: The Diamond Approach to Inner Realization.* York Beach, ME: Samuel Weiser, 1998.

*Almaas, A. H. *Luminous Night's Journey.* Berkeley, CA: Diamond Books, 1995.

Almaas, A. H. *Soul Without Shame: A Guide to Liberating Yourself from the Judge Within.* Boston: Shambhala Publications, 1998.

Davis, John. *The Diamond Approach: An Introduction to the Teachings of A. H. Almaas.* Boston: Shambhala Publications, 1999.

Shantimayi

Shantimayi. *The Gayatri Mantra.* Rishikesh, India: Sacha Dham, 2000.

Mata Amritanandamayi

Amritaswarupananda, Swami. *Ammachi: A Biography of Mata Amritanandamayi.* San Ramon, CA: M.A. Center, 1994.

Amritaswarupananda, Swami. *Awaken Children.* Vols. 1-8. San Ramon, CA: M.A. Center, 1989-1996.

*Chaitanya, Amritatma. *Mata Amritanandamayi.* Vallickavu, India: Mata Amritanandamayi Mission Trust, 1988.

Suzanne Segal

*Segal, Suzanne. *Collision with the Infinite.* San Diego, CA: Blue Dove Press, 1996.

INTERNET RESOURCES

Gautama, The Buddha
www.accesstoinsight.org/ptf/buddha.html
www.buddhanet.net

Hui-Neng
oaks.nvg.org/wm2ra3.html

Yeshe Tsogyal
pages.ancientsites.com/~Julia_Manach/yeshe.htm
www.indranet.com/spirit/meditation_images.html

Jalaluddin Rumi
www.armory.com/~thrace/sufi/

Disciple of Abulafia
www.geocities.com/Athens/Atrium/1281/abu.html

Saint Catherine of Siena
home.infi.net/~ddisse/siena.html
www.humanities.ccny.cuny.edu/history/reader/catherine.htm

Kabir
www.cs.colostate.edu/~malaiya/kabir.html

Gendun Gyatso Palzangpo
www.tibet.org.za/kundun.htm

Saint John of the Cross
www.karmel.at/ics/john/gen.html

Hakuin

www.ozemail.com.au/~ksolway/hakuin.html

Baal Shem Tov

members.aol.com/LazerA/baalshemtov.html
www.dlshq.org/saints/baalshemtov.htm

Baha'u'lláh

www.bahai.org/article-1-3-0-2.html
svr.eng.cam.ac.uk/~dp10006/bahai/history/bahaullah.html

Ramakrishna Paramahamsa

paramahamsadev.freeyellow.com/
www.digiserve.com/mystic/Hindu/Ramakrishna/index.html
www.ramakrishna.org/rmk.htm

Ramana Maharshi

www.prahlad.org/gallery/sri_ramana_maharshi.htm
www.ramana-maharshi.org/

Swami (Papa) Ramdas

www.anandashram.org/
www.sivanandadlshq.org/saints/papa_ramdas.htm

Mother Krishnabai

www.kfa.org/
www.kinfonet.org/

Paramahansa Yogananda

www.yogananda-srf.org/py-life/
www.crystalclarity.com/yogananda/chap1/chap1.html

Meher Baba

www.avatarmeherbaba.org/

Franklin Merrell-Wolff
www.integralscience.org/gsc/

J. Krishnamurti
www.anandashram.org/mataji.htm

Peace Pilgrim
www.peacepilgrim.com/pphome.htm
www.wakan.com/Documentary/PeacePilgrim.html

Gopi Krishna
web.stn.net/icr/gopikris.html
www.koausa.org/Kundalini/

Lester Levenson
www.sedona.com
www.releasetechnique.com/

Jean Klein
www.jeanklein.org/

Ramesh Balsekar
www.advaita.org/aframesh.htm
www.non-local.com/balsekar.html

Robert Adams
www.robertadams.org/

Bernadette Roberts
www.firedocs.com/carey/roberts.html

Deepa Kodikal
www.lifepositive.com/mind/personal_growth/transformation/
  transformation2_article.asp

Gangaji
www.gangaji.org/

Eckhart Tolle
www.eckharttolle.com/mainpage.htm

A. H. Almaas
www.ridhwan.org/almaas.html

Shantimayi
www.shantimayi.com/

Mata Amritanandamayi
www.ammachi.org/

Suzanne Segal
www.bluedove.com/books/b-collision.html
www.spiritualteachers.org/suzanne_segal.htm

INDEX

Robert Ullman, N.D., and Judyth Reichenberg-Ullman, N.D., M.S.W., are licensed naturopathic and board-certified homeopathic physicians in practice for nearly twenty years. Judyth received her B.A. in Spanish literature and master's in psychiatric social work. They are the authors of six books on homeopathic medicine, including the bestselling *Ritalin-Free Kids, Prozac-Free, Whole-Woman Homeopathy, Rage-Free Kids, Homeopathic Self-Care,* and *The Patient's Guide to Homeopathic Medicine,* and have published more than 300 articles on natural medicine. They treat patients in person and by telephone and can be reached at (425) 774-5599. Their Web sites are *www.mysticsmasters.com* and *www. healthyhomeopathy.com.*

Bob and Judyth began their spiritual search thirty years ago, long before they met. In the course of their spiritual journey, they have had the great blessing to study with a number of accomplished and realized teachers. Their love of travel has given them the opportunity to visit great beings and holy sites throughout the world, including frequent trips to India. They live in Langley, Washington, on Whidbey Island, near Seattle. They share their home with two lovable golden retrievers who are highly devoted to dinner and a very sweet cat who meditates on the meaning of mice.

Visit Our Website

Please visit our Web site, *www.mysticsmasters.com* or call (800) 398-1151 to order additional copies of *Mystics, Masters, Saints, and Sages* for family and friends. We offer pictures and additional information about awakened beings as well as a selection of books, audiotapes, and videos. Please check our schedule on the Web site for seminars, booksignings, and appearances in your area.

Send Us Other Enlightenment Stories

If you know of other enlightenment stories that you would have liked to have seen in *Mystics, Masters, Saints, and Sages,* we invite you to send them to the address below for a possible sequel to this book.

Robert Ullman and Judyth Reichenberg-Ullman
131 3rd Avenue North
Edmonds, WA 98020
mysticsmasters@hotmail.com.